Advance Praise for *EcoVillage at Ithaca*

The folks at EcoVillage have learned more than a little about creating an Earth-friendly community. Today, an ever-growing number of people are coming to the conclusion that our society is on a collision course with madness; they long for a way of life less alienating and more natural than the prevailing direction of our culture, but do not know where to turn.
In *EcoVillage at Ithaca,* Liz Walker speaks of the struggles as well as the joys of building such a community. I finished this book with a greatly renewed sense of hope and trust in humanity's ability to live with one another and the Earth.

— John Robbins, author of *Diet For A New America*
and *The Food Revolution*

Liz Walker's *EcoVillage at Ithaca* is an achingly beautiful and finely told account of a group of people — part of a larger movement — living as modern pioneers of a sustainable future. Walker and her dozens of companions are ordinary people called to an extraordinary adventure in our hyper-individualistic consumer culture — to trust one another, to cooperate, to work together, to make a "career" of living itself. I hope this book inspires you to be more neighborly at very least and perhaps to join the growing network of people living lightly and intentionally so that there might be many tomorrows.

— Vicki Robin, coauthor of *Your Money or Your Life,*
and cofounder of "Conversation Cafes"

Liz Walker's *EcoVillage at Ithaca* is a great contribution to the sustainability movement. Her personal, engaging account is an invaluable documenting of the process of creating one of the most successful alternative communities: EcoVillage at Ithaca. Liz Walker is honest about the frustrations and conflicts as well as about the joys of this social experiment. The lessons she has learned, and the example of sustainable, supportive living, are vital for anyone contemplating undertaking such a project. Thank you, Liz!

— Starhawk, author of *The Spiral Dance, The Fifth Sacred Thing, Webs of Power,* and *The Earth Path*

I had the good luck to stay at EcoVillage at Ithaca in its early days, and can still remember the heady sense of optimism, community, and verve. This fine book captures all that, and will serve as an invaluable tool for anyone with such subversive thoughts in the back of their own mind.

— Bill McKibben, author of *Wandering Home: A Long Walk Across America's Most Hopeful Region, Vermont's Champlain Valley and New York's Adirondacks*

Liz Walker's fascinating and touching story of the Ecovillage at Ithaca shows how two single mothers without financial means initiated and led the building of a model for a sustainable society. In the process, they not only reduced their ecological footprint by 40 percent , but also created community, trust and love among the participants. All future ecovillage projects will stand on the shoulders of their experiences. This is a place into which I would like to reincarnate as a child in a future lifetime. Ecovillagers are the true freedom fighters of our generation.

— Hildur Jackson, ecovillage designer, cofounder of Gaia Trust and the Global ecovillage Network, and author of *Ecovillage Living: Restoring the Earth and her People*

This thoughtful, candid look at a successful ecovillage by one of its cofounders is a must-read for anyone seriously interested in starting his or her own ecovillage or intentional community.

— Diana Leafe Christian, author of *Creating a Life Together: Practical Tools to Grow Ecovillages and Intentional Communities*

ECO VILLAGE at ITHACA

ECO VILLAGE at ITHACA

Pioneering a Sustainable Culture

LIZ WALKER

NEW SOCIETY PUBLISHERS

Cataloging in Publication Data:
A catalog record for this publication is available from
the National Library of Canada.

Cover design by Diane McIntosh. Cover images: Top photograph copyright
Laura Beck; bottom photograph copyright Laura Miller (www.lauramiller.net).
Back cover photo: Laura Beck

Printed in Canada.
First printing April 2005.

Paperback ISBN: 0-86571-524-6

Inquiries regarding requests to reprint all or part of *EcoVillage at Ithaca* should
be addressed to New Society Publishers at the address below.

To order directly from the publishers, please call toll-free (North America)
1-800-567-6772, or order online at www.newsociety.com

Any other inquiries can be directed by mail to:

New Society Publishers
P.O. Box 189, Gabriola Island, BC V0R 1X0, Canada
1-800-567-6772

New Society Publishers' mission is to publish books that contribute in fundamental ways to building an ecologically sustainable and just society, and to do
so with the least possible impact on the environment, in a manner that models
this vision. We are committed to doing this not just through education, but
through action. We are acting on our commitment to the world's remaining
ancient forests by phasing out our paper supply from ancient forests worldwide.
This book is one step toward ending global deforestation and climate change.
It is printed on acid-free paper that is **100% old growth forest-free** (100% post-
consumer recycled), processed chlorine free, and printed with vegetable-based,
low-VOC inks. For further information, or to browse our full list of books and
purchase securely, visit our website at: www.newsociety.com

New Society Publishers   www.newsociety.com

To my parents Alan and Margery Walker, for their
love and stellar example of lives lived with integrity;

to my partner Jared Jones, for taking a leap of faith
to join me in this fascinating journey,
and for offering me deep love and support;

and for my sons Jason and Daniel Katz,
who inspire me to work for a better world.

Contents

Acknowledgments

Although I write about the history of EVI from my own experience, clearly this entire project would not have happened without the creative and dedicated work of many dozens of people. I want to thank Joan Bokaer for so clearly articulating the original vision. My friends and colleagues on the Global Walk proved that you can reach a vision, one step at a time. The people who loaned money to purchase the EVI land took a big risk, and I thank them for their courage and, in some cases, for their extraordinary generosity in forgiving their loans. The dozens of people who served on the EVI Board over the years and helped to shape the nonprofit deserve a hearty round of applause. But most of all I want to thank the 160 people with whom I share this wonderful community.

I also want to thank my friends and family, who early on read drafts of the manuscript and offered words of encouragement: Irene Zahava (who helped me believe in my writing), Krishna Ramanujan (who offered excellent editing suggestions), and Elan and Rachael Shapiro (for supporting me throughout the process). Additional thanks go to Jalaja Bonheim, Tina Nilsen-Hodges, Margery and Alan Walker, Lars Walker, Rachel Cogbill, and Daniel Katz. Thanks to Phebe Gustafson for fact-checking, to Betsy Crane for emotional support, and to my women's group for their hugs. Thanks to Jim Bosjolie, Laura Beck, and Laura Miller for capturing the essence of this ecovillage in photos. Many thanks to New Society Publishers for accepting my unsolicited manuscript and working with me to create a book. Last, but far from least, Jared Jones has offered me steady love and encouragement to carry out my dreams.

Foreword

ECOVILLAGES:
SEEDS OF SUSTAINABLE SOCIETIES

by Duane Elgin

The human family has entered a pivotal time in history when we are challenged to make not superficial changes, but a deep transformation in our manner of everyday living. The great wisdom of developing more sustainable patterns and ways of living was powerfully declared in 1992 when over 1,600 of the world's senior scientists, including a majority of the living Nobel laureates in the sciences, signed an unprecedented "Warning to Humanity." In this historic statement, they declared that "human beings and the natural world are on a collision course . . . that may so alter the living world that it will be unable to sustain life in the manner that we know." They concluded that "A great change in our stewardship of the earth and the life on it is required, if vast human misery is to be avoided and our global home on this planet is not to be irretrievably mutilated." Roughly a decade later came a related warning from 100 Nobel Prize winners who said that "the most profound danger to world peace in the coming years will stem not from the irrational acts of states or individuals but from the legitimate demands of the world's dispossessed."

As these two warnings by the world's senior scientists indicate, powerful trends are now converging into a whole-systems crisis, creating the likelihood of a planetary-scale evolutionary crash within this generation. These "adversity trends" include growing disruption of the global climate, an enormous increase in human populations living in gigantic cities without access to sufficient land and water needed to grow their own food, the depletion of vital resources such as fresh water and cheap oil, the massive and rapid extinction of animal and plant species around the world, growing disparities between the rich and the poor, and the spread of weapons of mass destruction. The potential for "vast human misery" and conflict seems very great.

Another path is possible. Rather than pull apart in destructive conflict, the human community could choose to pull together in cooperation and work collaboratively to create a sustainable future. I am heartened by research that indicates public attitudes and behaviors seem to be shifting in favor of more sustainable ways of living.

A "World Values Survey" was conducted at the turn of the 21st century, which represented a majority of the world's population and covered the full range of economic and political variation. Strikingly, this survey revealed that, over the several decades prior to the turn of the century, a major shift in values has been occurring in a cluster of a dozen or so nations, including the United States, Canada, Northern Europe, Japan, and Australia. In these societies, the emphasis is shifting from economic achievement to post-materialist values that emphasize self-expression, subjective well-being, and quality of life. These emerging values are important in supporting a shift beyond a narrowly focused materialism to a broadly oriented concern for more sustainable and satisfying ways of living.

A similar shift in values can be seen in other surveys focused on the United States. They show that several generations have tasted the fruits of an affluent society and have discovered that, for many, money does not buy happiness; instead, it is producing a society of emptiness and alienation. Not surprisingly, millions of people are trusting their experience, pulling back from the rat race of consumer society, and moving toward a way of life that is richer with family, community, creative work in the world, and a soulful connection with all of life.

Overall, in the United States and a dozen or so other "post-modern" nations, a trend toward simpler, more sustainable ways of living has evolved from a fringe movement in the 1960s to a respected part of mainstream cultures in the early 2000s. These surveys show there exists a distinct subpopulation — that I would conservatively estimate at 10 percent of the US adult population, or 20 million people — that is pioneering a way of life that is outwardly more sustainable and inwardly more soulful and satisfying.

Although millions of people are seeking to move toward new ways of living, they face an enormous challenge — our current patterns and scales of living do not suit their emerging needs. The scale of the household is often too small and that of the city too large to realize many of the opportunities for sustainable living. However, at the scale of an ecovillage, the strength of one person or family meets the strength of others and, working together, can create something that was not possible before. To illustrate from my own life, for a year now, my partner Coleen and I have lived in a cohousing community (often viewed as a stepping stone to an ecovillage) of roughly 70 people, and we have seen how easily and quickly activities can be organized. From organizing fundraisers (such as a brunch for tsunami disaster relief), to arranging classes (such as yoga and Cajun dancing), planting the community landscape and garden, and creating community celebrations and events, we have participated in several dozen gatherings that have emerged with ease from the combined strengths and diverse talents of the community.

A new architecture of life is needed: one that integrates the physical as well as the social and cultural/spiritual dimensions of our lives. Taking a lesson from humanity's past, it is important to look at the in-between scale of living — that of a small village of a few hundred people. Great opportunity exists for organizing into clusters of small ecovillages that are nested within a larger urban area.

Looking more broadly at this inspiring vision of a sustainable future, I can imagine that a family will live in an "eco-home" that is nested within an "eco-village," that, in turn, is nested within an "eco-city," and so on up the scale to the bioregion, nation, and world. Each ecovillage of several hundred persons would have a distinct character, architecture, and local economy. Most would likely contain a childcare facility and play area; a common house for meetings, celebrations and regular meals together; an organic community garden; a recycling and composting area; some revered open space; and a crafts and shop area. As well, each could offer a variety of types of work to the local economy — such as the arts, health care, child care, a non-profit learning center

for gardening, green building, conflict resolution, and other skills —
that provide fulfilling employment for many. These micro-communities
or modern villages could have the culture and cohesiveness of a small
town and the sophistication of a big city, as virtually everyone will be
immersed within a world that is rich with communications. Ecovillages
create the possibility for doing meaningful work, raising healthy children,
celebrating life in community with others, and living in a way that seeks
to honor the Earth and future generations.

Ecovillages represent a healthy response to economic globalization
as they create a strong, decentralized foundation for society and a way
of living that has the potential for being sustainable for everyone on
the planet. Because they typically range in size from roughly one
hundred to several hundred people, they approximate the scale of a
more traditional tribe. Consequently, ecovillages are compatible with
both the village-based cultures of indigenous societies and post-modern
cultures.

With a social and physical architecture sensitive to the psychology
of modern tribes, a flowering of diverse communities could replace the
alienation of today's massive cities. Ecovillages provide the practical
scale and foundation for a sustainable future. I believe they will become
important islands of community, security, learning, and innovation in a
world of sweeping change. These smaller-scale — human-scale — living
and working environments will foster diverse experiments in community and cooperative living. Sustainability will be achieved through
different designs that are uniquely adapted to the culture, economy,
interests and environment of each locale.

In a shift similar to that which nature makes — for example, in the
jump from simple atoms to complex molecules, or from complex molecules to living cells — humanity is being challenged to make a jump to
a new level of organization: social, ecological, economic and cultural/
spiritual. We have never before *consciously* confronted the combined
opportunity and necessity of such an enterprise before.

Despite the importance of ecovillages to a sustainable future, and
despite a reservoir of interest numbering in the millions of persons,
there are only a relative handful of ecovillages in the United States.
One of the largest and most well-known ecovillages in the United States
is in upstate New York. EcoVillage at Ithaca or EVI was co-founded by
Liz Walker in 1991. Liz has lived within, and been the director of, EVI

since its inception and has worked on all aspects of the community's development. It is understandable that there is great media interest in the Ithaca ecovillage because, in it, we can see the seeds of our own future. As a pioneering experiment in sustainable living in the US, EcoVillage at Ithaca will surely be recognized as a catalyst, spurring innovation throughout the country.

What is the lived-experience of transforming these seed potentials into a practical reality that can be seen and touched, with real people co-creating community, resolving conflicts, building consensus, celebrating together, constructing a distinctive physical architecture, stewarding the land to walk upon, and eating food from the community garden? Liz Walker answers this and other questions by taking us inside the personal journey of creating, and living within, the Ithaca ecovillage. The journey she describes feels both ancient and familiar as well as modern and exciting. I believe this is a journey to which we are all being called.

Duane Elgin is the author of books including *Promise Ahead* and *Voluntary Simplicity*. His website is: <www.awakeningearth.org>.

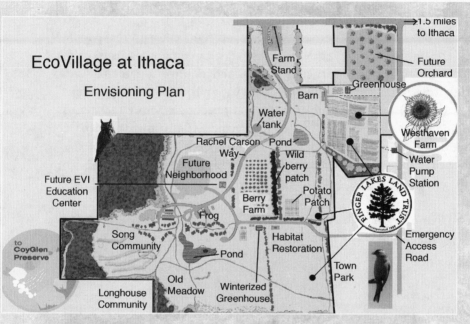

EcoVillage at Ithaca
Envisioning Plan

1.5 miles to Ithaca
Future Orchard
Greenhouse
Farm Stand
Barn
Water tank
Westhaven Farm
Rachel Carson Way
Pond
Wild berry patch
Water Pump Station
Future Neighborhood
Future EVI Education Center
Potato Patch
Berry Farm
FINGER LAKES LAND TRUST
to CoyGlen Preserve
Frog
Song Community
Pond
Habitat Restoration
Emergency Access Road
Old Meadow
Winterized Greenhouse
Town Park
Longhouse Community

Bill Webber
EcoVillage at Ithaca Envisioning Plan, updated 2004.

Introduction

Ecovillages are communities of people who strive to lead a sustainable lifestyle in harmony with each other, other living beings, and the Earth. Their purpose is to combine a supportive social-cultural environment with a low-impact lifestyle. As a new social structure, the ecovillage goes beyond today's dichotomy of urban versus rural settlements: it represents a widely applicable model for the planning and reorganization of human settlements in the 21st Century.

— Ecovillage Living: Restoring the Earth and Her People, Hildur Jackson and Karen Svensson, eds.

As a young boy my son Daniel loved to explore the outdoors. He sat for hours by streams, catching and releasing tadpoles and crayfish, oblivious to the cold water. He climbed gnarly apple trees and harvested the sour, scaly-skinned fruit with delight. When we took a walk together, his eye caught the darting grace of electric blue dragonflies or the green-stalked delicacy of a praying mantis without fail. His older brother called him "Nature Boy," with a smirk, but I thought it was a wonderful nickname, connoting the connection Daniel felt with the land and the beauty of its creatures.

One day Daniel returned home from school looking completely dejected. Traces of tears smudged his round cheeks. When I gave him a hug and asked what was wrong, he told me that they had just studied an ecology unit in his third grade classroom. He had been devastated to find out that species were dying out at a rate faster than at any point in the last 65 million years.

"Liz," he sobbed, "I wish humans would just die off and let the rest of the world survive." This was a huge and terrifying thought for

1

anyone, let alone an eight-year-old, to entertain. Although it shocked me that my son could wish for the demise of the human race, I could see his point.

At the beginning of the 21st century, we face a world that is falling apart at the seams. All major life support systems are in decline: the atmosphere, oceans and rivers, forests, and even the soil are showing signs of massive stress. Species are vanishing at a rate a thousand times faster than natural extinction rates. Worldwide one in eight plant species is endangered, and worse, one in four mammals is threatened. Global warming is finally being hailed as scientific fact, and its disastrous consequences are just beginning to be felt as glaciers melt and whole islands disappear under the ocean.

We face similar breakdowns on a social level: Our world is drenched in the blood of seemingly endless warfare. The centralization of wealth in the hands of a few perpetuates miserable living conditions for much of the world's population. And even as we are increasingly tied together (coal-fired plants in the Midwest create acid rain that kills off trees in the Adirondacks; pollution from US cars contributes to global warming that creates deserts in Africa), we seem to be further apart in understanding other cultures.

Although it is easy to despair, there is also cause for hope. I believe that we are in the midst of a remarkable global transformation. Increasingly people see that the old ways are no longer working. They see that it simply no longer makes sense to operate as isolated nation-states where "might equals right." It no longer makes sense to poison the planetary nest that is our home. It no longer makes sense to create laws that benefit multinational corporations while ignoring the needs of local people. If we want to survive as a species, we simply cannot continue on our current path of materialism, environmental destruction, and alienation from the life force in ourselves and in nature.

Now in the 21st century, we are rediscovering what indigenous people have always known: We are all interconnected; each action affects the whole. We need to shift to a paradigm that embodies the core values of love and respect for all beings, the fostering of cooperation, and the restoration of healthy ecosystems. We need to foster a sense of vibrant connection to the natural world, our spirits, and each other.

Some days I have great faith that we will make it. Other days I feel the way my son did and wonder if humans have a right to be on the planet we have so despoiled. But perhaps like Daniel, who is now immersed in Environmental Studies, our only choice is to be proactive and become solution seekers.

If we are to recreate a "culture of belonging," then we need to see working examples of it in action. Fortunately there is a rapidly growing, multifaceted movement focused on environmental and social sustainability. Some forward-thinking corporations are adopting the "triple bottom line," trying to balance the resources of the three "Ps" — People, Planet, and Profit. Some cities (such as Curritiba, Brazil and Portland, US) have adopted creative planning measures that create more livable downtown areas by concentrating development, preserving green space, and enhancing public transportation. Some innovative educators are developing school and college curricula that emphasize sustainability. And the United Nations has declared 2005–2014 to be the "Decade of Sustainability Education."

At the grassroots level, thousands of people in ecovillages and other types of communities around the world are striving to resurrect the best practices of traditional village life and combine them with modern lifestyles in practical ways that work. They are consciously beginning to embody the new paradigm — not as remote, abstract utopias but as living, breathing examples of reverence for life, all life. EcoVillage at Ithaca (EVI) is helping to forge this movement. Along with other ecovillages, and thousands of other cooperative projects focused on creating a life-enhancing culture, we could be called new pioneers — green pioneers in planetary responsibility.

As one of the largest and best-known ecovillages in the US, EcoVillage at Ithaca is committed to reaching mainstream, middle-class Americans and others who are open to positive change. EVI is a living laboratory that draws from the best alternative practices in land use, organic agriculture, community living, green building, and energy conservation. We integrate proven social and environmental systems to provide a glimpse into one possible positive future for the planet. And we are not just talking about it! We are immersed up to our elbows in learning and teaching about the multiple aspects of sustainable living. People are paying attention and using our example to create their own sustainable communities.

EcoVillage at Ithaca is recognized internationally. In 1998 EVI was one of ten finalists for the World Habitat Awards, and we have received delegations of visitors from China, Japan, Europe, Australia, and Canada. We have been featured on national television programs and in popular magazines in the US, Spain, and Japan and included in numerous books about sustainable communities. People are clearly eager to hear our message.

So what is it like to create a safe place for people to share their vulnerability and their joy? How do people transform over time? What does a community-build project look like? How do people deal with conflicts? What does it mean to connect with the land you live on? These are the questions we began with, and their answering continues to unfold in a beautiful and complex process.

When I moved across the country to help found EcoVillage at Ithaca, I thought the environmental aspects of the project were key: Sure, we would create a strong sense of community, but one could do that anywhere. A dozen years later, I find the cultural shift we create is more far-reaching than the details of which solar panels to choose or what organic farming techniques are the most up to date. A friend recently summed it up. "You're creating a culture of sustainability through the love you offer each other. There's nothing like it around."

In our best, most shining moments of community, I'm inclined to agree. The deep sense of caring, trust, and support that we often (but not always) share helps us grow into fully functioning human beings — for me, the essence of social sustainability. Those same qualities help us grow into better stewards and healers of the Earth. As we farm, parent, work, build, or educate, our efforts model important aspects of environmental sustainability. It is this profound integration of social cooperation and ecological practices, mixed with a healthy dose of wisdom, practicality, and deep caring that fosters a sustainable culture.

EcoVillage at Ithaca tells the human story behind EVI. It is not a comprehensive overview. It would take many books to describe our history, our individual stories, and our collective experiences from the last 13 years. I write from my own lived experience, and in some cases I use pseudonyms to protect the privacy of community members who share their vulnerable moments on these pages. The book will not show you how to create an ecovillage or intentional community. Nor will it explore our legal, financial, or organizational strategies. Other books can do that (for example, see Diana Leafe Christian's excellent book *Creating a Life Together* [New Society, 2003]). Instead I offer you

glimpses into our way of life and stories that illuminate our path —
from the original vision that set us upon this road to the joys and
struggles of living in community. And I invite you to hear about the
ecological features of the project and our participatory education and
outreach programs.

I believe that there is a lot in our particular experience that illustrates the human journey of living on the planet at this point in history.
As we struggle through resolving conflicts or celebrate life passages,
we are learning lessons that are universal. You don't have to live in an
ecovillage to create a strong sense of community or practice sustainability. You can begin anytime, anywhere. I hope this book will inspire
you to make changes in your own life, your own neighborhood, and
your own circle of friends — changes that celebrate life and point the
way to a positive, sustainable future.

CHAPTER 1

HOW IT ALL STARTED

The ultimate goal of EcoVillage at Ithaca is nothing less than to redesign the human habitat. We are creating a model community of some five hundred residents that will exemplify sustainable systems of living — systems that are not only practical in themselves but replicable by others. The completed project will demonstrate the feasibility of a design that meets basic human needs such as shelter, food production, energy, social interaction, work, and recreation while preserving natural ecosystems.

— EcoVillage at Ithaca Mission Statement:
Towards Systemic Change, adopted by the
EVI Board of Directors, 1994

The Global Walk

J oan Bokaer is a visionary — someone able to paint such a vivid picture of a possible future that people want to help make it a reality. Joan's vision of an ecovillage began while she was taking a long walk (in fact a very long walk) that stretched from Los Angeles to New York City. We called it "The Global Walk for a Livable World."

The year was 1990, some 20 years after Dennis Hayes had declared the first Earth Day. About 150 people from six different countries planned to walk across the US to raise awareness about the environment. The walkers were of various ages and from diverse backgrounds. The group included a Japanese Buddhist monk; a homeless man from Puerto Rico; European artists and activists; two Navajo men; a delegation from the former Soviet Union; middle-class couples; college students; my family (my sons were four and seven at the time); and many other fascinating people. I had spent the previous six months helping to prepare for the Walk by recruiting potential Walkers, publicizing the Walk, and fundraising.

When we all arrived at the starting point (in Simi Valley, outside of Los Angeles), I was dismayed to find that Joan, despite her vision and charisma, had no organizational plan. She shrugged her shoulders and gave the job to me. And, although I felt totally unprepared, I trusted my intuition and got to work. Drawing on my 14 years as a community organizer and activist, I convened the initial group meetings, put together a steering committee, organized work teams and committees, and taught people how to use consensus.

We had two weeks to prepare, and then we hit the road. We walked an average of 20 miles a day, six days a week. We stopped in 200 communities across the country to host "Livable World" fairs; hold teach-ins; plant trees; and meet with local schools, church groups, environmental activists, and the media.

Photo courtesy of Joan Bokaer

"The Global Walk for a Livable World" reaches Washington, DC, after walking across the US.

We were a traveling community that invented how to live together as we went along. We had an advance outreach team, mediators, solar-powered computers, a "Walk" newsletter, and much more. We held a daily morning circle to center ourselves. During times of conflict we held "talking stick" circles, which encouraged each person to speak from the heart as everyone else listened.

My kids mostly loved it. Although they only had the sporadic companionship of other kids, they rode high in one of our support vehicles to the next campsite and spent time with dozens of adult friends. They studied fossils with Ralph, a retired geologist, and learned how to create colorful friendship bracelets with Catia, a college student.

Jason, my intrepid seven-year-old, learned how to skateboard from Daveed. A young Californian with surfer-boy looks, Daveed would often skateboard to the head of the Walk, set up a tripod, and videotape our colorful procession as we walked by carrying the Earth flag.

Jason also learned to stand on his head and walk on stilts, and had decided to become a vegan. He refused to eat any animal products (but made an exception for ice cream). For the time being I gave up trying to home-school the boys and just accepted that they were learning more through their own experiences than they ever could through books.

A muralist traveled with us. In six cities across the country, he created spectacular murals of endangered species on the walls of multi-story buildings. We held ceremonies to dedicate these works of art, complete with original music from one of the three musical groups traveling with us. The handprints of local schoolchildren and the footprints of our walkers decorated the bottom borders of the murals, linking us all together in a visible way.

The Walk went through many hardships (including running out of money in the California desert in sub-freezing temperatures). But by our own creativity we survived and thrived. Minor miracles happened often, such as on the day our terrific cooks quit. How would we eat? Not everyone knows how to cook vegetarian meals for 150 people out of a mobile kitchen on a tight budget.

But lo and behold! As we walked down the highway that day, a van passed by. The driver looked hard, made a quick U-turn, and returned to our group. The man who stepped out had had lots of experience cooking for even larger groups, and he joined us on the spot. We came to expect this kind of miracle in our daily lives.

Everything was not so rosy, however. Jon (my common-law husband of 13 years) and I grew further and further apart during the Walk. We were both involved in key organizational roles, and it seemed there was almost no time in the day for us to stay connected. I convened the steering committee that represented the work teams, set the weekly goals for the group, and did constant problem solving. Jon was the key technological support person on the Walk. He made sure the solar panels, computers, and vehicles were running in top form. (Jon even built the Walk's kitchen from a converted racecar trailer, and set up satellite communication with environmentalists in Australia.)

In July, as we walked down the steaming back roads of Missouri, Jon confessed that he had fallen in love with another woman. After an agonizing month of confusion, we broke up. I spent many days crying on the shoulders of friends as we walked our 20 miles, trying to figure out what had gone wrong. It was an excruciatingly painful time.

Meanwhile the Walk went on. During the course of our nine-month trek, we visited a number of intentional communities, Arcosanti (near Flagstaff, Arizona) being the most famous. Paolo Soleri, an Italian architect, founded the community. Inspired by the Italian hill villages where he had grown up, Soleri had envisioned creating a city for 5,000 people in one huge interconnected building. Fertile gardens and wilderness area were to surround the settlement.

About 50 people lived at Arcosanti when we visited it. The members ran a successful Elder Hostel program, and a cottage industry produced Soleri's world famous bells and wind chimes. The buildings themselves were inspirational, with glorious vaulted roofs and passive solar design that kept them warm in winter and cool in summer. Joan was very taken with the concept of centralized housing combined with lots of open space. We did wonder, though, about the wisdom of having one person provide all the leadership in such a big undertaking.

As we traveled Joan continued to gather lessons and ideas from many sources. I remember her great enthusiasm one night as we sat by the campfire outside St. Louis. She showed several of us a book she had just bought: *Cohousing: A Contemporary Approach to Housing Ourselves*, by architects Kathryn McCamant and Charles Durrett (Habitat Press, 1988). The husband and wife team had taken a year and toured Denmark, staying with communities that shared many common spaces while retaining private homeownership.

"This is it!" Joan proclaimed. "This is the model we can use for the social part of the city I want to create." As Joan extolled her idea of building an ecological city of 50,000, I remember thinking, What a pipe dream. That's too big to ever happen.

As we talked I raised my doubts about such an ambitious project. "Maybe you're right," she reflected. "Maybe I'll start out with five thousand people." It still seemed far too big to me.

But the idea continued to develop and was eventually winnowed down to a village of 500 people. As the idea became more realistic, I grew more interested. But I was still reeling from my personal crisis and gave little attention to such a grand scheme.

MOVING ON

After the Global Walk, I went back to San Francisco, and Joan returned to her hometown of Ithaca, New York. When she gave an "EcoVillage vision" speech at the Unitarian church in May 1991, she was amazed to find an excited audience of about 100 people. She quickly laid plans for a five-day retreat near the end of June to build on that enthusiasm. I was asked to facilitate and accepted the invitation.

Then I received a second call from Joan. "Liz, will you move here from San Francisco to help me build this EcoVillage?" My heart thumping, I knew the answer was yes. But I asked for a little more time to think.

I climbed the Bernal Heights hill, just a few blocks from where I lived. The top glows with golden California poppies and other drought-resistant wildflowers. Its commanding view of the whole city includes the Golden Gate Bridge, Twin Peaks, and the blue East Bay hills that encircle the winding bay. After drinking in the grandeur of the view, I closed my eyes and meditated on Joan's request. The answer was crystal clear: Yes, this is my next step. This is the best way I can use my talents to create a better world.

At the same time as my spirit was saying yes, my mind was busy sorting out practicalities. What would it mean to move 3,000 miles away from home and leave my friends of the past 15 years? And what about all my colleagues in the peace and environmental movement? I would need money to live. It would be a huge change for my kids and me. What if the project didn't succeed? I felt as if I was poised on the edge of a cliff, being asked to fly.

I called Joan back and told her I would decide after the June retreat. I wanted to make sure that there was a large group of motivated people, enough money to pay me a small salary, and a strong likelihood that the project would succeed.

The Envisioning Retreat

The third week in June arrived, and I flew out from San Francisco to facilitate the retreat. We planned to bring together other people who were excited about building an ecovillage, learn about some of the possibilities, and begin an organization. Little did I know what an enormous job that would turn out to be!

About 100 adults and children from all over the country gathered under large white tents erected in a field a few miles from Ithaca. A few people stayed at the B&B owned by our hosts, but most camped out in colorful tents reminiscent of those we used during the Global Walk.

A wizard of all things technical, Jon was once again the key logistical support person. In fact he reused the kitchen trailer from the Walk, and we hired the same skilled cooks to make all our meals. Jon also used the 500-gallon (1,900-liter) portable tanks from the Walk to supply all our water, and he set up a simple graywater system for us.

We invited Philip Bennett (a local leader in the field) to lead a two-day workshop in co-counseling before we began the envisioning process. Co-counseling or reevaluation counseling provides a framework for people to express emotion safely and respectfully. Individuals take turns, supporting each other to experience and then release their feelings. Usually people find the process clears their minds and helps them make more rational decisions — a valuable outcome for any group work. Philip's workshop set a powerful tone of community for the five-day process that followed.

Presentations filled the first few days. Joan shared her vision of an ecovillage composed of densely clustered cohousing neighborhoods surrounded by plenty of open space and an organic farm. Italian architect Tulio Inglese inspired us with images of Italian hill villages with their strong sense of community, winding pedestrian streets, and nearby farm fields and vineyards. Marcia Forte, a black woman who ran a local community center, spoke powerfully about diversity and the need to include many types of people right from the beginning. Bart Conta, a professor at Cornell, introduced us to solar energy technologies.

People became restless, however, and a strong democratic spirit bubbled up. Nobody wanted to hear any more presentations. They wanted to take part in the action, to talk nuts and bolts about principles and values, decision-making structures, and the site plan. Most of all, they wanted the organization to be their own, not Joan's.

There was a low-key revolt, and the retreat energy shifted. As the sole facilitator I felt like a surfer. I had caught the big wave and was hanging on for dear life, trying to channel the excitement and energy in a productive direction.

In the end we scrapped the carefully planned agenda and improvised. Spontaneously formed committees met to talk about where to purchase land, how to craft a mission statement, and how to incorporate everything from green building technologies to organic agriculture. The committees then reported back to the whole group, and we debated some of our top priorities, including whether our proposal should include a health care facility or an education center.

By the end of the five days I was dizzy with exhaustion. But I was also grinning from ear to ear. An organization had been born! Joan Bokaer and I would serve as co-directors of the EcoVillage at Ithaca organization, along with Tim Allen as a staff associate. The whole enterprise would fall under the aegis of the Center for Religion, Ethics, and Social Policy (a nonprofit affiliated with Cornell University).

One man, a local attorney, stood up at the end of the retreat and said, "I don't want to go home." It was a common sentiment. Already a strong sense of community pervaded the

A pedestrian village would not only address most of the major ecological problems of our times, but could also improve the quality of our lives. A highly interactive social life of diverse people would flourish in a setting of clustered housing with some shared resources, a mixed-use human-scale village center and lots of open land. It would address many of the problems faced by modern families such as a chronic time crunch, isolation, and lack of care for young children and the elderly. In addition, energy-efficient housing, the sharing of many resources, the lack of needing to own a car, and the production of food on-site can push the cost of living way down.

— Joan Bokaer,
"The Ecological Imperative,"
EcoVillage at Ithaca Newsletter,
August 1991 ∎

group. We had listened and argued and made decisions together. We had prepared and eaten meals together. And we had camped out under the stars together for the week of the summer solstice, illuminated by the flashing, dancing lights of fireflies. What more could anyone want?

By now it was clear to me that I was meant to help create this ecovillage. My criteria had been met: A large group of dedicated people had coalesced into a community. And the project seemed poised for success. But what about the money?

I didn't need to worry. Just before the retreat Joan had received a $60,000 check from a local benefactor. Some of that money could be set aside for staff salaries for the two of us. Not only that, but when we asked for pledges at the end of the retreat, ordinary people who were strapped for cash came up with hundreds of dollars. One couple handed me a check for $1,200 and told me they loved the strong yet nurturing leadership that Joan and I provided. I knew then that the vision would carry itself financially.

FOLLOWING THROUGH

The next two months passed in a blur. The energy of the envisioning retreat continued in full force. Eight committees met weekly or biweekly, harnessing the energy and good ideas of many people.

Meanwhile Jon and I flew back to San Francisco, collected our kids from their grandparents, and began packing up our lives. Although Jon's love affair was over and we had gone through couples counseling, he had no interest in getting back together. We still maintained a good working relationship, however.

Jon was committed to helping raise the children, so he decided to move to Ithaca, too. He drove across the country in a 22-foot Hertz-Penske moving van loaded with our life's possessions and his plumbing, computer, and solar equipment. All this while towing his own van behind! I drove my ancient Toyota station wagon, carrying our two children and Lars (a Danish student), who helped out with driving and gas money.

Although there was a severe drought in the Northeast and the grass was turning brown in places, to me the landscape seemed moist. After the dry grasslands of California, the waterfalls and green trees were like a blessing. I drank it all in: the wetness, the greenness, and the sense of community and purpose in our fledgling organization.

Buying the Land

We held our next big meeting at the fall equinox (late September), a mere month after I had moved to Ithaca. Many committees put an enormous effort into preparing for the well-choreographed event. Sixty-six adults and 20 children from all over New York State got together at a local school for a weekend of information sharing and decision making. Bob Schloss from Westchester County and I facilitated. Aside from some tense moments, things mostly went smoothly.

As the children built an ecovillage out of blocks, we adults tackled more serious topics. We needed to adopt the proposed Principles and Statement of Purpose of the organization. We had to decide on a time-line for the development of the bylaws and the election of the Board of Directors. Most importantly, we needed to decide whether or not to make a purchase offer on 176 acres (71 hectares) of land on West Hill.

CHOOSING THE SITE

The land search committee had checked out various sites in and around Ithaca. Someone had even offered us a piece of land for free if we would build them a house. But the land was ten miles away from Ithaca. That would create more of a commute for future residents (an environmental issue) and make it harder for visitors and students to visit.

We also had an option to convert an old gun factory into an ecovillage. The factory sat right in the middle of the city, making it very accessible. But there would be no open space for farming.

The site committee itself preferred a large, open parcel of land a mile and a half from the city but still in the Town of Ithaca. The West Hill site had beautiful views, pockets of rich agricultural soil, and open rolling meadows. No

It is remarkable how this project is taking off. In my 15 years as a grassroots organizer and organizational consultant, I have never before witnessed such energetic growth combined with such a group of highly talented, passionately dedicated people. There is no question that the time is ripe, the place is right, and the people resources are superb. The fact that several other ecovillages are in the formative stages around the country shows that we are part of a cutting-edge movement. EcoVillage at Ithaca will have brother and sister communities, each unique, yet each sharing a vision of a vibrant new way of living on the Earth.

— Journal entry,
September 1, 1991 ∎

trees would have to be cut down to build homes — an environmental bonus, since some other proposed sites were densely forested and would have to be logged.

To help people clarify their ideas before making a decision, I asked everyone to participate in an exercise. First I drew an imaginary line down the long school hallway. One end represented rural sites that were five or more miles from Ithaca. The other end represented the gun factory site, right in Ithaca. The middle represented sites that were semi-rural, within one or two miles of Ithaca. Then I asked people to stand on the line where they thought we should build.

It was dramatic! Some 60 participants milled around for a minute and then stood still. Virtually no one wanted to build at the gun factory, and only one couple advocated building five miles or more from Ithaca. Everyone else had opted for a semi-rural site. The simple exercise pointed the way. While we were deciding to make an offer on the West Hill site, a janitor came by and told us we had to be out of the building in just five minutes.

Photo courtesy of EVI
The farm pond at EcoVillage at Ithaca.

A few vocal people wanted to talk more, but we were out of time. I knew that if we called another meeting, we would lose most of our out-of-town participants, who had traveled up to five hours to attend. I made a hurried executive decision: We had agreed to use modified consensus at the beginning of the weekend, and a straw poll showed that we had a clear mandate from more than 90 percent of the group. Therefore we had made a decision.

Looking back, the decision still seems right. Sadly, after the meeting, several people dropped out because they felt the process wasn't good enough. It was the beginning of a slow winnowing process. As the organization defined itself, some people became disillusioned and left. Yet the decision to buy the West Hill property unleashed a flurry of excitement and activity for the rest of us.

RAISING THE MONEY

The asking price on the land was $800,000. An interim Board member bargained the owner down to half of that, and we thought we had a great deal. (We found out later that the property was probably worth closer to $200,000.)

We agreed to put $20,000 toward the purchase price, using some of the large donation we had received before the envisioning retreat. The remaining $40,000 from that donation would cover attorney's fees and closing costs for the land purchase, as well as support an office and staff salaries for the following two years. That meant we'd have to raise $380,000. It seemed a monumental amount to someone like me, who was used to supporting a family of four on an activist's salary of about $10,000 a year.

Joan and I began strategizing about how to raise money. We had no organization to approach, but Joan had attracted a number of wealthy friends in the course of her national speaking tours on the arms race. And I knew a few people of means who might also help.

Joan and I used our co-counseling skills to bolster our confidence. We took turns role playing. First I pretended to be the fundraiser, approaching Joan as the prospect. Then we reversed roles. When it was my turn to make an imaginary call, I broke out in a cold sweat and shivered with barely suppressed fear. Joan, playing the potential lender, would give me a hard time. At some point we always gave up and howled with laughter. I don't think I've ever laughed so hard in my life. My stomach ached after these sessions.

After making a long list of possible lenders, we turned from imaginary calls to real ones. Joan had many more contacts than I did and raised the lion's share, but I was happy to help with the people I knew. In the end ten people loaned us the entire amount. And we did it all in the record time of just six weeks!

Now came the tough part — figuring out the appropriate legal vehicle to carry the loans. That took us another nine months. We ended up with two mortgages: one for $120,000 from a single source and another for $260,000 from a mortgage pool composed of the nine other contributors.

A toxic contamination scare changed our plans somewhat. A neighboring antique store that also stripped furniture had had a problem with an overflowing septic tank, possibly contaminating a portion of the land. The Board of Directors, after much consideration, decided to return an acre surrounding the septic tank to the owners of the store, with the stipulation that no buildings could be constructed on that land. That brought our total holdings down to 175 acres.

Mortgages and meetings weren't all I was thinking about during this period. I was working in the office when I received one of the most important phone calls in my life. A man from Santa Cruz, California called. He was setting up a cohousing community there and wanted to visit and find out more about our project. On the phone his voice was deep and resonant, and he spoke with passion about the need for community. I wanted to meet him.

Jared Jones arrived at the office a few hours later, and we had an immediate and strong connection. He was handsome, confident, and warm. After chatting long after everyone else had gone home, I had the brilliant idea of inviting him to the first meeting of our process committee. I also invited him to dinner at my house.

Jared, a true community trouper, was undaunted by the idea of going to a meeting that night. He came to dinner, helping to cook and do dishes after our casual meal. And he contributed good ideas at the meeting. We returned to my house and sat in front of the woodstove, talking until midnight about everything from Earth-based spirituality to men's and women's groups to backpacking adventures in the Sierras. My initial impressions were confirmed: Here was a man I could really love.

There was a problem, however. Although I was tantalized by the possibility that he might move to Ithaca someday, Jared lived in California and was involved with another woman. The timing obviously wasn't right. Still I couldn't shake my attraction.

Meanwhile a lot happened during the nine months it took to put our financing in place. In January 1992 EVI received nonprofit status, held its first Annual Meeting, and elected a Board of Directors to conduct the organization's business. Then in March 1992 our cohousing group held its first meeting, as 50 people crowded into the large living room of one couple's home in Ithaca. There were only a few cohousing communities in the country at that time, and none of us had ever seen one. But that did not stop our enthusiastic group. We met every other week to begin planning how we would form our community.

Finally on the summer solstice of June 1992, exactly a year after the envisioning retreat, the West Hill property was ours! Some of us camped out on the land that night. Others joined us in the morning, and we held a delightful ceremony. We sang, joined hands in a circle, and dedicated ourselves to the land. We wove ribbons into a net of dreams for the ecovillage and strung it between two trees. We feasted and gathered the first wild strawberries. I looked out over the meadows to the blue hills to the south and watched the mist rise. I felt in awe of this magical place we would soon inhabit.

CHAPTER 2

PEOPLE AND THE LAND

North Americans are probably the most mobile people who have ever lived. One-seventh of the US population — 10 million households — moves every year. The pioneer ancestors who pushed ever Westward to conquer the "wilderness" have left us a dangerous legacy. The wilderness is gone, but we haven't stopped moving. By now so many of us feel isolated or dislocated that it doesn't seem to matter if a strip mall goes in down the road or yet another subdivision gobbles up a farm. Without a sense of the land as sacred and with little or no connection to nature or a particular place, we lose a precious part of our souls.

Unlike most other North Americans, we are actively cultivating a sense of place. We are learning to slow down and sink our roots deep into the soil. This is our home. We are in place.

Once we had purchased the land, the next step was to figure out what to do with it. We had to decide where to build the village, where to situate the farm, and what acreage to leave untouched. We also had to pay off that whopping mortgage.

We entered an intensive and participatory land use planning process that involved many people, hours of research, and multiple meetings. Everyone felt the need to connect deeply with this place. And what a place it was!

Ithaca

The Finger Lakes region of upstate New York is spectacular. From the air it looks like the handprint of a giant laid down in wet clay: Lake

Ontario forms the heel of the palm, with long skinny fingers reaching southward. The striking blue of deep water fills the handprint, and lush greenery covers the steep ridges between the fingers.

Cayuga Lake, the middle finger, is the longest of the lakes and 435 feet (133 meters) deep. Carved out by a two-mile-thick glacier that retreated 10,000 years ago, the finger points to the small bustling city of Ithaca. Thirty thousand year-round residents and 24,000 students call Ithaca home.

Three hundred years ago the place was called Coreogonal and was inhabited by Tutelos and Cayugas — part of the Six Nations of the Iroquois Confederacy. Tragically in 1779 Continental Army soldiers destroyed Coreogonal and its people. Under orders to eliminate anyone who had supported the British during the Revolutionary War, the soldiers killed the inhabitants and burned their homes and crops. I imagine that the land still carries echoes of this genocide.

To my mind the Iroquois make good role models. They valued female leadership, used a consensus-based form of decision making, and became well known for their lasting pact of peace between feuding nations. Their innovative form of governance was even an important model in the development of the US Constitution. I feel proud to live near an early Native settlement and to carry on some of their traditions.

By 1790 the frontier had opened to pioneers — mostly soldiers who received large parcels of land in exchange for their military service. Apparently the early community of Ithaca was a lively place and was known as "Sodom" and "Sin City" for quite some time. But in 1817, when Ithaca became the county seat, it turned much more respectable. Businesses and churches popped up, and a commitment to education encouraged Ezra Cornell (with a fortune made from the telegraph industry) to create Cornell University on farmland located on East Hill.

Today Ithaca shines as a jewel in the Finger Lakes region. *Organic Style Magazine* called Ithaca "the best healthy city in the Northeast" (October 2003). Not only is Ithaca relatively unpolluted, says the article, but it also sports "a lively mix of academics from Cornell University and Ithaca College, vintners, organic farmers and preservationists, artists, musicians, and a community that teems with theater, politics, art festivals, and music." Even more impressive, in June 1997, *Utne Reader* ranked Ithaca at number one on their list of the "Ten Most Enlightened Towns in the US"

Remarkable scenery matches the lively and progressive local culture. Streams and waterfalls thread Ithaca's densely packed but attractively small downtown area. Bumper stickers proudly proclaim "Ithaca is Gorges" and "Ithaca, NY: 10 Square Miles Surrounded by Reality." There are more waterfalls here than people can even name. Some are truly amazing. Taughannock Falls, the highest free-falling waterfall in the East is even higher than Niagara Falls.

Steep hills surround the city on three sides. To the north the blue-gray waters of Cayuga Lake shimmer in the sun. On East Hill, Cornell University presides with its large green campus, historic buildings, and signature clock tower. On South Hill, the twin white towers of Ithaca College provide another seat of higher education. And on the brow of West Hill, just two miles from downtown Ithaca, EcoVillage sits amidst its 175 acres of rolling open meadows, streams, ponds, and woods.

EVI offers yet another form of education — one that includes an intense exploration of environmental and social sustainability for residents, students, and visitors alike.

EVI did not always grace West Hill, of course. Many people have expended a great deal of effort to develop our ecovillage to its present state. Back in our early days, when we first started to work with the land, we had to start from scratch.

The Land Use Planning Process

In June 1992, at the same time as we purchased the West Hill property, we formed a Planning Council. The Council met for three hours every Monday afternoon to research and plan how best to use the land.

Liz Walker

Waterfall at Tremain State Park, one of Ithaca's many beautiful gorges.

Ten people sat on the Council, including two local architects (one of whom, Don Ellis, we hired as a consultant), a landscape architect, a biologist, several Cornell graduate students, and a sprinkling of future village residents. I acted as chair. (Becoming chair was one of those scenarios that became typical in my career as Director of EcoVillage. I had no prior experience of the task at hand nor expertise in any relevant specialized field except group process. Yet somehow I found myself in charge of this group of diverse, highly skilled, strongly opinionated people.)

As it turned out, my intuitive and participatory leadership style served the Council well. Although Don Ellis had experience in the design process, our project was different from most. Our research and design process by necessity drew on multiple disciplines ranging from architecture to water management. My job became one of coordination, as together we gleaned ideas from the different disciplines and tried to synthesize them into a coherent program and a timeline.

Soon it became obvious that we needed to present our findings to the larger group. Not only did they need to be informed, but they also needed to take an active part in any decision making. So we decided to set aside an entire weekend to do just that, and the first Land Use Planning Forum was born.

I looked forward to having a finished land use plan in place by the end of the weekend. Was I in for a surprise!

THE FIRST LAND USE PLANNING FORUM

The first EcoVillage Land Use Planning Forum (or LUPF, as it was affectionately termed) was held on a weekend in late September 1992, just three months after purchasing the land. The result of major preparation, the forum was a smashing success. It brought together the members of the Planning Council, more than 60 participants from the EcoVillage community, and a wide range of local professionals.

For weeks beforehand, the Planning Council task forces feverishly gathered information on various aspects of the land, which we then organized into six topic areas: agriculture, natural areas and recreation, neighborhood siting, transportation, village siting, and water/waste management. A convenor was assigned to each topic area to organize relevant material and invite local experts to act as resource people. We also hired Steve Blais, a young architect, to produce a series of CAD maps (computer-assisted drafting) that would show the land's topography, soil types, wind flows, existing streams and ponds, and more.

Our goals were:

1. to educate the EcoVillage community by sharing information about the land and the issues involved in siting the various elements of the village (roads, waterways, neighborhoods);
2. to record areas of agreement and disagreement; and
3. to decide on a site for the 1993 EcoVillage community garden.

To meet our goals, we would ask participants to divide into six smaller interest groups to study the information (one group for each of the six topic areas) and come up with community-based decisions. Appropriate resource people would be on hand, and the beautiful CAD maps would be posted around the meeting room for reference. Linda Schade (one of the Cornell graduate students on the Council) would put together a crew to videotape the forum's proceedings, with a plan to show an edited version on our local public access TV station at a later date. Once the Council had come up with the "what" of the forum, the "how" of it was left up to the program committee.

The Facilitators

I planned to facilitate the weekend with Jay Jacobson, a research plant physiologist at the Boyce Thompson Institute (connected with Cornell University). We made a good team, even though our different styles sometimes made it challenging for us to work together. Jay is a very thorough and orderly man, whereas I tend to take a more intuitive and spontaneous approach. Jay finds it hard to be assertive, whereas I take charge easily. On the other hand, Jay's penchant for scientific detail grounds my enthusiastic energy. The program committee worked with us to put together an exciting and creative plan for our forum.

When the weekend finally arrived and I was checking off all the last-minute details, I was filled with a potent mixture of excitement and trepidation. Yet underneath the surface of my emotions was a soothing sense of calm. I felt that a larger purpose was guiding us at a crucial moment in our history.

The Weekend

The forum convened Saturday morning at the local Alternative Community School, which had graciously offered their facilities for the weekend.

After a rousing talk from Joan Bokaer about the vision of the village, each interest group made a brief presentation. Following the presentations, ecologist Chuck Mohler from Cornell introduced the basic ecology of the site. And Scott Whitham, a landscape architect, introduced the land use planning process. The morning's activities helped provide a theoretical context for the group to keep in mind as they took part in the more experiential activities planned for the rest of the weekend.

After lunch the interest groups carpooled up to the land to tramp the site and then reconvened inside for discussion. The process seemed to work well and sparked several key recommendations that would affect the overall plan for EcoVillage. My group, for example, which looked at neighborhood siting, recommended that we cluster all five neighborhoods in one area, limiting each to an area no larger than three or four acres (1.2 to 1.6 hectares). We knew that some other cohousing neighborhoods had successfully clustered 30 homes on just three acres. We tested our recommendation by taking a walk on the EVI land site and staking out circles of approximately the right size. It seemed cozy but doable.

The air has a biting freshness after a rainstorm on this cool fall day. Mist rises over fields of goldenrod. As a lone hawk circles lazily overhead, children shriek wildly at play. All the while six clusters of adults walk the land, talking intently. They are ecologists and architects, teachers and planners, students and parents. They carry maps outlining topography, soils, hedgerows, and watercourses. Even more they carry lifelong convictions about healing the Earth. Together this group is taking a giant step in the evolution of EVI.

— Journal entry
September 1992 ∎

The water group made another key recommendation when it suggested that water be the starting point for all other planning. Phil Snyder, the director of the Finger Lakes Land Trust, convened the water group, and under his direction the group looked at the land's water sources and how we could protect and enhance our water's life-enhancing properties. They suggested that we cleanse our water through a series of ponds and marshes. And they made the point that ponds could also be used for swimming, for raising fish, for irrigation, to mitigate the effects of droughts and floods, and as a home for wildlife. Ponds would also slow down the movement of water over the land, thus helping to recharge the aquifer below. (With his extensive knowledge of natural systems, Snyder also served as a mentor to Joan and helped to shape the overall land use plan.)

As the remaining groups reported back to the larger group, they added their varying suggestions and recommendations, too. The agriculture group, for example, which was convened by our young farmers Jen and John Bokaer-Smith, studied soils, microclimates, and slopes. They came up with a plan that would create a beautiful interplay of orchards, vegetable gardens, and hay fields.

As each group spoke, I had the sense that a weaving was in progress: Each report added a bit more color and dimension to the planning process. Each group had made use of background information and what they knew about EcoVillage needs and had added that to input from our expert resource people to expand their knowledge base. And each group had drawn on their kinesthetic experience of the site itself to help shape their suggestions for a program or set of desired elements specific to their topic area. The group discussions ended the afternoon portion of our first day.

On Saturday evening we enjoyed two presentations. The first was a video on Poona, India, a community that makes creative use of limited water resources. The second was an excellent slideshow by Phil Snyder, on the Filipino tribe known as the Ifugao. The tribe uses a highly sophisticated and carefully regulated irrigation system to water their terraced fields, a system that has enabled them to be self-sustaining for over 5,000 years. The two presentations added to our understanding of the importance of water and rounded out Saturday's activities.

Sunday morning we reconvened and held a "rotating fishbowl" to further discuss our plans for the land. We set up a semicircle of chairs in front of the large group — one seat for each of the interest groups, plus one representing economics and affordability. As facilitators, Jay and I added a fun touch: Each member of the "fishbowl" received a hat labeled with the name of their interest group. Then, whenever a member of the audience wanted to chime in, he or she would simply replace the member of the fishbowl by literally putting on the right hat. People were totally engaged in the process, and I couldn't believe how well the weekend was working!

Sunday afternoon we carpooled up to the land for a wrap-up of the weekend. In a final ritual, planned by future residents Pam June and

Monty Berman, the group came together in a circle, spiraling in and out as the sun reappeared after a brief cloudburst.

The forum had been an outstanding success. Tom Johnson, a Cornell professor in landscape architecture who had participated with five students from his landscape design studio class, called the forum "a triumph in creating a sense of shared meaning in the project through community participation." I had to agree. Clearly we had reached agreement on many issues. And clearly we had also just begun.

The Planning Council was charged with articulating the conclusions of the group. And my idea of having a complete plan in place in just one weekend turned out to have been terribly naïve. Even so, by the time the first LUPF was over, the next stage of our journey had begun.

THE GUIDELINES FOR DEVELOPMENT

Our first LUPF led to other plans, and over the next nine months we held three more weekend forums. I stayed on as chair of the Planning Council, which had oversight of six different subcommittees that continued to research affordability, agriculture, diversity, an education center, energy, natural areas, residential buildings, and water/wastewater.

Each subcommittee worked hard to figure out solutions appropriate to the EcoVillage site. For example, the agriculture committee held a forum on agricultural models. They wanted to know if the community would rather participate in a commonly owned farm similar to an Israeli kibbutz or develop a privately owned farm supported by members (community-supported agriculture, or CSA). In another project, the natural areas committee undertook a plant species survey with Chuck Mohler from Cornell. I remember sitting in the middle of a field and counting the number of goldenrod plants in a square yard. Our discussions and decisions as a group during this time seemed charged with electrical energy, and we felt the sheer creative power of invention.

Our efforts ultimately bore rich fruit. Nine months and four LUPFs later, in June 1993, the EcoVillage community came to consensus on a comprehensive eight-page document, titled "Guidelines for Development." A huge achievement, the "Guidelines" covered all aspects of life at our future EcoVillage, from environmental goals and objectives to broad social goals having to do with affordability, diversity, and community. (Other cohousing communities and ecovillages still in the formation stage have also used the "Guidelines" as a resource document.) Finally we had a shared community vision that belonged to all of us.

THE ENVISIONING PLAN

The "Guidelines" gave us a text-based reference document, but they only constituted part of a bigger record of our intentions. "The Envisioning Plan" (developed in a somewhat parallel process by Joan Bokaer, Phil Snyder, and local architect Pam Williams) provided us with a visual representation of our proposed development (see the frontispiece for an updated version of the original). Beautifully hand-drawn, the map set out the placement of all proposed development at EVI, including its several neighborhoods, West Haven farm, habitat restoration area, greenhouses, pathways, ponds, woods, education center, and more.

When I saw the "Envisioning Plan," I felt the power of an image to galvanize action. I thought of the famous photo of the Earth that was taken from space. That image, showing the blue and white swirling ball of planet Earth against the black backdrop of space, revolutionized how we looked at our planet and helped to catalyze the environmental movement. Pam's sensitive artistry and the work of the team had also produced a powerful image, one that became a wonderful icon for our project. The EcoVillage "Envisioning Plan" crystallized the intent of our vision and showed us what we were working toward.

With the land use planning process completed and the "Guidelines" and "Envisioning Plan" in hand, all we needed to do was move forward and create the reality. Oh yes, and pay off our huge mortgage.

Paying Off the Land

Our original payback plan didn't work. When we first purchased the land in 1992, EVI's Board of Directors met with a banker and a businessman to negotiate a schedule for repayment. At that time we agreed that our number-one priority should be to establish our first neighborhood before starting to make payments on the principal and interest — a period we estimated would take three years. Then, once the first neighborhood was up and running, we would make annual payments of $30,000 to the lenders. And, as each new neighborhood came onstream, it would help with the payments. The plan seemed reasonable and easy, but nothing went according to plan.

The First Resident Group (FROG)

We ran into massive cost overruns during the construction of the first neighborhood (September 1995 – August 1997). We held emergency meetings, considered firing our builder or scrapping our Common House or pond. Tempers ran high as people blamed the builder, who in turn blamed the Town for adding unanticipated infrastructure costs with its requirements for an extra-wide entry road and a seemingly unnecessary long emergency access road.

When tempers finally settled, it was clear that the first neighborhood (nicknamed FROG, for "First Resident Group") faced cost overruns of about $20,000 per house. They could not afford to put any money into repaying our lenders for the EcoVillage land. Instead EVI, the nonprofit, agreed to give FROG 35 acres for free, allowing construction to continue. FROG residents grimly tightened their belts and poured more sweat equity into the project.

The situation caused some unfortunate fallout. Although EVI contacted the lenders to explain the situation and assure them that their collateral (the land) had risen in value with the installation of the road, water, and sewer, a massive fault line had developed in the project. No longer were we blithely self-confident that everything would work out. The distrust between our builder and many residents never healed. And some highly vocal residents blamed the nonprofit for being in arrears on payments to the lenders — a startlingly unfair accusation, to my mind, since EVI had bailed out the resident group, but unfortunately the accusation stuck.

Generous Gifts

EcoVillage finances were alarming. Unbeknownst to us, though, some unexpected help was on the way from some of our members. Mary and Bill Webber were among the nine members of the mortgage pool who had contributed $260,000 toward the purchase of the land. The couple came from St. Louis and first heard of the EcoVillage concept when the Global Walk went through Missouri. (Mary walked with us for about a week, and I was impressed by her enthusiasm and dedicated work for racial equality and social justice.)

After Bill (a surgeon) retired, the Webbers decided to move to EVI. Soon after, Mary was hired as the Director of CRESP (the nonprofit that helped EVI get its start). And Bill, who loved volunteering for sweat equity construction projects, also became our resident videographer and newsletter production person.

When Mary and Bill realized how financially rocky EVI was they generously forgave their $130,000 loan, (see EcoVillage at Ithaca Timeline) plus all accrued interest. It was an amazing gift! And it came with one small string attached. They asked that in acknowledgment of their gift, 55 acres (22 hectares) of EcoVillage land (the equivalent portion of the land secured by their loan) be set aside in a permanent conservation easement.

The request was easy to fulfill, since it followed the EcoVillage philosophy of preserving land in its natural state or for organic agriculture. Under the terms of our agreement, EVI would continue to own the land and pay taxes on it. The Finger Lakes Land Trust would administer the conservation easement, ensuring that it remained open space in perpetuity.

The Webbers' gift led to a ripple effect. Over the following eight years, five members of the mortgage pool (including the Webbers) generously forgave a total of $165,000 of principal — an amount equal to 43 percent of EVI's entire land debt! Ironically the gift also caused a few people in the residents' group to feel resentful. They wondered why the couple should bail out the nonprofit and labeled the action as enabling behavior. Most people, however, recognized that the gift was intended to create a stable financial base upon which the larger EVI project could build.

THE "SOUL" PARTNERSHIP

Even with the Webbers' generosity, the nonprofit faced very difficult circumstances. The first neighborhood took not three years, but five years to build from the first meeting until the final nail was pounded in. We got into further financial trouble when one of our major lenders decided to foreclose on his mortgage.

Harry was one of EVI's original lenders but did not belong to the

This morning, with snow falling gently and steadily and a winter storm watch in place, I decide not to go to work. Instead I follow my heart's desire and ski out of my front yard and onto our pristine 175 acres of land. Yesterday's ice storm has encased each twig and goldenrod stem in a quarter-inch sleeve of ice. And each cluster of bright red rose hips on the multiflora roses is its own brilliant crystal, capped with fluffy white snow. I make the first tracks in this ocean of white, feeling perfectly at home in solitude.

— Journal entry
Winter 2003 ∎

mortgage pool. Instead he had secured his $120,000 loan through a separate mortgage and under a different set of terms. Despite the fact that he was a millionaire, Harry decided to foreclose when he received no payment after five years. A flurry of activity ensued.

As one of two staff people coordinating the nonprofit, I felt personally responsible for the crisis. I myself had never been in debt, never had a mortgage and, on general principles, had never even owned a credit card. I was mortified by our position and took on the role of trying to find someone who could buy Harry out. During this time, I remember going for long walks by the thundering Ithaca Falls, just a couple of blocks away from my rental house downtown. As I heard the cascading water, I felt my headache ease, my shoulders lift, and my sense of panic subside. Somehow, somehow, we would get through this crisis.

It took over a year to solve the foreclosure problem. Various people offered to loan money to buy Harry out, only to pull out at the last possible moment. Perhaps they realized it was a very risky venture. Or perhaps one or the other spouse in a couple objected to the investment. Whatever the case, three different loan packages came together and dissolved on the eve of signing the final documents.

As loan after loan fell through, I realized I had to buy us some time. I met with Harry and, after a difficult negotiation, he agreed to give me a year to pull a new rabbit out of the hat. He also reluctantly offered to forgo any interest on his loan, as long as he got back the principal. I was thankful for the reprieve and continued my search for a new lender.

The year was almost up, and I had just about given up hope, when a solution presented itself. Cisela (an energetic Swedish woman who believed in miracles) got a group together that was willing to help out. Dubbed "SOUL Partnership" (for "Save Our Unlimited Land"), five future residents offered to lend us $108,000. That left us only $12,000 short, and a non-resident man I talked to agreed to invest the remaining amount.

We were golden, and not a day too soon! On September 11, 1996 we all gathered in Jim Salk's office (our brilliant local *pro bono* attorney), to sign the papers. The crisis of the land debt had been temporarily averted.

Our money troubles were far from over, however. A few years later, a lender from the SOUL Partnership also threatened to foreclose. I had to cobble together some new last-minute loans and a fundraising campaign to bring his loan payment up to date. We clearly needed a more permanent solution to the land debt problem.

The Second Resident Group (SONG)

The one way to pay back the lion's share of the land debt was to build a second neighborhood (also part of our EcoVillage mission). The second neighborhood would purchase a chunk of land from EVI on which to build, and the money would be used to pay down the mortgage. I called a meeting of interested people in August 1996, before the homes in the first neighborhood were completed. About 15 people showed up, some from as far away as Pennsylvania.

I worked weekends and evenings for years, pulling SONG together. It would take three long years for this group to stabilize and grow to 20 families. Eventually Rod Lambert and I signed on as co-development managers, and the group hired an architect, developed a site design and building designs, and started to get Town approvals (see "FROG and SONG: Choices and Consequences" in Chapter Seven). And discussions began between FROG, SONG, and EVI (the nonprofit) to help determine a financial structure and come to agreement on how the three separate entities would share land and infrastructure (negotiations that would only begin to bear fruit several years later).

In 1999, three years into the process, the SONG group completely fell apart when its hoped-for affordable-housing funding did not materialize. Many people felt that they could not afford to put in the substantial risk money required to get to the building stage. Others lost trust in us as development managers when we were not able to produce money to subsidize the homes. When the dust settled only 3 of the original 20 families remained.

Things looked pretty grim. If we couldn't get a second neighborhood up and running, then there was a good chance that the whole EVI project would collapse. I could easily see the scenario: Angry lenders would foreclose on the land around the first neighborhood, and our little cohousing neighborhood would become an isolated pocket in a sea of tract housing. As co-development manager of SONG, I felt profoundly discouraged. Even my friends were telling me that what I was trying to do just couldn't be done.

But I knew in my bones that if we could just find some more investment capital, we could get SONG back on its feet and find new potential residents. And then, just as I was in despair not only over our finances but also over our very future, Chuck Mathei came to Ithaca.

THE EQUITY TRUST FUND

Chuck Mathei was the director of Equity Trust, a nonprofit organization whose mission is to encourage the formation of community land trusts (CLT). A CLT combines preservation of open space with affordable housing and organic agriculture. His work and our need seemed like a perfect match!

I set up Chuck's visit and, with co-sponsorship from many local groups, arranged speaking engagements for him at Cornell and EcoVillage. Chuck inspired all of us with his passionate reports about groups around the country who were using this relatively new model of land ownership. And he encouraged me to apply for a low-interest loan for SONG.

In October 2000, almost a year after SONG's original group dissolved, I was able to finalize a low-interest $100,000 loan from Equity Trust. Once some of the financial risk was taken away, SONG could finally take off. Wonderfully energetic and competent people from all over the country joined up, and by May 2002 SONG was well on its way to building EcoVillage's second neighborhood. And an agreement reached in 1998 would also soon come into effect.

THE ISLAND AGREEMENT

The "ISLAND Agreement" (the 1998 consensus decision named for

It is a cold spring day, and I am in despair. What went wrong? What if SONG doesn't get built? Will the mortgage holders foreclose? Perhaps this is the end of Eco-Village. Perhaps after all our work, sacrifice, and commitment we'll be left with one isolated neighborhood in a sea of tract houses and parking lots. I feel the dark mantle of failure rest heavily on my shoulders.

I pray for guidance, for help, for wisdom. I pray because I don't know what else to do. Surprisingly I hear a clear message: Your struggles are not over. It is going to take far longer than you ever imagined. But it is also going to be far better than you ever dreamed. SONG will unfold beautifully. Give it time.

I take off the dark mantle, shake it out, and put it back in place on a dusty imaginary shelf. I hug myself and rock gently back and forth, laughing and crying at the same time. Spirit is with us.

— Journal entry,
Spring 1999 ∎

"Infrastructure and Land") rose out of the lengthy negotiations between the two neighborhoods and the nonprofit, and spelled out how we would share land and infrastructure. The "ISLAND Agreement" put arrangements in place to deal with inflation and cost overruns, but more importantly would start to help out with our land debt. Recognizing that FROG had spent hundreds of thousands of dollars on infrastructure that would be used by the entire village, the "Agreement" called for SONG to spend an equal amount on land. The resulting monies could then be used to pay back a substantial portion of the mortgages. We were beginning to see light at the end of a very long tunnel.

THE "DEBT-FREE IN 2003" CAMPAIGN

Late in 2002, after I returned from a five-month sabbatical, I realized

that we were within spitting distance of paying off our loans — loans that had posed a tremendous psychic burden for years. When someone close to the project independently made an anonymous $30,000 gift to bring down the mortgage, it gave me the hope and confidence to launch a new campaign. I called it "Debt-Free in 2003" and put together a small committee of dedicated souls to help plan the campaign and a kick-off event.

When the day came for the Eco-Village Annual Meeting and the kick-off for the campaign, I felt excited and terribly nervous. Would the residents reject raising money for the nonprofit, as had happened with some in the past? Or would I be personally blamed (as Director of the nonprofit) for being in arrears on the mortgage payments? I didn't really know if the community would embrace the campaign, but I felt as if the future of the project rested on the answer.

Photo courtesy of EVI

An aerial view of EcoVillage, showing FROG (above), and SONG (still under construction.)

Our high-powered, fun event succeeded beyond my wildest hopes! The assembled crowd was thrilled to hear of the $30,000 contribution and even more thrilled by the fact that we had only $54,000 left to raise. The goal seemed achievable and the pledges rolled in. One woman, with few financial resources, contributed $1,000 on the spot. Another agreed to organize and cook two gourmet fundraising dinners. "Hilby, the Skinny German Juggle Boy," our resident professional performer (who had performed all over the world), agreed to donate the proceeds from one of his popular shows. One couple offered to donate double whatever money their son raised selling tickets for his school's spaghetti dinner. We were on a roll!

And the money kept coming. Over the next five months we raised an additional $23,000 from the sale of a one-acre lot on West Haven Road (a residential street bordering EVI land). I wrote our lenders to tell them about the campaign and about a Board member's pledge to donate $5,000 if they would forgive $10,000. And they did! The pledge spurred the Hepburns (a retired resident couple with the largest outstanding loan) to generously forgive $15,000. Four other lenders (Tad Baldwin, Monty Berman, Sara Pines, and Anne Zanes) together forgave another several thousand dollars.

I felt incredibly fulfilled. We had reached our goal of raising the full amount, and it was only June! I was reminded of what Goethe had to say about risk taking: "Whatever you can do, or dream you can, begin it. Boldness has genius, power, and magic in it. Begin it now." I keep this quote over my desk, and it has inspired me on many occasions to take the risk, no matter how unlikely the outcome may seem. Things looked good. But, as with many things at EcoVillage, the story wasn't over.

We still had some unexpected accounting issues to deal with. When one of the lenders prompted me to look more closely at the Excel spreadsheets for the loan, we discovered an accounting error of about $7,000 — and it was in the lenders' favor. And that wasn't all.

The cost of getting SONG up and running (time and construction costs) added up to more than what had been anticipated. Because the ISLAND Agreement accounted for cost overruns by splitting the difference between the three entities, the amount of money that SONG was scheduled to pay EVI suddenly dropped by about $16,000.

The upshot was that we needed to raise another $23,000 (plus interest for the year), if we were to clear the books on the land debt.

The task seemed monumental, given the fact that everyone who might be expected to give had already done so. Then a new proposal was brought forward, when someone suggested that we subdivide another lot on West Haven Road.

Although the idea caused some friction in the community, the EVI Board mostly loved it. Proceeds from the sale of a second lot could easily meet our remaining goal, and a few fundraising events could top off the remaining interest, solving our debt issues once and for all.

Some of the residents strongly supported the sale. Why not sell off peripheral land that was already on a built-up residential street? they asked. The land was outside of the farm fence and effectively blocked off from the rest of EcoVillage already. It would be the easiest, simplest solution.

But some of the residents did not agree. They argued that by subdividing and selling, we would be engaging in the very land use practices we were trying so hard to avoid.

Jen and John (our farmers) and Joan were all adamantly against the proposal. The first lot that had been sold bordered the farm, and when a modular house had suddenly gone up right next to the eggplants, some of the peaceful, rural quality of the farm was destroyed. They felt that another house next to the farm would further destroy the long views of the hills to the east. Once again, our community was deeply divided over a core issue. My heart sank, and my dreams of being "Debt-Free in 2003" gradually faded.

Another resident stepped into the debate with a compromise proposal. Deena Berke was a founding member, a former special education teacher, and had raised three children (now grown) as a single parent. She had recently inherited some family money, and had quit her job to pursue her real love — classical guitar. She would offer the community a $23,000 interest-free loan for up to four years. If each of our 60 households put in $8 per month over the four years to cover the repayment, then the money was ours.

Deena's proposal brought more controversy. Questions flew fast and furious. Why should the residents shoulder the burden of the last of the nonprofit's mortgage? For that matter, why should anyone be required to pay $8 a month? Especially in SONG, the repayment plan seemed like one more expense in an array of already uncontrollable cost overruns.

Stomach churning, I mapped out a strategy. The Board would delay its decision for a month, giving residents time to decide on whether or not to accept Deena's generous offer. (I knew the group, and a month was the bare minimum for creating consensus on a large financial issue that involved both neighborhoods.)

I asked each neighborhood group to discuss the offer at their separate meetings, and I introduced the topic at our quarterly Village Association meeting. Holding my breath, I also scheduled a special Village-wide meeting and issued an e-mail survey to test the waters.

I thought an agreement was a long shot, and I began to think about the long-term split that might develop between some of the residents and the EVI Board, should a second lot be sold. It seemed like a no-win position. But I was in for a surprise.

Things turned around at the special village-wide meeting. The people who were most vociferously opposed to Deena's proposal were willing to stand aside. One woman expressed strong opposition to the proposed monthly payment, feeling that it should be optional and not compulsory. Deena gave way on that condition, and we came to consensus. We would accept Deena's loan and work out the exact details later.

The decision was a momentous one. In a complete turnaround in attitude from the beginning of the EcoVillage project, our residents were taking responsibility in helping to pay off the land, and they were doing it by choice. Even though I still thought that selling off another lot was by far the simplest, easiest route to take, I loved the way that my friends and neighbors were stepping up to the plate and participating in shaping the overall project. To me, often isolated in my role as the lone staff person working for the nonprofit, the decision came as a huge relief. We were indeed Debt-Free in 2003. And somehow I felt that I was finally coming home.

On December 23, 2003, I wrote the final checks and paid off the mortgage. After almost 11½ years, the land was finally ours! Like a bird let out of a cage, the vision part of EcoVillage was free to soar.

CHAPTER 3

WEST HAVEN FARM

It is a clear summer day in mid-August. Jen and John work with a dozen helpers to bring in the day's harvest. They pick bright red and sun-gold tomatoes and three kinds of beans. Huge heads of romaine, green leaf, and butter lettuce overflow their containers. Zucchini, patty pan, and yellow summer squashes abound, along with purple shiny-skinned eggplants. The air in the barn is redolent with the aroma of herbs — dill, basil, and cilantro.

Everyone works quickly. Soon the farm's 179 shareholders will come to pick up their weekly allotment of organically grown produce. People will stop and chat with friends, as children play in the sandbox. And they will pick bright bouquets from the cutting garden to add color and scent to their homes. The bounty of this place will find its way to kitchens and tables throughout the EcoVillage community and beyond.

West Haven Farm was the first part of the EcoVillage vision to manifest. Established by Jen and John Bokaer-Smith, the 10-acre (4-hectare) farm is certified organic by the Northeast Organic Farming Association (NOFA). Unlike other farms, it will never feel the pressure of developers eager to create another subdivision, since it is protected by EVI's permanent conservation easement. The farm is also a Community Supported Agriculture (CSA) farm.

A CSA farm creates a web of connection between people and the land. By joining a CSA, people can enjoy organic seasonal food produced close to home at the same time as they help sustainable agriculture to flourish. Shareholders pay a portion of the farm's expenses and in return receive a weekly bounty of freshly picked vegetables, herbs, and flowers all through the growing season (from late May to early November). Farmers benefit by having a guaranteed market for their produce, and consumers have the satisfaction of eating well — a dynamic that is both reciprocal and personal. As Jen told me, "The relationships we develop with our members nourish us, just as the food we produce nourishes our members."

West Haven Farm is not only supported by its CSA members, however. Although 60 percent of the farm's crops do go to members, another 40 percent go to the Farmers' market, and 1 percent goes wholesale to EVI and Greenstar (a local cooperative store). That adds up to 101 percent, which accurately represents what the couple puts into the farm. All in all, West Haven Farm feeds about 1,000 people a week during the growing season. As a casual gardener, I find it astonishing that 10 acres can be so intensely productive.

Part of the secret of the farm's success has to do with the way that Jen and John nurture the soil. The couple literally feeds the soil by

Mary Webber

Jen and John Bokaer-Smith at the Ithaca Farmers' Market.

applying green and composted manure, planting nitrogen-fixing cover crops, and practicing crop rotation. Their efforts are restoring land previously depleted by years of poor farming practices. And healthy land produces healthy crops.

The land now produces veggies with exceptionally high nutrient values. In fact at EVI a popular folk remedy for colds calls for soup made from Jen and John's fresh produce. Eat the soup for dinner, the saying goes, and you'll feel better by morning. I've tried it and it's true.

As with many other stories having to do with the development of the EcoVillage community, the story of West Haven Farm intertwines with the story of the people who founded it.

Jen and John

Jen and John Bokaer-Smith first met in 1990 in a class on Urban Garden Ecosystems at the University of California, Berkeley. John remembers, "I was pretty awestruck by Jen's knowledge of soil chemistry and her ability to stand up in front of a large group of people and put out her political views."

According to Jen, "We sat in the back of the class and flirted." After briefly joining the Global Walk during its trek through the Navajo Nation, Jen and John finished their university studies and decided to move east to become part of the budding EcoVillage.

They became farmers because they liked gardening and the social and political aspects of bringing food to people. Then someone gave them free registration to the NOFA conference. "It was," Jen told me, pausing dramatically, "like finding God."

The couple's first exposure to a CSA came from working at Slack Hollow Farm in Argyle, New York for two months. "They paid us $40 a week for dawn-to-dusk work," John said. "Then we sat and picked their brains for farming information at every meal. We got by far the better end of the deal," he grinned. That was back in 1991. (The first CSA in the country had only started in 1990.)

I first became familiar with the farm while I was renting a house across the street from Jen and John in downtown Ithaca. At that point they were only farming 2 acres (0.8 hectares) of land, and our homes at EcoVillage were still in the design stage.

The couple kept a little greenhouse frame, enclosed in plastic, in the parking lot behind their home. There they raised their own seedlings and treated them like precious babies. Each seed was carefully planted first in a 1-inch (2.5-centimeter) pot. As the plant matured, it was transferred to a 2-inch (5-centimeter) pot, and then a 4-inch (10-centimeter) pot. The seedlings were sprayed several times daily to keep them moist. Never were plants better cared for than these.

Once the farm expanded, Jen and John were no longer able to keep up with seedling production, so they purchased what they needed from another farmer, several hours away. Once they finished building their large, permanent greenhouse in 2004, however, they were able to raise their own seedlings again.

Today the farm is a very successful operation. The couple farms 8½ acres (3.4 hectares) of veggies, 1½ acres (0.6 hectares) of fruit, and a 1-acre (0.4-hectare) apple orchard in a nearby town (which they work cooperatively with another farmer). They grow 250 varieties of seed, including about 50 types of flowers and just about every type of vegetable you can grow in the Northeast, except asparagus. They planted lots of fruit trees in 2001 — apple, peach, apricot, and plums — which will be ready in about five years. Knowing how delicious their strawberries are, I can't wait to bite into a succulent peach grown on our land!

Jen and John's farm has helped to form the backbone of EcoVillage, and yet for years I knew little about their circumstances or how difficult farming has been for them. A conversation I had with them opened my eyes.

Farming and Finances

Farming and financial difficulties seem to go together like bread and butter. I was curious about how Jen and John's experience of farming had changed over the years. Jen started the story.

"Well, our first vision was that we would be the EcoVillage farmers, and we would get a salary. The whole kibbutz thing. We had visited Israel. But it came clear pretty early on that there weren't other farmers at EcoVillage. And nobody to pay us."

Despite the fact that a CSA is all about cooperation, Jen and John still had the burden of running a privately owned business. Since they leased rather than owned land at EVI, it posed another set of problems. Jen expressed some bitterness over the financial demands.

"If someone had said you will have to pay for your own house and sink $100,000 in infrastructure into the farm, we would have had to think long and hard before doing it. We have student loans to pay back, and a mortgage. It's really hard."

Part of the problem, I found, was that when they want to retire or leave farming, it will be hard for them to sell the business, since they don't own the land. Even after all their hard work, they would have little equity.

As John said, "We barely make an income even with Jen teaching. We'd like to go back to the original vision of a real community-supported farm."

When I asked what they would like to see, John said, "On the financial level, we'd like to make thirty thousand dollars a year rather than ten thousand. The farm should be able to provide income for one of us, if not the whole family."

John went on to say that he'd like to see CSA members and EVI residents put more into the farm and build a sense of ownership. Jen pointed out that the farm greatly adds to the attraction of EVI and is one reason why people move here. She suggested that everyone in the community put in at least one work party per year or pay a small annual fee in lieu of work, regardless of whether or not they're part of the CSA.

Although the proposal sounded reasonable to me, I doubted that it would get complete support from the village. Many residents, like me, enjoyed all the benefits of the farm and felt it was a critical part of the whole vision of EcoVillage. For others, though, it was a peripheral part of their lives. I wondered if the ongoing financial strains were creating a major crisis.

"We're in this for the long haul," John responded. "We got through the first ten years on youthful vigor and idealism, but to be sustainable we have to make the finances work."

Now in their 30s and with a young family, the couple's perspective had shifted. Both of them worried about spending enough quality time with their five-year-old son Nate.

"In some ways, the farm work is relentless," John said emphatically. "The farm is like a freight train. It's either here or its not here. The spring and fall are crazy times, since I'm doing full time farm work and Jen is teaching."

"The summer is wonderful," Jen added. "But I'm tired in the summer, after teaching ten months a year."

Both of them said they enjoy connecting with people through food at the CSA and the farmers' market. John especially enjoys bringing in the harvest with his workers, who are mostly college students.

"It's a great social outlet. It's a short, intense, fulfilling thing to do a harvest. We have a high quality of life. I really thrive on that."

The couple's dedication shows. Jen and John's stall at the farmers' market is one of the most popular ones. They take great care in washing their veggies and select only the most beautiful produce for sale.

John bragged, "When we started out, organic food looked crappy. It was associated with hippies. It was dirty, yucky. One of our goals was to show that organic food could be just as beautiful and nutritious. And you didn't have to work that hard for it; it was just as it should be — natural."

While the two take a lot of pride in their work, farming has plenty of challenges.

"I love doing the farm," John told me. But he added, "The stress that it causes on the rest of my life is really hard."

Jen concurred. "I really miss working together. We can't both afford to work on the farm anymore. I used to love that."

Jen caressed her son's tow-blond head and admitted ruefully that their idea of getting Nate involved with farm work was not realistic. When they were working, he mostly just got ignored. "We used to work with headlamps on into the night," she continued. "With Nate, the farm just isn't as important as it once was. We set firm work hours, from eight in the morning until six at night. We don't work on Sunday unless something's going to die."

"I have residual disappointments about not doing more really groovy stuff," John added. "It takes so much energy just to break even. For instance, I'm really into bio-diesel. Ten years ago, I would have built a little barn to make the stuff. Now I'm just hoping that I find someone who can make it."

By now I was feeling the strain of their hard work and low pay and wondered how they felt about farming at EcoVillage. I secretly hoped that the answer would be positive.

Jen mused, "Other farmers are so isolated. The farmers we lived with didn't even get along with their nearest neighbors several miles away. It was very clear to us that we didn't want to live like that. For us as people, not just as farmers, it makes a lot of sense to live in this kind of setting." She laughed, "Even though we're weird and grumpy about it."

John smiled and added that as farmers they were far more sociable than most farmers. The conservation easement and the EcoVillage ·model brought the farm to the town and helped them to connect with people.

Jen concluded, "Having a farm right in town is great. There's no way we could do it on our own, since the land would be too expensive."

Jen and John's path has not been easy. They have both poured their lifeblood into achieving their dreams. And their work has helped create the very fabric of the EcoVillage. It occurred to me that with our enormous mortgage paid off, perhaps we could turn our fundraising efforts toward creating long-term financial sustainability for this couple who is helping make ecological sustainability a reality right here in our own backyard.

Working on the Farm

When I was growing up in northern Vermont, my mother kept a half-acre organic garden. She grew corn, tomatoes, squash, beans, peas, potatoes, and strawberries, and a few flowers on the side. The garden produced enough vegetables to feed our family of seven year round. We canned the tomatoes; kept the winter squash, onions, and potatoes in the root cellar; and froze the rest. I grew up thinking that nothing was real work unless you had dirt under your fingernails.

When I was in Eighth Grade, Mom took a month-long trip in the summer. Every other day, my brother and I picked several grocery bags full of beans, sweating in the hot summer sun. We dragged them uphill to the house, washed them, blanched them, and froze them. For years afterward neither my brother nor I would eat green beans.

Despite my childhood experience, I love gardening. And being a member of the CSA has kept me close to the land. But I decided it wasn't enough. In 2002 I finally decided it was time to clear out my life and make room for things that would bring me deep satisfaction. I had aspired for years to be closer to the farm. Now I wanted to get my hands in the soil and find out more about Jen and John's farming methods.

I took out a "working share" on the farm. Instead of paying $360 for a full share, I paid $180 and put in 30 hours of labor at $6 per

CSA Pickup

Today is pickup day at the farm. I take a large canvas bag out of my closet and fill it with recycled plastic bags. It is still an ungodly 95 degrees (35 Celsius), but at least today the humidity is bearable. The skies are clear and birds are chirping away in the hedgerows.

As I pass the chicken coop, about a dozen birds run out to greet me. They remind me of young schoolgirls, eager for a piece of candy. I can't help but chuckle at their antics. They rush after me in a flurry of excitement, all gawky tails and bobbing heads, cutting in front of each other and clucking, trying to reach me first.

"Sorry, gals, nothing for you today," I tell them and make a mental note to drop by Michelle's house for eggs. These chickens lay the best eggs I've ever tasted — with their bright golden yolks and fresh taste, the eggs outdo even the free-range eggs at the local natural foods store.

Turning off the dirt road, I walk along a mowed path that's covered in clover and pass the farm's potato field. The potatoes' purple, star-shaped flowers with golden centers are just starting to bloom. Elsewhere the grass is waist high and milkweed is coming into bloom, with large clusters of pink flowers that later in the season will turn into plump green pods filled with silky seeds.

The sight of milkweed brings up old memories and reminds me of a turning point in my life. When I was a child, I used to slit the ripe seedpods along one side, revealing polished brown seeds packed as tightly as sardines in a can. I pretended the pods were little cradles and the silky seeds were princes and princesses.

Later on, as a shy 13-year-old miserable with teenage angst, I remember holding a milkweed pod as I stood on the hill behind our Vermont house. I wished to be free and confident enough to engage with the world as an active participant instead of as a bystander. And then I blew the pod's silky parachutes all over the valley below.

As I watched the seeds circle and eddy in the wind, I knew I had the capacity to take risks and fly, too. By the following year I was happier than ever before and newly immersed in life. I smile when I remember that time. But milkweed is just one of the many plants that draws my attention today.

What I really want to know is, Are the black raspberries ripe yet? I spot the first rounded and ripe black berries at the tip of each cluster. Eager with anticipation, I pop a single berry into my mouth. Yes! As delicious as last year. I gather a hand-ful of the ripe globes, feeling somewhat smug. Apparently nobody else has ☞

checked out this treasure-trove yet. Should I let people know? No, I think. I'll wait a day or two and savor them on my own.

As I move on I glance up at the wild cherry trees in the hedgerow. Last year we had a bumper crop, which may explain this year's poor pickings. I notice that the birds seem to have gotten the best of what's here, anyway.

When I head across the rivulet that flows down into Cliff Park Brook, I startle a groundhog, which quickly shuffles off into its hole. I pause to watch the dragonflies hover over the little pool where the stream crosses the path. A black and white one skims over the water, as elegant as a dancer in a tux. Another looks like a brilliant turquoise dart. And, Oh look! There's a bright orange one — a kind I've never seen before.

Farther along, wild grapevines tangle over the bushes on both sides of the path, hinting at bounty to come. I pass the old shagbark hickory — the surviving tree of a pair that used to stand as stately sentinels on either side of the path. When lightning struck the other tree, we sawed up its trunk for wood and saved the stump for use in the playground. Now the remaining tree guards the path.

Just beyond the lone hickory, the farm comes into view. A tall deer fence surrounds the 10-acre (4-hectare) field, the result of a fundraising campaign to replace the original ineffective one. In the summer of 2000, deer almost decimated all the crops. Each week, the farm's newsletter chronicled the damage: "The deer jumped the fence again and ate about half of the lettuce and most of the strawberries." And then, "The snap peas were eaten to the ground."

In a heroic effort to save the farm, resident Martha Stettinius stepped forward to help organize two major yard sales, a brunch, and an auction to raise funds for a taller fence. Jen and John got the support of virtually all of their CSA member families. People donated goods and services, appliances, furniture, and even weekend getaways to destinations as far away as Las Vegas and Tucson. When everything was totaled up, there was $10,000, enough to have an 8-foot (2.4-meter) deer fence installed. So far no deer has dared to leap over.

Today the farm basks in the sun. John and Jen and two assistants are busy getting the irrigation system going. The system relies on 75,000 feet (23,000 meters) of drip tape set out between each row of crops. Since mice tend to chew on the hoses over the winter, every inch will have been checked for damage. As I watch, the long black snakes of irrigation hose sputter and come to life, spritzing water on the long rows of thirsty plants. ☞

Plants need an inch of rain a week, and with just a few spits of water from the sky, most of the water has to come from the irrigation pond. The system is very labor intensive, requiring tremendous effort to put in place, but it does conserve water — an important consideration, since the pond tends to run dry during drought years. It's good to know that the crops are getting what they need.

I step into the cool barn to pick up my produce. Pickup starts on Tuesday afternoons at 4:00 and runs until 10:30 Wednesday morning. I make it in just under the wire — it's 10:20 on a Wednesday morning. There is still a bounty of produce for me to choose from, however.

A small chalkboard proclaims, "2 pounds of lettuce, chard, and/or spinach (but no more than ¾ pound of spinach). One handful of cilantro and parsley. One quart of sugar snap peas and/or snow peas. Half a pound of garlic scapes." What on earth are garlic scapes? I wonder.

I'm glad to see I'm probably not the only one who's never heard of them before. According to the farm's newsletter, scapes are the tops of garlic plants that get picked off to encourage bigger growth of the bulbs. Like garlic greens, they make an awesome pesto, though it is best to add in some parsley, cilantro, basil, or spinach if you don't care to get too up close and personal with the scapes' intense flavor. You really can learn something new every day, I think, and move outside to where there are still some strawberries left for gleaning.

Laura Miller

CSA pickup at West Haven Farm.

I take a couple of pint baskets past rows of lettuce, spinach, carrots, and a large planting of onions to where 12 rows of large strawberry plants beckon. Other people have pretty much picked out the first few rows, so I choose a row farther down and methodically turn leaves over in search of an occasional juicy morsel.

Jen and John's strawberries are some of the tastiest I've ever eaten. Small and sweet, they pack a juicy punch when ripe. ☞

Avoiding any moldy or snail-bitten berries, I soon have two baskets full of rich red fruit, one for me and one for a friend. I turn back to the barn to get a set of clippers for my favorite part of the CSA pickup — flower-picking.

This week I pick stems of veronica — pink, white, and purple — and a small bouquet of pink, red, and white Sweet Williams. I even take a few fragrant stalks of lavender. When I get back to the barn, a woman and her two young daughters are sorting through the remains of the CSA veggies. Some of the leftover food will go to the Common House, but the bulk of it is set aside for the Friendship Donations Network (FDN).

Founded by EcoVillage resident Sara Pines in 1998, the FDN is a local nonprofit food rescue agency. When she was still a child, Sara's father was killed by a bomb, and for a while she lived homeless in the streets of Palestine. The experience left her with a deep-rooted desire to make sure that no one goes hungry and that no food is wasted.

Sara calls herself "a little old lady," but her volunteers call her "the Tornado." The winner of numerous awards for her work, 68-year-old Sara stands 4-feet-8-inches tall and has the tenacity of a bull. She and her volunteer-run operation feed about 2,000 people a week in the Tompkins County area. Bakeries, supermarkets, and a few farms (including West Haven), donate their "day-olds" or leftovers to the cause. And 200 people distribute a ton of food each day to local soup kitchens, food pantries, and work sites employing low-income workers.

What doesn't go to the FDN will go to the Common House. In fact I notice that Jen must have been in to set aside some cauliflower, lettuce, and snap peas for tomorrow night's dinner. She usually cooks for the Common House on Thursday and likes to use some of what's left after the CSA pickup. We're lucky to have the farm so close at hand. There's nothing like the crunch of crisp, organic lettuce or red tomatoes fresh from the vine.

My CSA pickup is over for another week, and I walk back across the fields with my canvas bag full of greens, garlic scapes, sweet strawberries, and flowers. I have often joked that my little walk to the farm and back makes me feel like a French housewife. I have just what I need to make a delicious dinner for my friends tonight, including fixings for strawberry shortcake. Now if the farm would just sell baguettes! ■

hour on the farm. A working share makes the CSA affordable to a wider range of people. Jen and John get help with the farm work, and work share members get a crash course in organic farming.

My working share wouldn't have been worth it if I hadn't thoroughly enjoyed the work — but I did. I found it profoundly satisfying to walk across the fields in the early morning, listening to the birds singing in the hedgerows, and arrive at the farm ready to become part of a bustling crew of other workers.

A Typical Harvest Tuesday

Share workers gather the harvest for the CSA pickup early every Tuesday morning. My coworkers were mostly graduate students from Cornell, pursuing various doctorates in philosophy, music, and ecology. One was working with an EcoVillage resident who was studying nutrient values in organic vegetables to optimize fertilizer inputs. They were friendly, energetic, and experienced workers.

The work itself was varied and required a great deal of attention to detail. On one typical harvest morning, we picked bunches of spinach with long knives and then moved on to cut garlic scapes — their beautiful curlicue tendrils reminding me of flourishing calligraphy script. By the time we plucked the top leaves off the basil plants to keep them from flowering, my hands had begun to smell like a wonderful salad.

Peas were next, and I ate one out of every handful I picked. We happened to be picking an edible pod variety, and they were sweet and crisp. I could have munched on them all day, but more work awaited us. And we were on a tight schedule. The CSA pickup would begin later that afternoon.

The eggplants needed weeding (something I did scooting along on my bottom, gathering dirt on my shorts, but saving my back from having to stay bent over). I was surprised to see that even the weeds — lamb's-quarters and purslane — were edible, though no one gathered them.

Later I worked with Alison in the cool barn, washing veggies. (Alison was a paid crewmember, nicknamed "the Flash," since she was so efficient and fast at whatever farm work there was to do.) We started with big vats of herbs: tendrils of dill weed and then cilantro, one of my favorites — setting aside the basil, since it doesn't take well to washing. It wasn't long until the whole barn was saturated with a lovely potpourri of herbal scents.

We also washed huge amounts of lettuce. There were great heads of romaine, light green heads of butter lettuce, and curly leafed red lettuce. There must have been ten bins of the stuff!

Spinach came after the lettuce, and it required three rinses in separate vats of water. No wonder I didn't have to worry about sand being in the spinach I got in my CSA share! Jen and John take such great care with washing that their produce always looks gorgeous and barely needs a rinse before cooking.

Once the washing up was finished, it was time for lunch. Our eclectic crew gathered in the barn to eat and do some socializing. Jen, John, and Nate were all there, as well as Nate's nine-year-old cousin Aviv and Caleb, a teenager from SONG who did the working share for his family. A neighbor and his teenage son, a couple of regular farm crewmembers, and the Cornell graduate students made up the rest of the group.

What a great mix! I had thoroughly enjoyed working with them all. And I was happy to have acquired some new skills. But I needed to get back to my other work. I said goodbye and headed back across the fields toward home.

The physical work had tired me out a little. And my hands and finger-nails were encrusted with dirt. But mostly I felt a sense of earthy fulfillment. It felt good to bring the harvest home.

West Haven Farm has been part of the EcoVillage vision right from the beginning. Jen and John are deeply connected to the land they farm and the ecovillage model. So are our residents. In fact the multiple connections that exist among us represent the essence of our cohousing community.

CHAPTER 4

LIVING IN COMMUNITY

Walking Iris

As Allegra and Sarah (aged 9 and 4) pass my house, I call them over to see something special: my walking iris has a beautiful, orchid-like bloom. "It only lasts for one day," I explain. "You can watch it unfold its petals in the early morning, and by nighttime the flower has shriveled up and died. When I lived downtown, it only flowered once a year. That day was so special, I would stay home from work to see it. But now that we live at EcoVillage, it flowers a lot. It likes the extra light it gets in my passive solar home."

Allegra is part Hispanic and has wide brown eyes and black hair. Sarah is Jewish, and her hair is a tousled golden mane. The girls lean toward the delicate white blossom with its bright purple center. "Mmmm," they murmur. "That smells so good!" The iris has a sweet almost spicy fragrance, as lingering as a gardenia. It is intoxicating. I offer each of them a cutting from the mother plant.

"Why is it called a walking iris?" Allegra asks.

"Because it is really a tropical plant that grows fast and sends out shoots like a spider plant. Each new shoot puts down roots, and then that sends out more shoots — almost as if it is walking forward."

The girls leave, and I reflect on the symbolism of the walking iris. When a walking iris sends out a new shoot, it also sends out a two- to three-foot-long stem, exploring new territory. If the shoot doesn't find soil or water, then the stem develops sticky scales and gradually dies back. If the shoot finds what it needs, then the whole plant develops fully.

When I first got my plant, it flowered so rarely that I hoarded the joy of its blossoms. Later, as the plant sent out more shoots, I gave well-rooted cuttings to my best friends. Now it is thriving, and I have several large plants around the house.

I have discovered that when I plant or give away a shoot from my walking iris, I am contributing to its overall health and growth. Likewise when I give freely of my love, my attention, my time, and even my money, I am contributing to the overall health and growth of my community. It makes me feel happy and healthy, too.

Such sharing is not a sacrifice but a celebration, an act of love that has an immediate ripple effect, sending happiness back to the giver, multiplied many times. Like the walking iris, our momentary, everyday acts of kindness permeate the community with a sweet and spicy scent.

At EcoVillage at Ithaca we have set up our lives to foster connection. We share meals together several times a week, participate in

Jim Bosjolie

SONG neighbors celebrate Jim Bosjolie's 60th birthday.

work parties, and create our own on-site entertainment. We get to know and enjoy our neighbors — without ever having to drive anywhere!

The Cohousing Model

The first cohousing community started in Denmark in 1968. As the idea caught on, people built small communities called *bofoellesskaber*, based on the premise that we need both privacy and a strong sense of belonging if we are to thrive. Members participated through all stages — from design and development to the ongoing maintenance of the community.

In a typical community 10 to 35 private homes were clustered around shared community space in a neighborhood setting. In a simple but profound shift of neighborhood layout, cars were parked on the periphery of the property, leaving pedestrian paths and park-like greenery between the houses.

Everything was set up to encourage frequent, informal interaction, including a central community facility called the "Common House." Typically cohousing residents used their Common House for several community meals a week, for children's play space, and for laundry

Laura Beck

The center of the FROG neighborhood.

facilities. The Danish-designed community spaces incorporated lots of wood and lots of light, creating an overall sense of cozy congeniality. Shared meals, celebrations, decision making, and work parties helped build the bonds that evolve into deep friendships over time. Soon cohousing became a popular alternative housing mode in Scandinavia and the Netherlands.

Twenty years later, McCamant and Durrett's book introduced the cohousing model to the US public (see "The Global Walk," Chapter One). By 2004 there were 69 cohousing communities in the US, with hundreds more in the planning stages. However, in 1991 (when we founded EVI) only two cohousing communities had been built in the US, and both were on the West Coast. So we had to imagine for ourselves what a cohousing community would look like.

Growing Pains

We invited McCamant and Durrett to give our budding group a workshop in 1992, and they gave talks to enthusiastic audiences both at Cornell and in downtown Ithaca. Later that year many of us attended a cohousing conference with scores of other people from newly forming communities. We had become part of a growing movement that was using the innovative, practical ideas of our Danish counterparts even as we forged a new American model of cohousing.

As a still-forming group we experienced a constant ebb and flow of people. It seemed as though every time Joan and I convened a meeting, we saw a different set of faces. Everyone seemed eager to live in community, but no one was ready to commit. After months of discussion, the group agreed to a minimum membership commitment of $250.

In a parallel process, the Board of Directors of the nonprofit engaged in a heated debate over what direction to go. Were we going to build impromptu yurts for the homeless, or were we going to create a more mainstream model? Some people felt strongly about offering housing to anyone, regardless of their ability to pay. Others held the view that since most new housing in the US served the middle class, it was here that we could exert our strongest influence. We hoped to lead by example and model a new direction in housing. Our densely clustered, community-oriented homes would be constructed to be super-insulated and passive solar, and we intended to set them in neighborhoods surrounded by plenty of open land. Over a very difficult six-month period, we made a key decision: We were aiming to reach middle-class Americans.

The decision led to a split in our fledgling community. We lost some people from the cohousing group, and several members dropped off the Board (including my ex-husband Jon). I felt sad to once again see idealistic members drop out. But at the same time it seemed to be the only realistic direction to take — our project had no track record for creating any kind of housing (let alone cohousing), and we had no money to subsidize anyone.

Painful as our decision was, once it was made those who stayed experienced a burst of energy and a new sense of direction. I personally recommitted to creating affordable housing with at least some of the units. At the time I was supporting myself and my two kids on $16,000 a year and knew how crucial it was to be as inclusive as possible. So when I received an unexpected windfall check of $500, I created an "affordability fund." We used the fund to hire a part-time affordability consultant.

ON THE PERSONAL SIDE

During the next four years, 1992–1996, I was scooped up into a whirlwind of activity. Between our first cohousing group meeting in the spring of 1992 and the first move-in during the fall of 1996, I took part in whole group meetings, committee meetings, meetings with the architect, and meetings with the Town Planning Board. It was typical for me to have meetings three nights a week and for a half-day or more every weekend. Decision making was endless, and every choice we made required consensus. I juggled my role as a new single parent with being an EcoVillage co-director. And I had become the coordinator of the First Resident Group (nicknamed "FROG"), as well.

EVI's formative years proved particularly stressful for the children and me. Jason and Daniel (aged 8 and 5 when we moved across the country) had to adjust to major changes: Jon and I had separated; the boys were traveling back and forth between two households; and they had left friends and grandparents behind in San Francisco. Not only that, they were living in a small town instead of a large city. And the considerably different climate included bitter winters.

My dedication to helping birth EVI meant that Jason and Daniel often stayed with a babysitter. On especially busy nights I sometimes didn't get home until midnight. I tried to make up for my crazy schedule by nurturing the children during my precious free moments. We hiked the gorges, picked apples in the orchard behind our rental house, and enjoyed craft projects. Reading became a favorite activity. The three of us would curl up together with a good book, and I would read to them until my voice was hoarse.

I was fortunate to have a roommate. Marcie Boyd was about my age, single, and she loved children. She was also a co-counselor and part of EVI. She offered the kids special attention at times when I was gone. The two of us laughed and cried our way through the difficulties of these stressful times.

I also discovered a new side of myself. When Jon had the kids at his place, I had some free time. I became an avid dancer. I went to contra-dances every Friday, took one class in swing dancing and another in contact improvisation. I lived for these times when I could flow with the music and the movement of my body, forgetting any nagging dilemmas from my life at work or at home.

In the spring of 1994, a window in my life opened. Jared visited me briefly before going on a long-anticipated five-month solo bike trip through Europe. We experienced the usual powerful connection. But when he told me he was still contemplating moving back to Ithaca, I would not let myself hope.

I told Jared about the book I was reading. *The Celestine Prophecy* (Warner Books, 1993) talks about finding spiritual lessons in life through a series of coincidences. Later that day (by coincidence), his sister-in-law gave him a copy of the same book, which he avidly read. We had several long, soulful phone calls before he took off for Europe.

Over the next few weeks I received beautifully written letters about Jared's travels. In them he spoke many times about the power of our connection. I sent off increasingly hopeful letters — to Athens, Istanbul, Rome, and Prague — tracing his route by US embassies.

Then I started receiving weekly phone calls at the office. (This was before e-mail or cell phones were widely used.) Joan and our volunteers would smile knowingly while I stretched the phone cord out into the hallway and talked for an hour or more. According to Jared, his heart told him to be with me. But his head argued that he had deep, satisfying connections with friends and his work as a hospice nurse in Santa Cruz. He had lived there for 20 years. He wondered how he could leave.

Jared spent several long weeks trying to decide what his next step was. Then, as he cycled along the bike trail by the banks of the Danube, it all became clear to him: He was meant to be my partner and to be part of creating EcoVillage at Ithaca.

I spent the next couple of months in a joyful dream. Jared and I were deciding to become life partners by transatlantic phone. At the same time I was totally immersed in the practical details of creating a cohousing community from scratch. And I was trying to decide what size of home to build and how many bedrooms I could afford. We were doing everything backwards — buying a house together before becoming a couple or getting married. But I didn't care. It felt gloriously right and I was totally alive.

In August 1994 Jared returned from Europe, cutting his trip short by a month in order to return to Ithaca. He spent a wonderful two months with me and became fully involved in EcoVillage activities, rapidly becoming an indispensable member of the process committee, the Common House design committee, and many others. Then he left for California to pack up his belongings and say goodbye to his friends.

I thought Jared would be back in a few months. But he didn't return until June 1995. He drove all night the last day and arrived at 6 a.m. on June 6. It was already 90 degrees and humid, but that didn't matter. I dove toward him and felt his loving arms surround me. The cottonwood trees rained cotton fluff on us, and I felt like a bride in a shower of white.

Moving In

In October 1996 (after four-and-a-half years of planning, designing, and building), the very first families moved into FROG, even though much of it was still under construction. A month later, when our family moved into our new home, seven families had already settled in.

Two weeks after our family moved in, we threw a FROG open house. We sent out press releases and invited the public to come and see this new "ecohousing." But before the open house got started, we got a group together to help our ninth family.

Rod Lambert, Julia Morgan, and their children came to us from the province of Ontario, Canada. They had decided that it would be easier to join us than to start an ecovillage project there. Unfortunately Julia fell sick with pneumonia on open house day, so it was especially important that we lend a hand to get the family into its new home.

The moving party went quickly, but I was still in sweatshirt and jeans when our first visitors started arriving (the open house was centered at our place). I served hot spiced cider and showed people around our lovely passive solar home. All in all approximately 120 eager visitors came to see what this crazy "ecovillage" was all about.

FIRE

We were congratulating ourselves on how well the open house had gone when someone looked out the window and yelled, "Fire!" We called the fire department and raced to find buckets of water or hoses. But the fire had already spread out of control. I ran outside with the others and watched helplessly as 70-foot-high (21-meter-high) flames spread from duplex to duplex and then jumped the 40-foot (12-meter) gap to the Common House.

Agonizing minutes passed before the first of eight volunteer fire departments started arriving. The fire spread as if it were a bonfire just getting started, feeding on the kindling of half-finished homes built of wood.

We had five minutes to vacate our homes and take any belongings we could. I stood in disbelief in the middle of my new, beautiful home, built after so many years of work, trying to decide what to take. The photo albums! I raced upstairs, only to find all our unpacked boxes in a pile on the floor. I had no idea how to find the right ones. Instead I got my winter coat and boots, a toothbrush and deodorant, and rushed out the door. (Luckily the kids were downtown with their dad.) I ran to the parking lot, dodging hand-sized burning red cinders, afraid that my hair would catch on fire. I jumped in my car, heart beating wildly, and escaped the burning chaos of the night. Once downtown, I joined a couple dozen other EcoVillagers who had gathered in one woman's apartment. We shared tidbits of news along with some hot soup. Thankfully no one had been hurt.

At midnight we received an incredibly welcome call: The fire had been put out and we could all go home. Over 100 firefighters, including the mayor of Ithaca, had responded to the call and worked for hours to control the blaze — one of the largest ever seen in Ithaca. The Common House and eight homes under construction had burned to the ground. Another six had been damaged but were still standing. None of the occupied homes had been affected.

As we drove back, I felt an odd mixture of shock and profound gratitude to be home. Jared and I picked our way through the debris, the acrid smell of burned wood searing our nostrils, to find our home completely intact. Later I would find out that our home, the next one in line after the eight burned ones, was within a minute or two of catching fire when the fire department managed to hook up to the fire hydrant by the pond.

In the following weeks we learned how the fire had started. One of the subcontractors had had a small engine fire as he was blowing insulation into the walls of our super-insulated homes. The fire was put out promptly, but a spark flew into the insulation hopper and was inadvertently blown into the house. Twenty-four hours later, the second fire burst into flames in the attic of the locked house. We received full compensation through our builder's risk insurance policy and gradually rebuilt the neighborhood over the next ten months.

Once all 30 households had finally moved in, we started enjoying the true benefits of cohousing: shared meals, shared celebrations, and an even stronger sense of community.

Famous Fried Tofu...

August 20, 2002 — It's my turn to be "Head Cook" again. Along with the rest of the team, I am responsible for planning and serving one of our three weekly community meals. (At EVI each adult volunteers two to four hours a week on one of six work teams — Maintenance, Outdoor, Finance, Cooking, Dishwashing, or Common House Cleaning. I enjoy cooking, so that's where I volunteer.)

Head cooking is a big responsibility. There is a lot of pressure to produce a good meal in a relatively short time. People with dietary restrictions have to be accommodated (simple meals work best, I find). And there are pitfalls — what if you misjudge quantities or timing, or burn the pasta? But I find it rewarding. I get to taste the results of my labors after two hours of intense hands-on work with people whose company I enjoy.

Planning is key. A week before our cooking night I post a meal sign-up sheet with my proposed menu: Liz's Famous Fried Tofu; Potato Salad; and Sliced Tomatoes and Cukes. Dinner will feature locally made tofu and produce from the farm — all of it bursting with nutrients and requiring little or no transport to bring to our table. Eighty people sign up, a much larger group than usual.

Our cooking day rolls around on a Monday. I find a stack of large plastic trays filled with ripe tomatoes on the Common House porch. Some are small and bright red, and still on the vine. The heirloom varieties are recognizable by their unusual colors and lumpy shapes. Still others are huge yellow globes that sit peacefully in their trays like round perfectly content Buddhas. And there are peppers, too, both red and green, each with a bad spot that can be easily removed. Jen tells me the veggies are free — leftovers from the Farmers' Market. Delighted to be able to use organic produce from our own land, I select a tray-and-a-half of tomatoes.

By midday the temperature hits 99 degrees Fahrenheit (37 Celsius). Julia, one of my assistants, wants to work early in the afternoon and has agreed to chop celery and red onions, and wash and boil the potatoes for the potato salad.

The rest of my helpers — Florian, Alison, and David (a visitor) — arrive at 4 p.m. Florian is French and, although he is married to a US citizen, has just received his green card after three years of trying. Alison, one of our newest residents, works as my assistant at the EcoVillage office. David, it turns out, is studying intentional communities. He is a Benedictine monk on sabbatical from his job as an English instructor. Within minutes the three of them are chopping vegetables and slicing tofu.

I decide to make 35 squares of tofu (based on our huge sign-up list), and hope there will be enough potato salad. David asks what we are making, and I explain the menu to him. "So how did your tofu get famous?" he queries.

"Years ago in San Francisco, I lived in a communal house. We loved this tofu so much that we made it several times a week. Our friends would drop over at dinnertime just to get a taste. The first time I made it at EcoVillage I decided, as a joke, to call it 'Liz's Famous Fried Tofu.' Visitors who thought they hated tofu asked for the recipe. One resident asked me to make larger quantities, complaining whenever I made it that there was never enough. Someone else joked that I could start a franchise selling this tofu."

As I'm talking to David, Elisabeth walks by. "I am so happy you're making your famous tofu tonight," she says. "I wasn't going to come to dinner, but now I will. And I've been telling other people, as well."

A few minutes later I notice Rachael, her son Gabe, and his friend Connor (both six years old). "Please, can we have a piece of tofu?" they beg her.

"Not right now, but we'll come back for dinner," Rachael tells them.

As they leave the Common House, the boys nudge each other. "Oh good! *Tofu* for dinner."

I smile and continue juggling the three frying pans on the stove that are filled with the first sizzling chunks of tofu. Our kids our growing up enjoying vegetarian food that tastes great and takes far fewer resources to produce than regular fare.

"Mmm, smells like bacon," Janet comments as she passes by. I'm beginning to feel that the "famous" tag may be justified.

I ask David to separate out the vegan potato salad and mix a dressing for it. By now Florian and Alison have cut up the rest of the tofu, prepared 15 bulbs of garlic that go into the dressing for the regular potato salad, and chopped up extra celery. They start slicing tomatoes, but I send Alison back to my house for my two good slicing knives and another frying pan for tofu. Florian carries on slicing, and the tomatoes glow with summer goodness, their bright reds and yellows mixing in the big bowl.

By a quarter to six we have only 15 minutes left before the crowds descend. Greg, Laura, and their three-year-old son Ethan arrive to help with setup. After quickly putting out plates, forks, glasses, and pitchers of filtered water, Greg offers to help cook. I decide to make another five squares of tofu, and together we fry it up. Alison's husband Peretz helps her slice the last of the tomatoes, and Florian slices cucumbers. Laura cleans the countertop for serving and arranges the kids' table. We need everyone's help to finish on time.

Liz's Famous Fried Tofu Recipe

Cut two large blocks of firm tofu into ¾-inch cubes. Pour a few tablespoons of oil into a large, heavy-bottomed frying pan. Toss the tofu cubes in the oil for a few seconds, over medium-high heat. Sprinkle tofu with ⅛ to ¼ cup tamari (depending on taste), then smother in ½ cup of nutritional yeast, tossing to coat. Continue to sauté the chunks of tofu, turning occasionally with a spatula, until they develop a crispy brown crust. Serves four. ■

At 6 p.m. I ask Ethan if he wants to ring the dinner bell. When he nods, Greg takes him out to clang the big iron triangle that hangs from the Common House porch. I calm myself after the flurry of getting the meal prepared. Soon the porch is bustling with people hungry from a day's work in town, out on the land, or at home with young children. People greet each other, ask a question, get a hug.

"Time for a circle," I announce. We hold hands in a large circle that expands as more people come in. Some kids join the circle; others continue to play. "Let's take a moment of silence together. Take a few deep breaths, and just relax and feel the strength of our community as we hold hands."

A deep and wonderful silence stills the group. I feel such gratitude to be part of this caring community, to have an abundance of delicious food prepared with many ingredients from our own land, and to have old and young living together.

When the silence ends, I ask if there is anyone who needs to be introduced. We have several visitors, including a couple from California who might want to live here and a student from Canada who is doing a senior thesis on women's roles in community. The mother of one of our residents is also visiting for the week. I am glad that our community is so open and welcoming to newcomers.

After introductions, I ask if there are any announcements. Megan (a recent arrival from New York City, with a background in graphic design) needs a work party to help spread landscape cloth on the beach after dinner. About four of us volunteer — not enough for a work party.

"Remember," someone chimes in, "this is in the water. You'll cool off." Six more hands shoot up, and the circle breaks up.

We form two snaky lines — one on each side of the 16-foot maple countertop. What a noisy, wonderful hubbub we make! The "village" in EcoVillage is growing, and it is an exciting time, with new neighbors moving in on a weekly basis. As I move down the line, I chat with two members whose homes will be ready soon, then move out to the patio and sit with five other friends.

It is still hot out, but I can feel a cool breeze as I look out over the pond to the lush meadows and blue hills beyond. We settle in to eat. Jared arrives, sweaty from his five-mile bike ride home from work. I give him a kiss and the plate of food I've saved for him. Everybody makes room to squeeze another chair up to the table.

Just then thunder sounds from the dining room: Children and adults alike are drumming on the tables. The noise builds, and then comes a loud cheer — "Yaaaay, cooks!"

A broad grin spreads across my face. That cheer is a welcome ritual and can be started by anyone who feels inspired to begin the drumming. One toddler who thought cheering was standard practice tried it at his first restaurant meal, much to his parents' surprise. I think he was right. Cooks should be appreciated.

... and the Beach Party

A couple of dozen people gather at the pond after dinner — some are there to work and some just want to sit in the shade and talk. A bulldozer has already carved out a large flat section for the beach, and kids have been running across the muddy spots, glorying in the wet messiness. But now it's time to put down the landscaping cloth.

We roll the black cloth out in long eight-foot-wide sections, overlapping the edges as we go. Once the cloth is laid, it needs to be anchored. And that's where the fun begins. We must tap five-inch-long staples through the cloth and into the ground. We have a couple of mallets and a few hammers, but most of us use whatever comes to hand — namely rocks. The staples often bend, making the task a challenge. It is like stitching together a large sloppy dress, complete with a hem where the fabric folds over at the edge.

The day cools down to a very pleasant 75 degrees (24 Celsius), and a brilliant cream-colored fingernail moon appears, with a single star beside it. We work alone or in pairs, moving along the beach.

I look around at my workmates and think of the diversity of people who live here now. Niruja, for instance, dressed in a bright orange and yellow sari that accents her dark skin and wide smile, is originally from Nepal. Ram Saran, the adopted son of one of our deceased members, used his inheritance to return to his village in Nepal and marry her. Following Nepalese tradition, the two met for the first time a day before their wedding.

When Niruja first came to EVI, she spoke hardly any English and followed Ram Saran at a respectful distance of several feet. Now her English is improving and she is overcoming her shyness. I am impressed. It's hard for me to imaging doing the same thing — moving to a different country, learning the language, and fitting in with a new set of customs.

And Niruja is only one of many residents who have come to EVI from other cultures. Eriko is Japanese; Hilbig is German; Todd comes from Trinidad; Ben is second generation Chinese; and Krishna is second generation Indian. This diversity helps to give us a broader perspective and make us feel connected to people all over the world.

By the time we finish it's really dark. But the landscape cloth is quilted to the beach. Like our community itself, we've made something new out of ordinary materials. We gather up the mallets and hammers and stack our stone tools. As I head home, I feel an inner glow from the camaraderie of cooking, eating, and working with my community.

Invented Celebrations

One of the most fulfilling aspects of our community life is celebrating together. And it doesn't take much to spark a party — just someone with an inspiration and the energy to organize. Add some shared food or drink and a little music, dance, or ritual and voila!

We celebrate Easter with an egg hunt and Channukah with potato latkes (cooked by the dozen). Other Jewish holidays, Christmas tree decorating, a big Thanksgiving feast (complete with the option of vegan turkey), and occasionally a Buddhist-inspired ceremony or Earth-based spirituality ritual all take the spotlight during the year. We have corn roasts in the fall and a strawberry festival on the summer solstice. Birthday parties happen year round. And we don't stop at ordinary parties. What makes our community extraordinary is that we often invent our own celebrations, drawing from many traditions — or creating a new one. We live for these times of creative and meaningful fun.

Pond and Beach, Summer 2004

Today if you look across the stream separating the two neighborhoods of FROG and SONG, you'll see that our large pond has grown up some. Cattails and large pink lotus flowers stir in the breeze and gentle movement of the water. Thousands of frogs, dozens of small-mouthed bass, a family of muskrats, and a family of ducks live here now. And, most days, a great blue heron fishes here early in the morning on its daily rounds. Further along, adults and children swim or wade in the water by our carefully constructed beach. At the pond the animal world and the human world peacefully coexist. I like to think that someday that will be true everywhere.

■

The Winter Spiral

December 21, 2002 — A hush blankets the Common House as people file in, whispering to each other and leaving candles on the table. It is winter solstice, and The Winter Spiral is about to begin.

Katie plays a single note on the recorder, and the waiting adults and children settle into a deeper silence. The room is dark. In the lulls between the simple tunes that Katie plays, we can hear the sighing of the wind outside.

Lori Freer, in a long white dress, presides as the "Starry Guide." She greets the children and beckons them with an outstretched arm to walk the spiral of dark pine boughs laid out on the floor.

Lori's daughter Zoe (age 5), who begged to be first, walks the spiral in silence with her mother. When they reach the middle, Lori helps Zoe light her very own candle from the central candle on the altar. Zoe's face is aglow as Lori bends over her — a mother and child lighting their way in the darkness. Once it is lit, Zoe places her candle on bricks near the pine boughs, resting it between a brass fairy and some pinecones and seashells that decorate the spiral. Then she returns, walking out of the spiral looking transformed.

One by one, each child takes a turn, leaving behind a burning light where before there had been darkness. Indulgent laughter ripples as a 15-month-old stumbles forward, getting his sea legs in this ocean of greenery. A 9-year-old swaggers through, big boots clomping, and lights his candle himself. Soon all 15 children have taken a turn. They amaze us with their silence and their ability to keep the mood of expectation.

Then it's our turn, as adults. We stand in line, clutching our candles, filled with the mystery of this darkest night and waiting for the light to return. As I walk the spiral in my stocking feet, I look around at my blessed community, at parents and children ranged on the floor around the spiral, faces bathed in candlelight. I see people leaning over the kitchen island and people sitting on chairs. I see retired couples, lesbian couples, and single adults. We are all united in the magic of this special ceremony. I light my candle and walk back through the spiral, entranced. I place my candle in a little niche near a crystal in the pine boughs. I want my light, among these many lights, to shine out brightly.

We sing: "Light is returning, even though it is the darkest hour. No one can hold back the dawn. Let's keep it burning; let's keep the light of hope alive. Earth Mother is calling her children home." I fill with love and joy and a very deep sense of gratitude. This ritual has filled a place in me that longed for connection and meaning in this time of holiday rush and stress. I hope we do this every year.

GUYS BAKING PIES

August 8, 2002 — Early August, and the blackberries drip off their branches. One section of the EcoVillage land had a huge blackberry bramble on it when we bought it. The farmer who hayed the fields that year mowed a careful path around the brambles. "That's a keeper. That'll have good berries," he told us. Sure enough, that bramble alone often produces many gallons of purple, juicy berries.

Jared puts out an e-mail to alert people that Saturday will be EVI's seventh annual "Guys Baking Pies" day. On Saturday Jared and a motley assortment of neighborhood men and boys troop down to the berry patch. The wise ones wear old jeans and long-sleeved shirts, despite the 95-degree heat. The less experienced wear shorts and sandals and are soon covered with long red scratches.

Jared Jones

Guys Baking Pies at EVI.

The crew picks berries all afternoon, then assembles piecrusts and fillings. Occasionally someone will ask a woman for advice on the right texture for a piecrust or how to make a latticework crust. But mostly these men and boys know what they're doing. Finally the pies go into the Common House ovens.

After people go home for a quick supper, the whole community (plus friends and family members) gather again at the Common House. Jared presides over a ceremony that includes the singing of songs specifically written or modified for the occasion (for instance, who will ever forget the hit, "When the moon hits your eye like a big berry pie, that's cohousing...."?).

People recount the major events of the past year. Jared reads a special poem he has written about berry picking.

Then it is time for the procession. About 15 men and boys of all ages proudly parade their pies through a gauntlet of waiting admirers. Each pie maker presents his masterpiece in turn. "This pie has a combination of blackberries and bananas, and I've carved a face of a pirate on the crust," says one young man.

The rest of us eagerly await the moment when we can dig in. We have 15 beautiful pies to choose from, along with vanilla ice cream, whipped cream, and tofutti (a vegan ice cream). We sit at long tables and compare notes

Mouth or Bucket?

Mouth or bucket?
For a few precious hours
my life simplified to this.
In the bramble I am the Buddha
my mind's chatter banished
by senses chasing away past and future.
All else falls away as my eyes lock on
a black jewel, protected by the maze,
morphed by sun, wind and rain,
facets swelling with earth flavors...
Oh, steady now! The fingers navigate the treacherous channel
OUCH! They won't give up their treasure easily
I acknowledge a grudging respect.
The fingertips caress it
a gentle squishiness, fully and deliciously ripe,
drops into my hand
an oral receipt for the price I've paid.
I study this black bulbous gift from the soil
but only for a moment:
Mouth.

— Jared Jones (excerpted from "The Jewel in the Berry") ■

on our purple teeth and tongues. (Did you know that only wild black-berries dye your mouth? Commercial berries have somehow had this characteristic bred out.) We eat and grin wild purple grins at each other, enjoying another successful "Guys Baking Pies" day.

WOMEN GOIN' SWIMMIN'

August 9, 2002 — Not to be outdone by the men, Sandy Wold organizes an event called "Women Goin' Swimmin.'" A group of girls and women (aged 9 to 60) gather at the pond at dusk. We sit on logs around a campfire and tell stories about our bodies. We each share something we love and something we don't like about ourselves.

I feel shy as I talk about my severe varicose veins — the worst he'd ever seen, one doctor told me. But they haven't stopped me from leading an active lifestyle, with lots of biking, hiking, and walking. Another woman talks about a congenital condition and wonders if her daughter has inherited it. It feels primal to share like this, with the firelight calling forth our deeper selves.

Then it's time to go swimming! We remove our clothes in the soft dark night and plunge into the cold water, shrieking with the cold. Tendai (an African anthropologist) notices the flash of a shooting star, the first she's ever seen. We swivel our heads, looking for more.

When we get really cold, we scramble back to the bonfire. Skins and souls washed clean, we warm ourselves to the bone by the flickering firelight.

OAFS BAKING LOAFS

February 22, 2003 — Jared decides that we need a big winter celebration to counterbalance the late summer "Guys Baking Pies." Someone suggests making bread, and he's off and running. Jared and I test bread recipes the week before the event, and my mother's classic whole wheat turns out to be our favorite.

Making even a couple of loaves with Jared brings back wonderful memories. When I was growing up, my mother made 13 loaves of bread every Saturday morning. She had a big, old-fashioned iron bread bucket, and we kids took turns turning the dough on an enormous hook, straining with all our might to mix the heavy mass.

I often helped my mother with the kneading. Her rule of thumb was to knead the dough 300 times. I loved the feel of the warm, fragrant dough as it got more and more elastic under my hands. I always patted the floured loaves, as cute and warm as a baby's belly, before I covered them with a clean dishtowel to rise.

Then there was a big rush when the bread came out of the oven. Before the bread was even cool enough to cut, my playmates and I would tear open a delicious loaf, grab a handful of hot, earthy bread, and slather it with butter. Yum! I am glad that Jared is bringing this kind of experience to the men and boys in the neighborhood.

"Oafs Baking Loafs" makes its debut on a snowy Saturday in the dead of winter. Jared carts bread pans, bags of flour, yeast, raisins, oil, and other ingredients to the Common House. About 15 men and boys gather around the large kitchen island, along with a handful of friends from outside EVI. Some have made their own bread for years, and a few have used bread machines. Many have never made bread in their lives.

While the guys make bread, a bunch of us go off to Cornell. They're running a matinee of *The Sound of Music*, and participation and costumes are encouraged. I've never been good at costumes, but just for fun I dress up as a snowflake (inspired by the line "snowflakes that stay on my nose and eyelashes"). Chris dresses as a moonbeam and Marcie in a white dress with a blue sash. Marcie's Austrian friend Erich arrives in full regalia of green leather lederhosen and knee socks, and Doug goes as a brown paper package. Once at the theater we get to be outrageously silly along with hundreds of other Ithacans.

When we arrive back at Eco-Village, we find a bustling dinner

Mom's Whole Wheat Bread Recipe

11 cups flour (I use half white and half whole wheat)

½ cup margarine (or oil)

6 Tablespoons sugar

4 teaspoons salt

4 Tablespoons baking yeast

4 cups water

Dissolve yeast in hot water; add margarine and sugar. The yeast will begin to grow. After the water/yeast mixture cools, add salt, then flour, and stir together. Knead dough 5–10 minutes, until it is springy and elastic. Put dough in a greased bowl and let rise until doubled in size. Punch down, and knead well. Divide dough and put in greased loaf pans. Let rise until dough rises above lip of pans. Bake at 325° for 45 minutes. Enjoy! ∎

underway in the Common House. The women and children who were not part of the bread baking have made soups and stews to go with the bread. (They try to bill their contribution as "Ewes Making Stews," but it doesn't catch on, and other suggestions just don't seem clever enough.)

The soups and stews are great, but the breads are gorgeous! Some men have braided their loaves to produce a crusty work of art. Others have made raisin bread or rye. Some loaves are lumpy; others look perfect. But whatever they look like on the outside, they're all steaming hot and delicious on the inside.

When we've eaten our fill, Jared rings the announcement bell and cries, "It's time for a celebration of our talents as a community."

Julia (age six) starts out with a solo recorder piece. Her brother Dylan (age nine) follows with a violin solo. Although their performances include some shaky notes and squeaky parts, overall they show a lot of promise. Like indulgent relatives at a family reunion, we clap heartily when they finish.

Our motley crew is next. Still wearing our silly costumes from *The Sound of Music*, we stand up and sing "My Favorite Things." I'm both embarrassed and gratified to be part of this performance. Somehow wearing a costume frees me to reveal a silly streak that otherwise rarely shows. Our song leads to a community rendition of "Doe a Deer" and other favorites.

One of EVI's renters brings out her guitar and sings a couple of her own songs. They are not polished or professional but contain such honesty and flashes of fiery passion that we want more.

Sara Pines sums up the evening. "This reminds me of the days before television, when people still knew how to entertain themselves."

She's right. Our homemade celebrations have an earthy, soul-satisfying, down-home quality. Our time together fills us up like homemade whole wheat bread: Nothing fancy — but oh so nutritious!

LABOR DAY

September 2, 2002 — For most Americans, Labor Day weekend is a time for families to connect, for picnics, for a last hurrah for summer. EcoVillage is no exception. Take the weekend Elissa Wolfson got married, for an example.

Elissa and Steve's wedding is small, attended only by family and close friends. But then Elissa and Steve invite everyone at EVI to a potluck brunch at the Common House the day after the wedding. The celebration turns into a casual, joyous event.

The beaming newlyweds arrive at noon. Throngs of wedding guests and villagers mix as they lay out fruit salads, bagels, French toast, wedding cake, and homemade goodies. People spill out onto the Common House porch overlooking the pond, helping themselves to the fresh fruit smoothies Sara is making. People eat and schmooze in the warm afternoon.

After an hour or so, Sara rings the announcement bell and asks for six volunteers to help with cleanup. A variety of EcoVillagers and guests raise their hands. By 2:30 the guests have wandered off, the dishes are washed, and the Common House has been swept. A great party!

Our next celebration unfolds later that day with a community meal. Doug Shire, an engineer originally from California, is head cook for the night. (Doug works at Cornell on cutting-edge techniques for curing blindness.) His menu is varied. We have a spread of potato salad, spinach salad, tofu salad, sautéed fennel, and specialty breads left over from Elissa's brunch to choose from. But delicious fresh-roasted corn is the primary attraction. People take turns at the fire pit by the pond, watching over the corn. Some is barely cooked, and some is charred. But we don't care.

We spread out on the grass, on logs, or on chairs. Neighbors catch up with each other on their latest summer trips. Nancy Brown (a resident in her late 70s) had been stopped at the Canadian border without her passport and not allowed to reenter the US until a neighbor found it and sent it to her by FedEx. My friends Elan and Rachael had their van's engine blow up as they were returning from 10 relaxing days in Cape Cod. Despite these adventures everyone seems happy and relaxed, and pleased to be home again.

After dinner we all roast marshmallows. Marcie sits at the keyboard she has set up behind her house. She and Sarah Gasser (age 12) belt out tunes from *Oklahoma!* Others join in, and soon there's an impromptu singalong of tunes from other musicals — definitely a cohousing moment. I join the cluster around the keyboard, and we put our arms around each other, swaying as we sing.

The sunset dashes the sky with orange and red streaks that reflect in the pond. The children poke at the fire with their marshmallow sticks, and a small group talks quietly on the grass, clapping at the end of each song. As the sky darkens, we reluctantly put away the keyboard.

Just then the danceable tunes of the Supremes and Aretha Franklin burst out of the Common House. Soon people of all ages are dancing in a circle on the Common House porch, taking turns doing fancy dance steps to the clapping of their cohousing fans. Little Julia (age five) kicks her feet to the rhythms, and Morgan (also five) trounces across the circle. Some children stay with their parents; others spontaneously join in without them. What a delightful end to a delightful day!

The following morning I am in the Common House preparing to cook when Petra comes in. She has stopped by to wash the Common House napkins and towels, and is upset. The Common House floor is filthy, and the compost — consisting mostly of corncobs — has not been broken into the bite-sized pieces needed to make good compost.

In a community like EVI everyone has different standards of cleanliness, and unfortunately the lowest common denominator often prevails. People who have lower standards don't see what the fuss is about, and people who have higher standards feel angry and resentful because they end up cleaning up after others. Petra and her husband Richard form the backbone of the Common House cleaning team, and the work is truly never-ending (much like trying to keep a kitchen clean with a house full of teenagers).

I empathize with Petra. But I am also happy that the two Labor Day parties had been so much fun. (Of course the brunt of the cleanup hadn't been on my shoulders.) As Petra and I talk, I pluck dead leaves off the vines growing across the Common House trellis — one small step to show that I, too, care about order and beauty in our common spaces.

THE TUNE CAFÉ

The Tune Café is another hit EcoVillage celebration. Every three or four months our family invites the community to our place for an evening of music. Everyone brings a potluck dessert and at least one CD cut of a favorite piece of music. The result is delicious and eclectic.

We have had as many as 60 people show up in our small living room (and once there were only 5 of us). We take turns listening to wonderful music — an opera, world beat, a solo vocalist, or a drumming group. It doesn't really matter. The kids play in the middle of our compact living room with whatever toys are on hand. Adults join in or curl up on the couch, blissfully enjoying the music. Some of us dance. We eat dessert, savoring homemade brownies, melting ice cream, grapes, or other goodies. Every evening unfolds in its own mysterious way, and somehow we are all satisfied.

At EVI meaningful human contact is the norm and not the exception. I consider myself blessed to live here. I can maintain my privacy when I need to, but also have plenty of opportunity to form and develop my connections with my cohousing neighbors. Indeed I think that living in community fills the deep longing for human love and connection that is shared by our whole species.

CHAPTER 5

IT'S NOT UTOPIA —
COMMUNICATION AND CONFLICT

*Being in community is a lot like being in a primary rela-
tionship. Most of us bring a somewhat romanticized and
starry-eyed idealism to the beginning stages. That wears off
after a while, especially once everyone settles in to live together.
Cracks in the dream picture begin to emerge. You see that
some people are more responsible than others. Some people do
their chores; others do not. Some people are full of good ideas
but don't follow through. Others may be less imaginative
but steadily get things done. You may get annoyed at different levels of cleanliness and order in the common spaces.
You have your first community-wide fight, and suddenly
the future doesn't look as rosy. You wonder if you really
want to spend the rest of your life with these people.*

*Then something shifts. A special connection happens
between friends. A child celebrates her first birthday. Or
you come back from a trip and see the friendliness and
profound sense of community with fresh eyes. You remember,
Oh, so this is what it's all about. It's like having a special
date with your partner. The magic is rekindled.*

Many people who visit EcoVillage assume that we either have created
or are trying to create a fairy tale-like utopia in which people will
live happily ever after. The truth is far richer, deeper, and more complex.

Communication

Communication at EcoVillage has many layers. I like to think of us as
a rainforest ecosystem. In the canopy or top layer, the intertwining

branches of the trees look like a single, unbroken ocean of green. EVI looks like an integrated whole, too, if you look at us at the community level.

The middle layer of a rainforest is a little more differentiated. The trunks of the trees are distinct, yet vines lace up and down and cross between trees. Howler monkeys hoot to each other. Coconuts, mangos, and bananas thrive. We have many subgroups at EVI, too — friends, interest groups, and committees, all creating webs of connection and meaning with each other.

The forest floor of a rainforest teems with action. The brush is dense with many species of plants and animals, each with their own niche. Likewise the many individuals who live at EVI — 102 adults and 60 children — each occupy a unique place in the whole.

In a rainforest nothing occurs in isolation. Everything that happens affects the entire ecosystem. At EcoVillage, too, every interaction ultimately affects the entire community. Communication takes place with each of these layers as a backdrop — the rich buzz of individuals as they go about their daily lives, the friendship and work groups that meet frequently, and the overview of the community as a whole.

Martha Stettinius
Morgan and Orion share a quiet moment.

Conflicts can arise at any level among the inhabitants of a rainforest. The same is true for communities. That is why effective communication is crucial if the whole is to remain healthy and strong. Most of us know how to carve out our individual niches — our society teaches us those skills as we grow up. Most of us even know how to communicate well with individual friends and colleagues. But we may not do so well at the group level. And that is precisely where the most challenge lies, and the greatest potential for conflict.

INTERACTION BY DESIGN

The entire layout of a cohousing neighborhood is designed to increase face-to-face communication and interaction. And indeed it does. As I walk to the Common House, pick up my laundry, or walk to my car I inevitably see at least one or two neighbors. On a sunny summer day, I may meet up with a couple of dozen people. Sometimes we'll just smile or exchange a Hi, how are you? At other times, depending on the mood or the weather, we may chat for a while or even have an impromptu meeting. There's a word for this kind of thing.

"Ratcheting," in cohousing slang, refers to the spontaneous interactions that cohousing promotes. For example Jared may ask me why it has taken me an hour to take out the compost. My response would be that I got "ratcheted." During that hour I may have talked to a couple of friends about our children, helped someone move a ladder, had a cup of coffee with a new neighbor, looked at someone's newly painted kitchen, as well as taken out the compost. Of course ratcheting has the potential to get out of hand. Which is why, over time, we have all become more attuned to each other's nonverbal cues. Usually it's pretty clear if people are in a hurry, or if they want to slow down and talk.

House design also supports communication. Design elements as simple as room and window placement make it easy for us to stay in touch. All our kitchens face the pedestrian street, so we can look out our windows and see what's going on. We can keep tabs on which kids are playing together or see who's out gardening or sitting in the sun.

It's easy for us to call out to our neighbors, join them for a visit, or lend a hand with some chore. For instance one winter day I looked out my window and saw Alan shoveling the paths. Although my plan had been to go cross-country skiing, I noticed that he was lobbing huge clumps of snow from drifts that were up to 15 inches (38 centimeters) deep. I remembered that many people were out of town over Christmas vacation. So, trading one form of exercise for another, I grabbed my shovel and joined him.

After 40 minutes of heavy work, we were about to go inside when my friend Rachael (a therapist) came down the path and hailed us. She had clients due at the Common House in 10 minutes, and the doors wouldn't open. She wondered if we knew where there was another shovel.

I directed her to borrow Jay's shovel, which was sitting outside his front door. Together the three of us dug out the Common House steps and porch. And we were in the nick of time too, finishing just as Rachael's clients stepped out of their car.

Alan and I were too tired to work any longer. But as I walked back, I noticed that another neighbor, Ben, and his young son had come outside and were widening the paths. Without EVI's layout to provide us easy visual access to our neighborhood, it is unlikely that our shared snow removal efforts would even have happened.

E-MAIL EVOLUTION

Face-to-face interaction may be the easiest and most preferable form of communication, but what happens when you need to share information with the whole group? Thirty families in a single neighborhood and 60 families in a village make a lot of people to "talk to." You need an effective and streamlined way to contact everyone, and that's where e-mail steps in. But we didn't always have it.

At the beginning of the project no one had e-mail. We used phone trees, which were cumbersome and often broke down, or held group meetings. And we mailed a lot of information. When I was FROG coordinator, a couple of volunteers and I spent most of one day a week on mailings for our members, many of whom still lived in different parts of the country. We copied all the minutes, agendas, proposals, and surveys on a little personal copier that could only handle one page at a time. Each mailing package often contained an additional 16 double-sided pages (or more) of background material as reading for the next meeting. It all had to be printed and collated, stapled and folded, put in envelopes, stamped, and mailed.

And there were problems. The mailings didn't get to California for five days, which put our West Coast members under a lot of pressure. They had to read and absorb everything and then, if they had serious concerns, respond by telephone before the next meeting. At the end of a typical workday, my ear would be sore from hours of phone calls as our many members tried to share information. Keeping everyone informed in the early 1990s was really very complicated.

The advent of e-mail revolutionized communication at EVI. By the time we moved into FROG in 1996, all but a few members were online. We could hold important discussions online, saving valuable meeting time (and my ears, since I had to field far fewer phone calls). We could generate ideas for discussion or ask each other for help — sometimes with almost instantaneous results. (Today it is not unusual for someone sending an e-mail at 10:00 asking for a ride to town to be picked up at 10:15.) And with one keystroke we could share pages of topical information with the whole group that previously would have taken hours, if not days, to assemble and distribute.

Of course most of us didn't have a clue about e-mail etiquette in the early days. That led to problems, especially when we were dealing with difficult topics. With no way to read each other's facial expressions or hear nuances in tones of voice, a simple statement could come across like a sledgehammer blow. And one such "flame" could start several brush fires as others leaped into the fray. After a year or two of such painful encounters, we wised up and put together some informal guidelines for e-mail use. By the time people had settled in at SONG, inappropriate e-mail use was mostly a thing of the past.

However, the very thing that makes e-mail so useful can also make it overwhelming. We typically post upwards of 45 group e-mails a day on several different internal listservs. If you don't keep up with them, then you can feel as if you are behind in the information flow and discussion. If you miss weeks or months of e-mail (as I recently did), it can take several days of sitting in front of the computer to catch up.

People cope with e-mail overload in different ways. Some only subscribe to the "announce" listserv, to catch the most important business items. Others drop e-mail altogether. However, for most EcoVillagers, e-mail remains a very significant form of interaction.

Beyond E-mail

E-mail isn't the only way to get people's attention. We also hold group meetings twice a month. And many of us post an attractive notice on the Common House door when we want to let people know about an upcoming event. Or we ring the bell at a Common House meal to make a quick announcement. I sometimes think, though, that the only way to truly reach everyone is to make use of all of the preceding methods, *plus* tape notices on everyone's doors.

SETTING LIMITS

You may wonder how we keep from being inundated with the details of each other's lives. Just think of all the thoughts, emotions, and relationships — not to mention the day-to-day organizational demands — of so many people living in such close proximity! At times it can be overwhelming.

While much of the rest of society has to deal with the clamoring call of Me first!, we sometimes have to deal with too many community demands. We may not have enough time for solitude. Or we may sacrifice valuable time with our families in order to attend a meeting. Task upon task can pile up. At the end of 2003, when we were at the height of new member move-ins, we set up an informal community-wide discussion to discuss the "EcoVillage Overwhelm" factor. But we had so few sign-ups that we cancelled the salon — people were simply too overwhelmed!

The constant balancing act between being involved but not too involved is like strengthening a muscle that needs exercise. You have to learn how to say no and to set limits that honor your own rhythms and needs. Limit setting is a healthy choice and can lead to tremendous personal growth.

DEALING WITH DIFFERENCE

Living in community makes us take a long, steady look at ourselves and at others. When we look, we can't help but notice some often-profound differences — in our values, our personalities, our lifestyles, and our income levels, among other things.

Examining our differences provides an opportunity for each of us to grow and change over time. Sometimes another person's actions are inspiring. At other times, they can make us uncomfortable. Often our discomfort is a sign that some personal growth is called for.

I often tell visitors that the single most important aspect of living in community is learning how to communicate effectively. Good communication includes the ability to listen well, to speak one's truth, to remain flexible under stress, to look for solutions that benefit everyone (rather than just the individual), and to work with others to resolve conflicts. Good communication demands a great deal of energy, and at times it can feel exhausting. Of course we don't always succeed — we really aren't living in a utopia here. However, at EcoVillage, we have found that the more energy we put into the important work of communicating well, the more good energy comes back to us, enlivening the whole community and all its individual members.

Conflict

Learning to deal effectively with conflict is the hardest part of living in community. Our society teaches us early to avoid it. When I was a child I often heard the adage "If you don't have something nice to say, don't say anything at all." It was all right to say mean things behind someone's back (gossip), but it was not all right to say them face to face.

Fortunately my Quaker family sent a different set of messages, including "There is that of God in everyone" and "Speak truth to power." I took my family's messages to heart and found that if I speak to the "good side" of a person and am sincere and honest, then it is much easier to communicate. This approach to conflict respects everyone involved. As my friend Poppy put it, "What we're really trying to do here is be honest and stay close at the same time."

Conflict has been part of community life since EVI's inception.

Child-Rearing at EcoVillage

Child-rearing in our cohousing neighborhood differs from the mainstream. Most kids seldom if ever watch TV — they are far too busy participating in the day-to-day activities of the village community. At EVI children learn conflict resolution skills from the earliest age. And 6- to 12-year-olds participate in a "Kids' Council," where they take part in developing their own behavioral guidelines and doing fun projects, such as building a bike trail.

Parents, on the other hand, have to deeply examine their own values about child-rearing. As part of our larger but closely integrated community, they must learn to cope with the differing parenting styles of their neighbors. And they have to deal collectively with the problems, such as exclusionary behavior, that arise among the children. As with many aspects of life at EVI, we try hard to communicate values effectively in our individual families and in our larger family of EcoVillage neighbors. ∎

Sometimes the conflicts are very personal and only involve a couple of people. But there are also group-wide conflicts. For me, as for most others in the community, even the word "conflict" creates stress. (I'll find myself clenching my teeth and tightening my belly, as if to ward off a blow.) The only thing that helps all of us to relax and let go of the tension is to talk openly about the issues — not an easy thing to do! But worth it.

A PERSONAL CONFLICT

I fell into a personal conflict shortly after Sue moved into the other half of our duplex. We shared a common wall, with my kitchen and living room adjacent to hers and separated by about a foot of well-insulated space. We had rarely heard any noise from our previous neighbors, despite the fact that they were raising a young child, so all seemed well. And it was, until the summer rolled around.

Sue loved to turn up her music to full volume and rock out to the Indigo Girls. Many times while I was working at home, trying to concentrate and with my writing materials spread out over the kitchen table, Sue's music would take over the house. Sometimes I could hear the lyrics but mostly my concentration was broken by the Thump! Thump! Thump! of the bass line.

I was surrounded by sound — impossible to ignore and not of my choosing. It was as if powerful vibrations beyond my control were invading the quiet sanctuary of my home. Or as if someone was thumping away with a jackhammer in my front yard, refusing to stop. The very ground of my being felt threatened.

Confronting Sue was the last thing I wanted to do. Doesn't she have the right to play her music? I'd ask myself. Why should I censor her? Or I'd think, I don't feel like talking to her about this again. I've already brought it up five times, and it's still happening. She'll just get mad. Or I'd say to myself, I'll just try to ignore it. Surely she can't listen very long without going deaf.

In the meantime, my whole body was tense. Hands over my ears, I would try to concentrate, reading the words on the page out loud in an attempt to understand them. I'd be shaking with the effort of not getting angry, but I was really seething inside. How could she be so insensitive? I'd protest. She knows that turning up the bass really reverberates in our house.

Anywhere from ten minutes to half an hour later, my patience would wear thin. I'd pick up the phone and call Sue, telling her that her music was really bothering me and asking her to turn it down. But she rarely answered the phone when she was listening to her music, so her answering machine would record my irritated voice. My next step was to knock on her front door. Sometimes she would answer and sometimes not. Even after my teenage son pointed out that it was the extra bass function causing the problem, Sue's music still occasionally broke the sound barrier in my house.

Things came to a head one morning in September. I was in a bad mood. My older son who was away at college suddenly asked me for a big chunk of money. He wanted to change apartments — for the third time in four months! I felt he was treating me like his private bank, with limitless credit, and I was upset and irritated. So when Sue's music came on, I didn't wait. I ran over to her house and knocked loudly. When I got no response, I opened the front door and stepped inside.

"Sue, I'm absolutely furious. Why don't you turn down your f... music? It's driving me crazy!" I yelled in her face. Sue, to her credit, stood her ground. Her face turned beet red.

"Don't ever talk to me like that! It's not okay for you to just barge in and yell at me. I'll never turn down my music if that's how you treat me!"

As her words sank in, I felt totally embarrassed. Was this really me, the ultimate mediator, losing my cool? Had I really sworn at her? I apologized for my behavior and slunk out — although a part of me felt justified for getting so upset.

There was no more audible music the rest of the day, and I was profoundly grateful for that. I still felt rubbed raw, though, and realized that other circumstances in my life were pushing me past what I could tolerate. I determined to talk to Sue the next day, apologize, and make up for my unacceptable behavior. At the same time, I hoped that she would mull things over and look at her own behavior.

The next day, Sue called to me as I walked past her house. She said she'd been so upset by my outburst that it had kept her awake all night. I told her I was sorry, and she apologized to me, too. And then she told me that she might be facing breast cancer. She said that listening to her music at top volume was the only thing that helped her forget her fears. But she also said she realized she shouldn't be disturbing me. She had plans to put up some soundproofing on her side of the common wall to help deaden the sound. And she promised not to use the extra bass function again. I gave her a jar of wild blueberry jam that I had lovingly made from berries collected on my last trip to Vermont. We hugged and both felt enormously better. Since then Sue's music has never disturbed me again. And thankfully, Sue's cancer scare was just that — a scare.

Fortunately most conflicts at EcoVillage do not escalate to this degree. However, I think that my conflict with Sue illustrates some good points:

1. Both parties have to be willing to listen to each other and to speak for their own needs. I find it much easier to listen than to speak out. Rather than confront Sue, I seethed in silence until my anger built up to exploding point. I think the reverse tends to be true for Sue. She easily speaks up for herself but finds it harder to understand someone else's point of view. We are all programmed a little differently, but it is crucial to be able to both listen and speak up.

2. People don't always behave well when strong emotions are involved. It helps to have a cool-down period. Talk to other friends about the conflict, or wait until you're in a calmer frame of mind to sort out what is going on. When I lost my cool, I ended up yelling and swearing at Sue. And she yelled back. But we both thought about things overnight and talked them through the next day.

3. The conflict may not always be about the people involved in the conflict. Conflicts can kick up deep-seated emotions that may be rooted in past or unrelated events. Some of my anger was really about my son's behavior. And some of Sue's actions rose out of her worries about her health.

4. People actually become closer when they work through their conflicts. It took a crisis for Sue and me to really talk to each other. When we did, we came to understand the larger context of each other's lives. We could empathize with each other. And we found solutions that met both of our needs. Having passed the difficult hurdle of working through our conflict, we became genuinely friendly neighbors.

5. Success breeds success. Once you have worked through something that felt like an impossible situation, you can relax and let go of tension, knowing that you have the ability to cope with whatever comes your way. Future conflicts may not upset you quite so much.

COMMUNITY-WIDE CONFLICTS

If personal conflicts are hard, then community-wide conflicts can be excruciating. It's bad enough having two people involved in a disagreement, each with their own baggage. (I picture each person holding a bulging suitcase full of their personal history, unique way of looking at the situation, relationship with the other person, and strong emotions — all needing to be sorted out in relation to the issue and the other person.) But if you multiply those two people by five or ten, then the number of interrelationships and amount of baggage grows exponentially. Add some unpredictable group dynamics and a few dysfunctional personalities, and you end up with a big, seething, chaotic mess.

We've experienced plenty of community-wide conflicts at EVI. Not only have we survived, but we've also learned how to better manage conflicts and to reach solutions more easily.

Jared Jones

Pam and Jay share an intense moment.

Family Friction

One community-wide conflict at EVI arose between three of the original families in FROG and the larger community as a whole. Families A and B were very close friends. The men were MIT graduates — brilliant, analytical thinkers and also both stay-at-home dads. The women were medical professionals — a doctor and a nurse-midwife. The two families had checked out several other cohousing groups and decided that ours had the best group process. In fact they moved to Ithaca together (in 1995) to become part of EcoVillage. Needless to say, it felt like a coup to have them choose our group and bring their combined talents to our young community.

Family C was a local family with two children. Both parents worked — one at Cornell and the other at a local publishing house. The two brought experience with alternative technologies, such as solar panels and composting toilets. And they brought a can-do attitude.

It soon became apparent that none of the three families was very happy with EVI. We make decisions by consensus, a process in which all points of view are taken into account. Objections get discussed and solutions are proposed to address them. Facilitators help us work toward achieving a "group mind," in which commonly held values lead to a clear consensus. After much discussion the community as a whole comes to a decision with which everyone can agree. Sometimes an individual may disagree with the decision but still agrees to abide by it — an acceptable choice within the consensus process. If someone feels very strongly that a group decision is wrong, then the consensus process allows a person to "block" it. Since proposals only come to the floor for a decision after weeks of discussion, proposal writing, and committee meetings, blocking a decision is a very serious step. And usually a very rare one.

As we went about conducting the community's business, we found that more often than not, one of the three families would block a group decision. The men in particular seemed to block if a decision was not going the way they wanted it to, or if it would not bring personal benefits to their families. Conflicts occurred around spending money, but lifestyle issues arose, as well.

The tactics the three men used were very hard to deal with. Consensus-based decision making takes faith, trust, and goodwill — qualities the three seemed to lack. They reminded me of rambunctious young boys on a playground who had not yet learned to be team play-ers. Tom used his considerable intellect to put down anyone who disagreed with him. He spoke at length and was able to talk circles around other people who were less articulate. Upon closer examina-tion, though, his arguments were almost always self-serving. Because people found it hard to interrupt him, or to be the butt of his acerbic put-downs, the group as a whole stood by and watched rather than set limits on his behavior.

George worked hard and put in lots of time on the neighborhood finance team. He rarely spoke up at meetings, but when he did, he expressed a lot of anger. Like Tom, he frequently used put-downs and often blocked consensus.

Henry almost never spoke. He was very shy, with an occasional slow sweet smile. A strict vegan, Henry became disillusioned when we decided to serve meat occasionally at Common House meals. Intended to meet the needs of those members who felt that meat was an impor-tant part of their diets, the decision came about only after months of meetings to discuss dietary preferences. We established cooking proto-cols to deal with the change that would suit our vegetarian and vegan members: There would always be a vegetarian and a vegan main dish at each Common House meal. Cooking pots and utensils used for cooking meat would be kept entirely separate from the rest of the kitchen equipment.

Henry came to one or two discussions, but withdrew from the decision-making process early on. He had a firm idea of what he wanted. When the group decided on something else, Henry did not block the decision but made a vow never to enter the Common House again. When asked to talk about his feelings, he refused. Gradually Henry withdrew more and more from social contact, leaving for work from his back door and hardly ever interacting with anyone outside his immediate family. His moral stand was rigid and unbending — difficult to handle and out of synch with our diverse community.

Aside from taking issue with EVI's decision-making processes, Tom, George, and Henry also saw my leadership as a threat right from the beginning of the project. And their distrust and hostility was particularly hard to bear. With Joan, I was a co-director of the whole EVI project. But for several years before our first set of homes were completed, I was also hired to act as FROG's coordinator. In that role

I convened a steering committee that set each week's agenda, published minutes, oversaw subcommittees, and worked closely with our development managers Jerry and Claudia Weisburd. I worked hard and conscientiously to keep information flowing, identify issues needing to be resolved, and help the group move through the myriad complexities of designing and developing a cohousing project. I saw myself as a professional organizer, someone who could make sure that we accomplished our goals.

Most people appreciated what I did. But Tom, George, and Henry thought that I had too much power, despite the fact that every decision was made using consensus. The three treated both Joan and me with hostility and frequently criticized us in meetings. And it seemed that everyone else was too afraid to defend us. I had seen that pattern in other groups, and it scared me to see such a toxic dynamic developing here. Since I had no desire to dominate the group, the accusations and criticisms really hurt my feelings. And I became very cautious about taking any kind of initiative.

By the time we had lived in community for two years (1998), the tension between the three families and the rest of the group was becoming unbearable. Mistrust and hostility were rampant. The families felt isolated and unhappy and looked mostly to each other for companionship (even though several individuals in FROG did reach out and cultivate friendships with them). Meetings seemed filled with acrimony. Here we were striving for a strong sense of community, and yet no matter how many special process techniques we tried, a yawning chasm was widening between this subset of families and the rest of the group.

Our process steering committee (devoted to planning and facilitating group meetings) took action. Why not train the whole community in conflict resolution? We selected two outside facilitators, set dates, and began in earnest.

The whole FROG community met with the facilitators six times over the following year. At first the sessions focused on simple skill-building exercises, such as "active listening." We learned how to attentively listen to each other's viewpoints and then repeat them back. Other exercises taught us how to empathize with each other.

We also learned about some basic healthy group dynamic principles. Our facilitators showed us the importance of having each person take responsibility for expressing his or her own viewpoint rather than remain a bystander. And they cautioned us not to scapegoat people who were perceived as different.

The community divided into conflict resolution groups made up of four or five adults. Groups got together twice a month to practice conflict resolution skills, focusing on any conflicts (even minor ones) between members of the group. As we practiced, our skill levels gradually increased.

Then our facilitators moved us into scarier territory. I'll never forget the night in 1999 when I sat in the hot seat as 60 of my friends and neighbors peppered me with questions about my leadership and the actions I had taken over the previous eight years as a director of EcoVillage at Ithaca. It was a very direct way to dredge out people's unspoken criticisms and fears about leadership. Despite the fact that my heart was galloping like a racehorse, I felt that I answered well. I was able to clarify quite a few misconceptions. By the end of the meeting I was sticky with sweat, but that didn't stop me from giving and receiving a lot of hugs. I certainly felt clearer in my role as leader. Paradoxically I also felt more a part of the group than ever before.

Conflict resolution training changed our behavior. We started challenging dysfunctional behavior in our meetings. Different people spoke out when disrespectful comments were made. But despite our best efforts, things didn't seem to change much.

Meanwhile the three families stayed on. I remember realizing that they would probably be here for the rest of my life — unhappy, unwilling community members who might verbally attack me or other members at any time. By this time two of the men refused to say hello or to even make eye contact when we passed on the path. The third refused to take part in any kind of mediation or conflict resolution.

Then, at about the same time I finally accepted the situation, things miraculously seemed to shift. Each of the families came to the conclusion that they would be happier leaving the community. It was a huge relief to have them leave and take all their anger and hostility with them. Sadly no one offered to throw a farewell party for them — a harsh reminder of how little connection they had made with others in the community.

Our experience with the three families also changed how we orient prospective members. We now emphasize how important it is to be flexible and willing to talk through differences. And we particularly highlight the role that effective communication plays at EVI. In my view cohousing simply will not work for people who are not dedicated to these principles.

Water Tank Talk

Another community-wide conflict arose over a water tank. In the spring of 2002 Dan Walker, town engineer for Ithaca, approached me with a proposal. The Town needed to find a site for a water tank and was thinking of using EcoVillage land.

My ears perked up. Perhaps a water tank would provide us with pressurized water. Then we wouldn't have to pump water uphill from the last residential street below EVI land. Or perhaps we could use the tank as a source of emergency water for our proposed third neighborhood and Village Center. Perhaps the Town would give us a large donation to compensate for the acreage they would use. And perhaps the tank would be as ugly as sin and the Town wouldn't pay us anything.

Dan and I talked. He made it clear that the Town had the upper hand — they could use eminent domain to force us to take the tank. The tank could not provide us directly with water. Any water would have to flow downhill to be pressurized enough to use, and the lay of the land precluded that. And the Town was unlikely to pay any cash, though they might do us some in-kind favors, such as putting in a sewer line where we needed one. Apparently the tank (75 feet [23 meters] in diameter and 30 feet [9 meters] tall) would largely benefit the residential area below us. But — and this was the big carrot — the tank could be used as an emergency water source for future EVI development.

Water had been a perennial issue between EVI and the Town. First the Town had asked us to hook up to city water and sewer, rather than dig wells and use composting toilets. Then it had told us we needed a 60- to 90-foot (18- to 27-meter) water tower if we wanted to build housing on the hill. Depending on where it was placed, the $300,000 – $400,000 tower would have dictated where we could site the neighborhoods.

Our development managers Jerry and Claudia Weisburd went to bat for us. They convinced the Town to let us use a simple pumping station on West Haven Road to supply domestic water to FROG and SONG (and possibly a third neighborhood). They also persuaded the

Town to let us build a one-acre pond for fire protection. We were allowed to install residential sprinklers in the Common House, even though it was considered a commercial building and would have no pressurized water source until a tower was built. FROG dutifully built the pond and the pumping station and installed the sprinklers.

When SONG came along, we held our collective breath to see if we would be required to build a water tower. Rod Lambert and I, serving as development managers for SONG, met with the fire chief and the assistant fire chief to talk about fire protection. The two agreed that the existing one-acre pond would be adequate but insisted that we install an extensive "dry hydrant" system to allow easy access to the pond's water.

Later on fire protection officials required more hydrants, and a "wet well" system that was both more complex and more expensive than a dry hydrant one. And they insisted that we use iron pipes, rather than much less expensive PVC pipes, to carry water to SONG. Our hydrant system was tested several times, and each time the fire department wanted more bells and whistles added to it. All told it took approximately two years to get them to sign off on the expensive system. Since we had all experienced the fire, we knew that safety was important, but it came at a higher price tag than we had expected.

Time passed as our two neighborhoods established themselves. All the while I dreaded the thought of having to secure a source of emergency water for a third neighborhood. Would the Town finally require that we build that 60-foot water tower? Or would we be able to sink another pond that would have an adequate water supply? Or would we be stymied from building anything else at all?

Now the issue was coming to a head, but not over a third neighborhood as I had expected. People were more interested in building a Village Center to provide recreational and performance space than in building a third neighborhood. Considering EVI's ever-present water needs, the option Dan was offering us was a huge plus and a potential win-win situation.

Everything quieted down for a while, and we wondered if the Town had changed its mind. But then Dan Walker called Greg Pitts (resident, SONG consultant, and EVI Board member) to say that the water tank issue had surfaced again. I knew this was a pivotal moment. I asked Greg to call a meeting with the Town.

A week later, we got together with representatives from the Town. Dan was there in his role as town engineer. So were the chief town planner, the town supervisor and assistant supervisor, and the assistant building inspector. Greg Pitts, Rod Lambert, and I, along with Mike Carpenter (the SONG construction manager) and Marcie Finlay (an attorney on the EVI Board) represented EVI. It was a watershed meeting.

Both sides were doing a bit of a dance. The Town was involved in site negotiations with the Eddy family who owned open land across the road from us. And it had backed off from making "good and valuable considerations," such as paying us for acreage used, putting in the sewer line, or paying for moving our pump station.

Those of us from EVI surmised that future development would be hard if not impossible without having the tank on our land. But we knew that the issue would be controversial in our community. Some of us wanted the tank, while others did not.

The discussion went back and forth. Although we received no definitive answers, it seemed clear to me that, despite the lack of financial remuneration, the water tank would be essential for future development. Therefore, at the end of the two-hour meeting, I made it clear that I supported the tank and would ask the EcoVillage Board to vote on the matter at our next meeting. There was an audible sigh of relief from the Town. But I knew that not all members of our team were equally as happy.

Back at EcoVillage I presented the information to the group via an e-mail describing the meeting and presenting the facts as I knew them. I set up a forum for residents on the topic, and invited EVI Board members to attend. I also invited Dan Walker to join us. A few people e-mailed me back — even some who had been previously opposed — to say that they supported the rationale for the tank. I felt confident that people would see it was in our interest to accept the tank.

When Dan Walker arrived on meeting night, we got right down to business. As the light faded, we turned on one of the high-intensity lamps to show maps of potential sites for the tank. And over the following hour-and-a-half the group grilled Dan, literally making him sweat in the spotlight.

Dan handled the questions well and made a number of concessions in EVI's favor. At one point he told us that the Town's tanks usually have a chain-link fence topped with barbed wire around their perimeter. There was a group intake of breath and an exchange of worried looks around the room. Was the water tank area going to look like a military camp? But then he added, "Well, at EcoVillage we probably wouldn't need that. You people are always around. You provide your own security. I know every time I go up here, someone politely asks me what I'm doing. I don't think you'll need the fence." We let out a collective sigh of relief.

Then we questioned him about the road. If the Town sent in 20 concrete trucks a day for 40 days to build the tank, it would really chew up our already fragile dirt entry road. I pressed Dan on this point. He agreed that the Town would repair any damage.

"Would you take photos before and after?" persisted another resident.

"Yes," said Dan, still in the spotlight.

"What about the farm? Would you have to take down the deer fence around it? How would you repair that?" asked John, the farmer.

"Yes, we would take down the deer fence, and we'd pay to repair it. We'd also work with you to scrape off the topsoil, then return the soil in good condition," Dan stated. One by one concerns were raised and addressed, almost entirely in our favor. The meeting ended on a good note, and I thought the rest of the process would be easy. After all at least 20 people had attended the forum, including those opposed to the tank.

Zach Shahan (our intern) took minutes and sent them to me for corrections the next day. I e-mailed out the corrected minutes to the group a few days later. I took care to represent all sides of the issue and included one section on benefits to EVI and another on outstanding concerns. I also asked if we should have another forum to discuss the location of the tank, since at least one resident was uncomfortable with the Town's preferred site. That done I went away for a three-day weekend with some friends to a very relaxing yoga center and came back Sunday night, deeply refreshed. At least I was until I checked out my e-mails.

Oh, my God! There was a veritable torrent of e-mails about the water tank. "It will destroy our property values!" "It will look awful!" "Don't trust the Town, they're just taking advantage of us!" The list went on and on. I counted 25 new e-mails on the topic, most of them filled with the potential horrors of accepting the tank.

The energy of the group felt like a sheet on a clothesline as it flapped wildly out of control in a gale force wind. My carefully garnered relaxation from the weekend drained away. We were clearly in crisis. I had not seen the community so upset and divided more than a handful of times through our whole history. Would our community be ripped to shreds over this issue? What should I do? My inner voice told me to wait 24 hours before trying to tackle this mess.

I'm glad I waited. Bill Goodman, an attorney and SONG resident, came out with a rather astonishing e-mail the next day. Standing up for civic responsibility in the midst of negative feedback, Bill's e-mail was headed "Two thumbs up for the tank." Not only did Bill make good points about the advantages of the tank, but he also waxed eloquent about its beauty. He boldly suggested that we could paint a giant turtle on top of the tank, as a symbol of unity with the Native Americans who once lived on this land, and call it "Turtle Island." Coming from an attorney, this was unusual language indeed. But it created an opening in the debate.

I sent out a community-wide e-mail on Tuesday, carefully debunking some of the misinformation. First, property values were unlikely to go down. Libby Long, the appraiser who had worked with us for years, had specifically told me that in her view the tank would not affect property values. Nor would the tank be environmentally unjust. Poor aesthetics, the tank's main drawback, would be more than made up for by its usefulness, since it would enable us to fulfill our whole vision for EVI.

The battle lines had been drawn in the digital sand, and the storm raged back and forth during the next week. I called a second forum for the following Monday, hoping our community could make it until then without serious damage.

And then I had a crisis of confidence. I began to wonder if I had the strength to lead us through the situation. In a co-counseling session with my friend Betsy, I sobbed my heart out. "I'm not sure that anyone will speak to me after this, no matter what the outcome. If the tensions are that bad, I may just have to leave the community. I'm caught smack in the middle between the EcoVillage Board, which keeps the overall EcoVillage vision alive, and the residents, many of whom are tired of change and just want the status quo."

Tears coursing down my cheeks, I contemplated abandoning everything I had worked for. And all because of that stupid tank. I knew that if we had to import water in the future, the hundreds of thousands of dollars in up-front capital would probably prohibit future development. I thought of our dream of a third neighborhood, of a Village

Center, and an Education Center. Why did the Town have to bring up this divisive issue, anyway? Betsy, as a good co-counselor, assured me that I would find the strength to lead the group through the mess. Her faith in me brought fresh sobs. I still felt helpless.

As it turned out our co-counseling session was a turning point. By expressing my deepest fears, I was able to face them down and open my mind to fresh, creative thinking. Most importantly I was able to act on my most deep-seated intuition and let go of the outcome. After all, if the group definitely didn't want a water tank, who was I to foist it on them? Sadly I let go of our dreams of further development and accepted the reality that the group, and not I, would make the final decision.

Meanwhile the second forum was fast approaching. Although I asked for support, no one was available to help me plan this critical meeting. So instead I gathered helpful suggestions from several people and created a simple questionnaire. I sent it out through e-mail on Friday, polling the group for their thoughts on whether or not to accept the tank and, if so, at what location. I also wrote up a two-page fact sheet on the tank, since the e-mails that were circulating were becoming increasingly inaccurate. Several key people had even signed off on reading or writing any more e-mails on the subject.

On Saturday night, after another a long day spent working on the issue, my family went to a friend's house for dinner. On our way my teenage son Daniel and I distributed hard copies of the poll to all 45 households. Everyone would have ample opportunity to look at the few simple questions and respond — either through e-mail or hard copy. When the Board came to vote on the issue, it would be imperative that it take the wishes of the community to heart.

The make-it-or-break-it night of the second community forum rolled around on Monday. I had worked out a very simple agenda. I would give an information update, we'd all walk the three potential sites, and then we'd come back to the Common House for a "talking stick" circle. I had purposefully not invited Dan Walker to this meeting. It seemed to me that more than anything else, we simply needed to talk and listen to each other in a respectful way as we aired our various opinions. Would I find myself facing an angry mob of neighbors? I wondered. Strangely I felt calm and peaceful, and ready to accept whatever happened.

I called the meeting to order as a couple of dozen people crowded into the sitting room. I began with the information update. I had talked to David Herrick (an engineer with a local firm), who had served as a consultant to EVI numerous times. In Herrick's view, there was insufficient surface water to sustain another pond, should we decide to dig one. We could sink wells that would feed a pond, but the water table was quite low at the top of West Hill, and there were no guarantees that we would find enough water. And each test well could easily cost us $10,000. As an engineer, Herrick strongly favored the water tank. I also reviewed the three potential tank sites on a map. And then we all went walking, heading out to tramp the three sites.

It was a beautiful May evening. Birds were singing and the hedgerows were alive with the blossoms of wild cherry trees. There was a festive feeling about going on a walk together — it almost felt like we were on a treasure hunt. It was only a short walk to the first site, and we all thought that it was too close to the village for comfort.

At the second site we stopped and spread out to form a circle with a 75-foot diameter. I was shocked. Was the tank really that massive? We discussed the pros and cons of this option, which was the Town's preferred site. Most people were happy that it was so far from the sight lines of the residential area, even though the tank would rise high above ground level.

Finally we visited the site behind the neighborhoods. The area was already staked, and someone from EVI had placed a white flag on top of a center pole to mark the center of the circle. At this site the tank would be almost completely buried, with the central dome rising 7½ feet (2.3 meters) above the ground. Although the tank would be visible from the upper windows of the FROG homes, landscaping would easily hide it after only a year or two.

We all trooped back to the Common House and settled in for the remaining hour-and-a-half of the meeting. I took a minute or two to set the guidelines for the talking circle. We would begin with a moment of silence.

Jim Bosjolie

The Town constructs a water tank on EVI land.

Then we would speak one at a time, as we felt moved, passing the "talking stone" that had come from the land from person to person until everyone who wanted to speak had spoken. I asked that we all speak our own truth and not interrupt or question the person speaking. The time we would share here was for listening, not for debating or dialogue. My heart was beating rapidly as I spoke. But then I felt a deep calm come over me — this felt like sacred, healing time.

After an initial silence, one woman came into the center and took the stone. She said she felt happy to have a chance to talk. And she did not want to see the tank, or the massive disruption and earth-moving its construction would entail. She and her husband had moved to EcoVillage from New York City, mostly for the quiet enjoyment of the natural surroundings, and she felt the tank would be a blight on the landscape.

A man took the stone next and spoke of his ambivalent feelings. On the one hand, he realized that future development would be a lot easier with a tank, but he questioned whether enough research had been done on the alternatives. Surely we could find another way to support future water needs without it. At the very least, he thought we should get the Town to guarantee that placing such a tank would satisfy our requirements for the future.

Another man took the stone. It would be nice to have guarantees, he said. But in practical terms he believed it was almost impossible for anyone to say what the future would bring. In everyday life we take risks based on the best information we have available and, in his opinion, this issue was no exception.

Another man, who had cancelled a rare date with his wife to attend the meeting, took the stone next. He was definitely in favor of the tank. Not only would it help us to fulfill the whole vision of EcoVillage, but it would also help out the Town of Ithaca. He saw it as an opportunity to show some civic spirit. Rather than taking a Not-in-my-backyard (NIMBY) attitude, he advocated a Yes-in-my-backyard (YIMBY) approach. In his view a water tank was fairly innocuous. Other communities had had to accept sewer treatment plants or coal-fired plants. We would be getting off easy.

The stone went around the circle for over an hour. As some people left others came in to speak. The tone was quiet and respectful, and I noticed that everyone was listening intently as people spoke.

I was the last speaker. I noted that the stone, which had been cold, was now throbbing with warmth. I said that I felt very grateful to have this opportunity for us to listen deeply to each other. I said that I felt passionate about the overall vision of the EcoVillage, yet respected those who had strong reservations about future development.

After the circle was over, I shared the results of the survey. Of the 36 people who had responded, 0 were neutral; 6 were strongly opposed; 8 were unhappy but could live with it; and 22 supported saying yes to having the tank. The results could be read a couple of different ways: Either 83 percent were mostly in favor (22 in full support, plus the 8 who were willing to live with it) or 40 percent were mostly opposed (6 strongly opposed and 8 unhappy). Either way it was obvious that the community was still split.

The evening ended on a positive note. As people filtered out, many seemed happy to have had their voices heard. One friend who opposed the tank wrote me an e-mail the next day that said, "Regardless of how I feel about the water tank, the forum was wonderful. Liz, you're who I want to be when I grow up." I smiled, gratified that I had intuitively chosen a process that worked so well. Once again, the magic of listening with an open mind and heart was healing emotional rifts, despite strong disagreements.

The EcoVillage Board met several days later at its second meeting in two weeks on the topic of the water tank. It was a typically busy evening at the Common House. Ithaca College students were upstairs giving a final presentation to the community on a landscaping project, while the EVI Board and five or so residents met in the basement crafts room.

After some information sharing, the group did a go-round on the topic, What do you think about a water tank on EVI land, and why? People spoke briefly and eloquently, with Board members mostly in favor and residents more or less equally divided in their opinions.

Jay Jacobson (a FROG resident and Board member) reported that he had been undecided when he came to the meeting. But after hearing people speak to accept the tank, he had decided to oppose it. He said he was concerned about the rush to develop more of the EVI vision before we had, in his view, learned how to live sustainably in the neighborhoods we had.

Jay's comments ended the discussion portion of the meeting, and John Schroeder, the Board chair, called for a motion. The Board voted almost unanimously to accept the tank, with Jay casting a lone vote against.

It felt very odd to have a split in the vote — something that had only happened once before in the entire history of the EVI Board. I was glad that the Board had chosen voting over consensus to decide the issue, or we could have been deadlocked for months. And I was relieved that we had finally come to a decision. But I also felt sad and somewhat numb, since the Board was usually of one mind in its decisions.

The following day I sent out the minutes from the Board meeting. I also requested that we have a third and final community forum to decide on the site for the tank. (This decision would be entirely resident driven.) And I invited Dan Walker to attend. As it turned out, it was good that I did.

The forum was set for a Monday night. Dan explained to me on the morning of the meeting that if the Town built on its preferred site, they'd save a lot of money in building costs. And he said that the Town was prepared to split the difference with us. That night, at the meeting, one woman asked Dan to be specific about the amount. According to Dan the amount was $90,000. And the town supervisor had said that we could have half of that back in cash.

We were thrilled! The Town would pay us $45,000 cash up-front. It had already agreed to deal with our road and the farm, repairing the one and minimizing the impact on the other. The site they were talking about was well out of sight of the neighborhoods, although it would be in clear view from the entry road. Clearly this site option would be strongly preferred. And that is the option the 15 people present at the meeting recommended to the Board.

In the ensuing days, the Town zigzagged back and forth on its promises. At first it wanted to give us an all-cash payment. Then it offered less cash but more in-kind services. Then, apparently, it wanted to offer us less of everything.

In a final Board meeting later that week, we decided to agree to the Town's preferred site, along with a few provisions that would need to be written into an easement (most of which I had already negotiated with Dan Walker). We agreed to accept the $20,000 in cash and $20,000 in road improvements that Walker had committed to in writing. But we also wanted an additional $10,000 to pave the first 40 feet

(12 meters) of our dirt road, since this would get substantial wear and tear from the concrete trucks.

Greg, my fellow negotiator, was not present at the Board meeting, and I asked the Board for their opinion. Should I tell the Town up-front what we wanted? They all agreed to go with my candid negotiating style on this one. So John Schroeder incorporated the changes that the Board had made to the provisions, and I sent the whole thing off to Dan Walker. And then Jared and I left for a four-day weekend at a dance festival in Cape May, New Jersey.

While I was away I had trouble sleeping. In one troubled dream I was in a pristine landscape. Suddenly a new road gashed across the green fields, opening a quick and easy access to a new development. In the dream I appreciated the practicality of having a road but mourned the scarred earth. Was the future development worth it?

Another night I tossed and turned, wondering if I had done the right thing by putting all our cards on the table. Greg and I differed in our negotiating styles. He had advised me to not divulge the details of what considerations we wanted but to get the Town hooked on the concept first. Greg had far more experience than I did, with his background in corporate negotiating and government contracts. On the other hand, my up-front, candid approach seemed to work well with our local Town officials.

The Town Board held its meeting the night I came home. Greg and I showed up on time and then waited for over an hour to speak. When we did, it was surprisingly quick and easy. Greg said we were willing to accept the tank. Not so much for our own use, but because the Town needed a place to put it, and needed to increase water pressure for the rest of West Hill, including the local hospital. We would receive an indirect benefit, however, by having a source of water available for fire protection in future development at EVI. The Town supervisor appointed Dan Walker to further solidify the details with us, and the Board moved on to the next business item. And that was it.

After a month of sweating over the whole issue, I felt that I could rest at last. I was proud of the whole community. The water tank issue had put many of us at odds. But we didn't shut down or stop talking about things. People were willing to participate in good group process and use it to resolve their differences. It wasn't utopia. But it was a pretty good place to be.

CHAPTER 6

THE CYCLE OF LIFE

*The next Buddha will not take the form of an individual.
The next Buddha may take the form of a community; a
community practicing understanding and loving kindness,
a community practicing mindful living. This may be the most
important thing we can do for the survival of the Earth.*

—Thich Nhat Hanh

Our community has learned a lot about living, working, and cele-brating together; about communicating effectively; and about resolving conflicts. But I think we really shine when we're celebrating an important milestone or when we're supporting someone through a crisis. We are a large group, and milestones and crises happen with surprising frequency. People graduate, get married, birth babies, lose jobs, experience breakups, or lose their parents. As we witness each other's lives, we find in ourselves a larger capacity for loving and giving than we knew existed. We grow larger as human beings.

What we do at EVI is not new. People have lived in close-knit communities for thousands of years, whether in Australian Aboriginal groups or small New England towns. The basis of our success, as with theirs, rests in strong relationships between people. We are reweaving the web of our togetherness as we learn to create a culture of deep caring and sustainability. The pain or joy that one person experiences reverberates through all of us, calling forth a deep response.

Birth and Death at EcoVillage

Cohousing attracts many families with young children, and EVI is no exception. Cohousing neighborhoods meet the needs of growing families, offering a strong community spirit, other children as built-in playmates for the kids, not to mention the convenient opportunity to share childcare. Over the years, a total of seven children have been born at EVI — four at FROG and another three at SONG.

A BLESSING WAY

Midsummer 2003 We are holding a "Blessing Way" to honor Poppy and Alison before they give birth. The two women from SONG are round and full and due within two days of each other. Poppy is very tall and dark haired — a beautiful woman with great presence. At 42 she already has one daughter, named Simnia, who is 20. An artist, Poppy has her own part-time business, creating a beautifully designed line of organic cotton bedding.

Jim Bosjolie

Expectant mothers Alison and Poppy.

Alison is in her 30s. Although of medium height, she is substantially shorter than Poppy, but they share the same dark hair color. Like Poppy, she also has one daughter, named Emma, who is 3. Alison has a beautiful smile that lights her face from within. She practices Buddhist meditation and offers tremendous support, wisdom, and love to those around her.

I am struck by the beauty of the two women — one tall, one shorter — as they sit side by side, both beaming, both with ripe bellies as round as watermelons. Wreaths of wildflowers gathered and woven by Sara encircle their heads. The white and pink flowers against their dark hair make them look like goddesses.

The rest of us, 12 women in all, sit on pillows around a special dark red cloth that is sprinkled with flowers and the images of strong women. Laura and Sara, who have organized the ceremony, begin by leading us in a ritual. We call in the spirits of the four directions and light candles for East, South, West, North, and center. Special music that was played during another friend's Blessing Way and labor fills the room. I look over at this friend and see that her eyes are wet.

One by one, as we go around the circle, we offer a blessing for the expectant mothers and string a special bead on a necklace for each of them. I have brought two shells from a white sand beach in Costa Rica, and memories of a day of complete relaxation.

One shell is large and convex. It reminds me of Poppy and her round belly. "It is big, bold, and beautiful. Just like you," I tell her.

Alison's shell is a lovely spiral, with an intricate gold and white pattern. "This represents your spirit," I tell her. I hope the women will carry the same sense of peace and calm into the days ahead that I felt on the day I picked up the shells from the beach in Costa Rica.

After the blessings we bathe the expectant mothers' feet in rosewater and massage their heads, shoulders, hands, and feet — six caring women to each woman. "This is like heaven," Poppy sighs.

One woman starts crying. "I wish I had had something like this when I was pregnant," she weeps.

I know that her experience — especially her first birth, which was a miscarriage — has been traumatic. The hospital staff had not allowed any friends to come into her room, and the baby's father was long gone. She had labored alone, knowing that her child was already dead in her womb. And to add to the tragedy, her recovery room was right across from the maternity ward, where smiling mothers rested with their healthy new babies.

"This Blessing Way is for all of us, for all women," I say, and the others agree.

We are touching something primal, recreating the art of women supporting women. We could be in ancient Egypt or a traditional village in Russia or a Native American longhouse. And our newly created necklaces — with their special beads, shells, and tiny dancing women made of clay — connect us to our ancestors, stretching back over thousands of years. We have stepped into the healing waters of Mother Earth to celebrate the creation of new life, as women have done since the beginning of time. We open the circle and release the four directions as we chant, "Blessed be."

We make "belly casts" out of plaster to honor the fullness of our friends' pregnant bodies. Poppy and Alison look magnificent, glowing with health as they sit side by side in armchairs that we've draped with tarps. Their breasts rise full and ripe above their naked bellies. We take turns slathering their skin with petroleum jelly and crisscross warm, wet plaster strips over their rounded abdomens.

Halfway through the process, Sara lets out a horrified gasp. "We're out of plaster strips!"

Laura calls the local craft store (due to close in ten minutes) and explains the situation. Half an hour later she returns triumphantly with enough material to finish the job. "The woman waited outside the closed store for me," she grins. "I guess she knew it was important."

The casts dry quickly once they're finished, and Poppy and Alison have tangible mementos of their babies while the babies are still in the womb. The three-dimensional casts look like works of art — and to my mind, they are.

BIRTH

I am delighted when Poppy invites me to be with her during her baby's home birth. "So many times I've seen you think creatively and lovingly when someone is having a hard time. I'd like you to be part of my support team," she tells me.

Poppy's labor and delivery is a long-anticipated event. Alison gave birth five days after her due date, and Poppy is now nine days overdue on hers. She is restless and becoming increasingly annoyed by people's teasing, "Hey Poppy, haven't you popped yet?"

July 17, 2003 — Poppy comes over to borrow some good books and lies on my bed, looking like a tall and stately queen as she chats and leafs through a pile of books. She says she is feeling a lot better since the midwives checked her and told her that her contractions have been doing some work. She is already somewhat dilated, though not yet in labor.

July 18, 2003 — Sara calls. "The midwives say to come over, but please don't come into the room until Poppy asks for you." Sara is an obstetrical RN training to be a midwife and will be at the birth, too.

I hurry over and creep up the stairs, trying to be quiet and unobtrusive. I sit by the low wall of the kitchen and look into the living room where Poppy is laboring. Two midwives, Sara, Poppy's husband Matthew, and their daughter Simnia all hover around her.

Time blurs. Poppy grunts and makes deep primal sounds through the contractions. And my body remembers the intense sensations of birthing my own two sons. I watch and wait and breathe along with her, supporting her even though I am across the room. I am tied to thousands of years of births and to the thousands of women who bring life into the world through this everyday, seemingly impossible miracle. For how else can birth be described?

Rain pours down outside, and Poppy's contractions surge through her in wave after enormous wave of effort. Between contractions she manages to climb into the birthing tub and sink into its warm water. We all sigh and wait for the next wave to take over her body. And take over it does. She pushes and pushes as hard as she can, but still the baby does not emerge.

Hillary (one of the midwives) checks, and finds that the baby's head is pulling down the lip of Poppy's cervix. Hillary can pull it back, which will be very painful, or Poppy can pant through her contractions (even though her whole body aches to push) and wait for the lip to retract on its own.

Poppy finds it excruciating to have Hillary touch her. So she spends what seems to be an eternity panting and blowing through the waves of contractions. Ann (the other midwife) coaches her, squatting at eye level and blowing directly into Poppy's face. Their joint, focused concentration is amazing.

Matthew holds his wife so that she can remain in a squatting position, but Poppy is obviously uncomfortable. She gets out of the tub, tries other positions. And although Matthew is young and strong, he is laboring, too as he holds up his six-foot-tall wife.

I decide that I can help by holding Matthew while he supports Poppy in a deep squat. The shift seems to work. Gradually the cervical lip disappears and Poppy starts to push again. But we can't sustain our positions for long. So Matthew moves against the wall, with Poppy leaning up against him.

The baby's dark head appears, draws back, and appears again. The room is electric with Poppy's effort and the imminent birth. Leslie holds a mirror so that Matthew and Poppy can see what's happening. It becomes clear that Poppy needs to move again — she is squatting too close to the floor, and there is no room to deliver the baby. Matthew, Diane (another friend), and I grab Poppy under her arms and heave her up. It takes all my strength to help hold her. But then I look down over her belly.

A powerful contraction grips Poppy's body, and the baby's head emerges, swollen and dark purple. Moments later the rest of the baby slips out, curled in a fetal position and still attached by its blue, unearthly umbilical cord. Poppy slips down onto the floor and cradles her newborn, exhausted and suffused with joy at the same time.

Watching them I can't quite believe that this live, complete human being has really arrived. I marvel at the little purple toes that gradually change to pink and the squinched-up face that has worked so hard to be born.

July 20, 2003 — I have been reflecting on how privileged I am to have witnessed the birth of Poppy's baby. Birth, like death, connects us both to our animal natures and our spiritual selves. Yet our culture shields us from these gateways of human experience. What if we could all see children being born and the labor of the women who birth them? What if we could reclaim this human passage and bring it home to the community? What a gift that would be. I believe it would help reconnect us to the natural cycles that are such an essential part of our existence and return us to a wholeness that we long for.

The same holds true for death. While birth is a time of great rejoicing, death brings cause for mourning. But the process of dying can itself be a way to profoundly affirm life. Pamela Carson, the only EVI resident to die thus far, taught us how it is possible to live and die with dignity, openness, and courage.

DEATH

Pamela was diagnosed with terminal stomach cancer shortly after she moved to EcoVillage in 1996. Stomach cancer is usually a swift killer, cutting down its victims in six months to a year. But Pamela fought long and hard. She had her stomach surgically removed, went through several rounds of chemotherapy, and managed to live for three years after she was first diagnosed.

The community stepped in to help Pamela all along the way. In fact, she often said, "I'm alive today because I live in this community." When chemotherapy nauseated her and she couldn't eat much (causing drastic weight loss), Seagull cooked tasty meals each day to tempt her. Marcie, a professional folksinger, serenaded her during her chemo treatments (amazing the nurses!). Sandra provided weekly Reiki treatments, and Suzanne gave massages. Many others visited, helped with transportation or shopping, or just looked in to make sure she was all right. And I met with her once a week for a delightful hour-and-a-half of creative writing.

Pamela was taking a women's writing class in Ithaca but often couldn't attend. So the instructor sent assignments home. We wrote for an hour or so and then read to each other from our work. It was a great way to get to know each other better. And I got to see a bawdy, zestful side of her that was not otherwise apparent.

Pamela was a remarkable woman who accomplished a lot in her life. In her highly successful first career, she opened a major flea market in Boston. Then she started a top restaurant, called Friends and Company. But she didn't stop there.

Pamela dropped out of the fast-paced life and studied Zen Buddhism in Japan for two years. On her trip home, she stopped in Nepal and was appalled at the poverty — especially the condition of its many street children. So she adopted two Nepalese boys off the streets of Kathmandu. One of the boys, Ram Saran Thapa, came to the US to live with her when he was 14. And though he struggled to fit in with American society, Ram eventually became a chef, specializing in ethnic cuisine (see Chapter Four). For Pamela the two adoptions were the start of a much bigger effort.

Pamela's strong sense of justice and caring led her to start a non-profit, which she called Educate the Children (ETC). ETC's original purpose was to raise money from donors in the US to sponsor impoverished children in Nepal, but soon women's empowerment programs became part of its mandate, too. Handcrafted sweaters, jewelry, and other Nepalese goods were sold to raise money for programs that taught women how to read and write and acquire some simple business skills. ETC continues to this day, directly benefiting thousands of women and children. And it all arose from Pamela's simple, generous impulse.

For someone who was dying, Pamela packed a lot of punch. When she knew her hair would fall out from the chemo, she decided to cut it all off. But she did so in the best Zen Buddhist tradition, following the custom of head shaving practiced by Buddhist monks. We were all invited to the ceremony.

It was summer, and the yard was decked out with colorful Tibetan prayer flags. A dignified Pamela sat facing us in a wicker chair that stood behind a low table covered in flowers. The ceremony began with some Buddhist chants. And then Pamela handed the scissors to a close friend of hers from the Zen monastery in Rochester. As Karen snipped off Pamela's beautiful curly white hair, I felt grief, knowing that my friend did not have long to live. But I was also very moved by the beauty of the event.

Pamela was turning a deep loss into a devotional act. She was letting go, releasing her attachment to her looks as a sort of precursor to letting go of her physical body entirely. She was also modeling a way to maintain her center through her frightening illness and reclaim her power to be fully alive and alert while facing her imminent death.

Pamela did not confine herself to a private event, either. She believed in making the most of publicity if it meant that what she had to teach would reach a broader audience. So it was that a report of her strikingly original ceremony made the front page of the local paper, complete with an article and accompanying photo.

A few weeks before Pamela's death, her friends organized a living memorial for her in the Common House. The whole community showed up, although Pamela herself was too ill to attend. People brought their favorite foods and dressed up in elegant clothes for the occasion. Her sister Gail, a former opera singer, sang beautifully. Someone brought a video camera and interviewed people about Pamela's special qualities. Once dinner was over we gathered in a circle to share stories, some lighthearted and some serious.

It was a poignant evening, knowing that we were gathering together our memories of Pamela and celebrating her life while she was still alive. And that, like Huck Finn, our friend

For the Children

Pamela always seemed to know what to do. When her dog Ashley died, Pamela held an elaborate ceremony for the entire neighborhood. The children, who loved the dog, gathered to pet it one last time. They wept as they reminisced about Ashley, and then covered the grave with flowers. The pet funeral was a gift, preparing all of us, but particularly the children, for Pamela's approaching death. ∎

could watch her own memorial. In fact Gail took the video home and reported that Pamela enjoyed watching it many times.

By October Pamela was dying, and I went to visit her at her home one last time. She was no longer conscious, and a thin line of spittle ran down her chin. Her breath rasped in and out of a body that looked white and waxy. She looked like she had aged 20 years. Tears coursed down my cheeks as I held her hand and whispered my last goodbye. Her eyelids flickered, and I hoped that she could still hear me.

How many of us ever see someone as they are dying? Even in her last hours, Pamela was modeling tremendous openness, giving us the gift of witnessing her death. I left and went for a walk on the land, feeling fully alive and in tune with the world. As I walked I was thinking, This is a good day to die. A few hours later Pamela was gone.

But that was not the end of the story. Pamela, organizer that she was, had planned her own elaborate memorial service. She had arranged for the church, pre-printed programs, chosen people to speak, and picked the songs she wanted sung. The service was held several weeks after she died.

Photo courtesy of EVI
Pamela's Zen Buddhist haircutting ceremony.

Ram Saran Thapa, looking elegant but uncomfortable in a suit and tie, offered a most moving eulogy. Normally Ram was extremely shy, but he overcame his shyness to speak with eloquence in front of hundreds of people at the church. His dark face grimaced as he spoke of his childhood, filled with abuse, on the streets of Kathmandu.

Ram had been a beaten, starving, and homeless nine-year-old when Pamela first met him, he told us. Pamela took him and his friend to a local restaurant and fed them a good meal. They begged her to come back, and she did. Eventually Pamela had adopted him and brought him to the United States. It hadn't been easy for him to adjust to his new home or for Pamela to adjust to being a single parent. They had had plenty of ups and downs, but from the way Ram spoke, Pamela had clearly been his saving angel.

Pamela's memorial was beautiful. And, as usual, her capacity to do the right thing extended even to this final act of her life. Her service gave the whole community a chance to come to closure over her passing.

Two years after Pamela's death, her legacy had come full circle. Gail (Pamela's sister) and her partner Barbara had inherited Pamela's house. Ram Saran had used his inheritance to return to Nepal, marry Niruja, and bring her home (see Chapter Four). The two couples were sharing the house. Groups of Nepalese friends were gathering periodically in the Common House, and Niruja had mastered English, acquired some computer skills, and gotten her driver's license in time for her 22nd birthday. Pamela would have loved it all.

Life Passages

Over the years the community has stepped forward many times. Sometimes it lends its support to someone who is working through health problems or relationship issues. At other times it acts as a witness as people mark important changes or transitions in their lives.

TIMES OF CRISIS

Sometimes our members face a medical crisis. Julia, for instance, recently suffered a serious accident. The mother of two young boys, Julia suffers from epilepsy. When her husband Rod came home one day, he found her at the foot of their stairs, unconscious and with a cracked skull.

Julia was airlifted to a hospital specializing in neurosurgery. The surgeon who operated on her said that he had never before removed such a big blood clot from a living human being. Internal bleeding had severely compressed Julia's brain, and it was likely she would die or at least suffer permanent mental or physical impairment.

Our community mobilized an outpouring of love and support. We held silent prayer vigils every night. Someone accompanied Rod to the hospital (over an hour away) every day. Others cooked dinners for the family, ferried the boys to and from school, or provided after-school care. One neighbor offered to clean the family's house and wash the daily dishes. We made up a photo-board — covered with pictures of Julia, her family, and friends — signed it with our get-well wishes and took it to the hospital for her. We visited regularly. People gave her massages, took her flowers and videos, or played soothing music for her. Almost everyone helped out in some special way.

To the amazement of her doctors, Julia got out of the hospital just two weeks after the accident. She seemed to have recovered her full range of motion and, although she still felt disoriented, her mind was sharp. Her recovery was truly a miracle — one that Julia ascribed, at least in part, to all the loving care from the community.

Julia's crisis is not the only one we've weathered at EVI. A few years ago my partner Jared suffered a severe depression. Through the loving, steady help of many friends, he recovered quickly and completely.

The Power of Love

It was a dramatic moment. I was talking to Laura Beck (a prospective resident from Austin, Texas) in the Common House. Julia and Elan were standing nearby. Suddenly Julia's eyes began to roll, and Elan stepped forward and hugged her tightly.

As Julia went limp, I explained to Laura that Julia had epilepsy and experienced seizures, sometimes as often as three or four times a day. She had recently discovered that if someone gave her a firm hug right as a seizure began, it could alleviate the symptoms and even prevent her from fully losing consciousness. That's why Elan had stepped in.

Within moments Julia returned to normal consciousness, without having entered a full-blown seizure. Later, Laura would refer to this incident as pivotal in her decision to move to EcoVillage. She said it had been inspiring to see love conquer illness. ∎

In another instance, the 18-month-old son of some friends contracted meningitis and was sent by ambulance to an intensive care unit an hour away. No one knew whether he would live or die. Community members made many trips to Syracuse to visit him and his parents, shared childcare for his older sister, and welcomed him home after his miraculous recovery.

Our community's caring — whether we are giving or receiving it — is to be treasured. It creates a safety net that, unfortunately, is not available to most of our society. We know that help will be there for us during the most traumatic moments of our lives. I like to think of it as "community life insurance."

DIVORCE

When we first moved into EcoVillage, I näively assumed that we'd all be here for the rest of our lives. Was I wrong! Some people moved away because cohousing did not suit their lifestyle or values, others because they thought it was too expensive. And four FROG families decided to build homes in SONG. But divorce took its toll, too.

Cohousing families are certainly not immune to stress. Cohousing can provide a wonderfully supportive environment, with shared meals, shared childcare, and friendly neighbors. But it can also increase the stressors in our lives — endless meetings, committees, and the strains of building a home *and* developing a neighborhood demand a lot of attention and work. If a marriage is already shaky, then this additional stress can push things over the edge. Three couples out of the original 30 families at FROG have divorced, and another couple split up for a time and then reunited. And two couples from SONG separated within the first year of that neighborhood's existence.

What is it like to get divorced in a community? Initially, it can be very hard. One woman dreaded having people ask her how she was doing. She said she knew she'd just burst into tears. And one man didn't want everyone knowing his business. But despite the difficulty of having one's private affairs on public display, community can also provide rock solid support for each member of the couple. "I can't imagine what it would have been like to split up if I didn't have friends I could talk with every day, and cry on their shoulders," one woman put it. "Community makes all the difference." And that seems to be true. Take, for instance, the situation with Laura Beck and Greg Pitts.

Laura and Greg first visited EcoVillage at Ithaca when their son Ethan was a baby in a backpack. I was very impressed with this couple from Austin, Texas. Greg studied up on EVI and was able to help me lead a large tour the second day he was here. Laura came with us and took the first of many stunning photos of the tour and West Haven Farm (some of which are included in this book). The two were clearly talented professionals and committed environmentalists. I also found them very engaging.

When Laura and Greg moved to EVI a year later, we became good friends. The two put their shoulders to the wheel. Greg got very involved in SONG, putting his background in project management to good use. Laura strongly advocated for affordable housing and helped to administer the SONG affordable-housing program (a very difficult and time-consuming task). And they worked hard on designing and helping to build their own home.

We started getting hints that all was not right in the couple's relationship. Even so, when they told us they planned to separate, we were shocked. Laura moved into the downstairs of their house. Greg took the top floor, and they shared the main floor with its beautiful open kitchen and living room. Ethan, then four years old, had a bedroom on each floor. The two were so committed to remaining at EVI that they maintained that arrangement for a year, until Laura could buy her own home in FROG.

In many ways Laura and Greg's was a model divorce. They remained supportive and understanding of each other, despite the difficult circumstances. And when they each started exploring other relationships — some of them within the community — they worked through the hard parts and continued to stay close.

When asked, Laura told me how it had been for her as she went through her divorce. "It was excruciating at times for the lack of privacy. At the same time I can't imagine that we could have done this anywhere else. It felt like being in community gave us the permission and the courage to ask hard questions."

Laura went on to describe the witnessing power of the community. It provided her the safe place she needed as she moved through this painful stage of her life. Of course some people jumped to conclusions about their situation. But Laura found that when she communicated her needs directly, people were very responsive. "I felt that we were held by the community, that there were loving arms around us, around Ethan, at all times. It made it really easy to follow my own compass and not feel compelled to play the 'at-odds' couple. It gave me the confidence to move through this major life passage on my own terms."

There have been other, more painful breakups at EVI. But Laura and Greg's experience offers hope for other couples, showing that clear communication and loving intentions can ease the transition of divorce.

RITE OF PASSAGE

Sometimes we are called upon to help mark an important life event. Cynthia, for instance, created a special ritual to honor her menopause and asked our women's group to witness it. More than a year had passed since her last period, and she was officially through "the change."

Cynthia was a little nervous as she faced us and started to talk. She explained that it was hard for her to ask for extra time in the group. But it was also very important that she honor this transition in her life. She laid out a special cloth and set eight candles on it in a circle, each representing a different stage in her life.

"This candle is for when I was an alcoholic," she began. "I was in a fog, just trying to cope. I was sexually promiscuous, always trying to find love in the wrong places." She lit the first candle. "I'm sending healing energy to that part of myself that was so lost."

There was a candle for her son who almost died in a drunk driving accident and who had been sober now for three years. She lit a candle for her husband, for his lifelong devotion and love.

As she moved from candle to candle, Cynthia honored all the events and patterns of her personal history. Women around the circle sighed appreciatively or nodded as she spoke. The depth and trauma of her experiences moved us all, as did the commitment she had to her own growth.

Finally she lit the last candle. "This one is for my future," she said, "and finding my niche in the work I want to do." Candlelight illuminated Cynthia's face. And it burnished the faces of the women in the circle, revealing eyes shining with love.

GROWING OLDER WITH PANACHE

Sometimes we are asked to help celebrate a milestone, as when Monty invited us to his 75th birthday. One of our original residents, Monty was still very active, convening a Bikram yoga practice at the Common House several times a week, and taking long daily walks with his dog Ria, no matter what the weather was like. Monty worked part-time with university students and actively participated on FROG's process steering committee. Perhaps most impressively, he had coped with prostate cancer.

Monty was not an easy person to get to know. He had an intense interest in personal growth and an allergy to chitchat, preferring deep soulful talks instead. Recently divorced from another community member, Monty, I knew, had sometimes felt lonely and isolated. But as he grew older, he had softened his edges and opened himself up to more people.

Monty's birthday party was simple, fun, and engaging. At his request, we each wrote a haiku for him and brought it to the party. (A haiku has a total of 17 syllables: 5 in the first line, 7 in the second line, and 5 in the last line.) Most of us had never written one of these three-line poems before, and it was challenging but fascinating to try our hands at it.

But how do you sum up the essence of a friend's life in just three short lines? Well, we found out at the party. The haiku form invites clear focus. As we read our poems out loud, we discovered that we had each honored some aspect of our friend that made him special. Consider Pamela Willett's piece:

> Seeing that baby
> In nineteen twenty-eight, who
> Imagined Monty?

And what about the lovely image Karryn Ramanujan evoked?

> In Tree Pose, my friend
> Turns seventy-five years old.
> Rooted, yet skyward!

And then there was Monty's son David's understated piece, shared in a letter.

> Seventy-five years
> Of constant refinement makes
> A skinny Buddha.

Monty's birthday party was inspiring. It gave us all a chance to show him that he made a difference in our lives. And it invited us to follow his lead and enjoy growing older with style.

At EVI, regardless of whether we are lending our support or witnessing an important passage, our active engagement with each other is part of what helps us grow in understanding and loving-kindness.

Personal Transformations

EcoVillage supports growth and change. I like to think that each of us is like a stone in a stream. As the stones' rough edges tumble against each other, they gradually wear away and take on a polished, smoother finish. A similar process can happen with people in the supportive climate of our community. People bring all their unresolved issues with them when they come to EVI and inevitably come up against the group. Those individuals who take responsibility for their learning, take risks, and grow begin to lose their sharp edges. As they confront their issues, work through them, and come to resolution, their transformation becomes obvious — they begin to glow with an inner beauty.

TRANSFORMATION THROUGH COMMITMENT

Jay is a member of the EVI Board of Directors and could be considered a founding member of FROG. But Jay is cautious and refused to commit to the group, even though he attended meetings for a full year and served on committees when EVI was forming. Only after Joan sat down with him and said, "Jay, it's time to join and write a check" did he overcome his reluctance. Since then he has been one of the most committed members of the community.

A retired plant physiologist, Jay has documented the more science-based aspects of our project. He has calculated our electric, gas, and water consumption over the years and kept track of the pond level. And he has represented EVI at the Ecovillage Network of the Americas meetings.

Now, at age 67, Jay has taken another enormous leap. After being single for over 10 years, he has started a relationship with Pam, a community member in her 40s. Jay has moved from committing to our group to committing to an individual — surely an even more profound experience.

Transformation into Leadership

If I introduced you to almost any of the 160 members of EVI, each one would have a story to tell of how the support and challenges of living here have changed their lives. Jay's transformation was a personal one, but we can experience transformation in our professional lives, too. And that is what happened to me.

When I first started working at EcoVillage in 1991, Joan Bokaer was the director and I was the associate director. But we quickly evolved a shared leadership role and combined our different skills. Joan was the main fundraiser, public spokesperson, and visionary. I was the one with more organizational savvy, the facilitator skilled at getting things done. Together we made a formidable team.

In early 1996 Joan tired of the stress and daily grind of working for the nonprofit. She told me in her usual directive style, "It's time to close the office." Her words struck me like a sharp knife, and I was surprised to hear myself emitting gut-wrenching sobs. How could she abandon something that was just starting and had so far to go? If she left how could I keep the office and the forward direction of the project going by myself? Our funding was very precarious, and I didn't think it was possible for me to assume the role of director and also be the only staff person — it was simply too much for one person to take on. But if I didn't do it, who would?

I knew deep down that I had met my destiny. All my years of working for peace and environmental groups had honed my skills for this major project. Yet I had a terrible fear of being shot down, as I had seen (and experienced) other leaders being targeted for abuse by the very people they sought to serve. It is a surprisingly common group dynamic, in which individuals relinquish their power to a perceived authority figure, who then becomes a convenient scapegoat for whatever issue is controversial. I had seen and experienced that dynamic at EcoVillage already (see Chapter Five). I had to conquer my fear, and trust that if I were ever at odds with the group, I would be given the strength to know what to do. My decision was gut-wrenching, and I prayed for guidance. The message that came back was clear: Keep the project going. And that is how I decided to become the director of this quirky and brilliant nonprofit. It is a decision I have never regretted.

I had the opportunity to take on even more leadership in 1996, when we started to organize SONG. Our fledgling group searched for a good professional development manager to lead the cohousing project. Our first manager (who worked with us for about a year) was local and had substantial project management experience. But he was unfamiliar with cohousing and had other time commitments that didn't fit well with us.

We decided to give a budding cohousing development firm from Virginia a try. But their fees exceeded our budget, and they knew less about the dynamics of cohousing than we did. Besides that they were quite a long way from Ithaca, New York.

So we tried yet another option. We hired a very part-time development manager from a cohousing group in Massachusetts. Again he was too far away from EVI to be a good fit. I came to the reluctant conclusion that SONG would not get built without a local development manager, yet no one was available.

I thought about the possibilities of teaming up with Rod Lambert. Rod had experience designing and building homes and had coordinated a group-built Zen retreat center. Rod and I would not be an easy match — we often held strikingly different viewpoints — but his engineering and building background did complement my community organizing and strategic planning experience.

After several sleepless nights of contemplating whether or not I could take on this huge new task, I invited Rod to go for a walk. We talked frankly about each of our strengths and weaknesses and how we could bring the SONG neighborhood to the point of construction. And by the end of walk, we decided to propose that we become co-managers in charge of developing our second neighborhood.

Our partnership worked. Despite our personality differences we supported each other as we took the big leap of faith — believing in ourselves, each other, and the project. And, yes, the road was often rocky. But we did manage to build an innovative cohousing neighborhood that is filled with wonderful neighbors.

Not all transformations are dramatic. Some are made up of many small steps that take place gradually over a long period of time. These day-to-day insights often emerge in support groups. Over the years people have generated a men's group, a women's group, a parenting support group, a co-counseling group, a daily meditation group, a self-employed support group (including retirees), and a SONG dads' group. They all offer support to the individual and, like fertilizer, a medium in which to enhance personal growth.

"Deepening Relationships" Groups

By 1997 all 30 households in FROG had moved in, and our Common House was completed. Many of us had been working together for five years and had long anticipated that moment. We assumed that we would automatically feel a strong sense of community as we ate together in the Common House, landscaped the neighborhood, or passed each other on the paths. But we were wrong.

We knew a lot about going to meetings together but very little about living together. Most of our interactions over the years had been related to organizing EVI. During the thick of the work, we had group meetings every Sunday afternoon. And some of us attended several committee meetings during the week. There was a never-ending river of decisions to make, and despite great preparation in committees, it always took a while for the whole group to reach consensus.

Certainly we knew each other's meeting styles intimately. We knew who talked a lot and who had to be encouraged to share their point of view. We knew who liked problem solving and who was unhappy making almost any decision because it closed down possibilities. We knew who listened well and who argued a point well. But in terms of really knowing what was going on in each other's lives, the situation left a lot to be desired. That lack was soon to be rectified.

Joe and Michelle Nolan, a young couple from California, had the distinction of being the first couple to join EVI overnight. They arrived at a FROG meeting during a cross-country motorcycle trip and signed up the next day. After living at EVI for about six months, the two went back to California to visit friends who lived in another community there. When they came back they brought a new idea with them.

Michelle called a meeting to propose forming a type of support group known as a "deepening relationships" group. The response was tremendous. Michelle had clearly tapped into a strongly felt need. We met in one of the larger homes — about 35 adults squeezed into the living room to sit on couches, pillows, and the floor. Four groups formed and decided to meet twice a month, usually on Saturday mornings from 9:00 to 11:00 a.m.

The "deep" groups were very popular and organized along similar lines. In each group six to eight men and women met together and talked. Everybody chipped in for childcare. Some groups rotated facilitation; others were more free-form. Some groups took on challenging topics or fun exercises for personal growth. In one exercise that eco-psychologist Elan Shapiro led, for example, people in our group all took journals and went outside. We spent about half an hour finding a special niche for ourselves on the land and then drew or took notes on what we were experiencing. When we came back together, we shared the results.

People had been drawn to very different places — some to trees, some to open areas, and some to the pond. Each choice somehow spoke to us or symbolized some aspect of our lives. One woman enjoyed wading in the pond, among the cattails. Her choice represented her desire to immerse herself in life, yet keep some areas mysterious and hidden. In contrast I loved my overview perch as I sat on a large stone overlooking the pond and enjoyed the sunshine on my face. Elan's simple exercise helped us take the time to connect with our souls, the natural world, and the people in our group.

No matter what activities any one group explored, they all set aside time for in-depth check-ins. Check-ins gave us a terrific opportunity to learn more about each other. Typically each person had five to ten minutes of uninterrupted time to talk about what was going on in his or her life. So we learned things like how someone felt about having her parents visit, what it was like being unemployed, how someone coped with their son's difficult behavior, and whose marriage was experiencing stress. Good ground rules ensured that people's boundaries stayed intact. (All sessions were confidential, and people agreed to remain respectful and not interrupt whoever was speaking.)

I can tell you that there is nothing quite like having the undivided, supportive attention of a group of peers. The attention alone was transformative — like having a favorite friend listen to you well. It challenged me to look clearly and honestly at my own life, recognize patterns, celebrate the good things, and ask for support for the difficult times. I found it a real joy to share at this level with people whom I also saw in many other contexts, and whom I expected would be part of my extended family for the rest of my life. And I'm not the only one who benefited.

At the height of the "deep groups," fully half of the adults in EcoVillage participated. When we rotated membership in the existing groups after a year, some people dropped out and others joined. Now only two small groups continue to meet. Perhaps, once we got to know each other better, we didn't need them anymore. Or maybe our close friendships gave us the depth of relationship the groups once offered. Or perhaps, like many other aspects of life in community, our needs will wax and wane and the deep groups will come around again sometime in the future.

Our community has a long way to go before we become the "next Buddha" that Thich Nhat Hanh describes. But we are getting better at bringing love and respect into our interactions. And if we — with all our quirky personalities, diverse socioeconomic backgrounds, and varied spiritual traditions — can practice loving-kindness, then I have great hope for the world.

THE "ECO" IN ECOVILLAGE

"Hi, welcome to EcoVillage at Ithaca," I say, enjoying the opportunity to show off our project to a group of architecture students.

"Is that a solar panel on the roof?" asks one. "I assume you're off the grid."

"No," I admit.

"Well, do you have composting toilets?"

"No, we're required by the Town to hook up to city water and city sewer."

"Well," comes the challenge I've gotten used to, "then what makes you so ecological, anyway?"

I wrote that vignette, a composite of many personal experiences, when FROG was completed but SONG was not yet built. The question is valid. And its answer is not a quick and easy one.

The Big Picture

EVI takes a pragmatic approach to ecological sustainability. Rather than opt for the sexiest (and often most expensive) appropriate technologies, we put our money into energy reduction measures first. Some of those measures are not easy to spot (super-insulated homes that have been oriented for maximum solar exposure are less visibly "ecological" than are windmills and solar panels, for example), but that doesn't mean they aren't effective. Taken together they add up. We are building a "green" community and culture, rather than individual state-of-the-art "green" buildings. And it's working: Our ecological footprint is much smaller than the typical footprint of most US households.

LOCATION

EVI's location is one of our biggest energy savers, because it helps keep our transportation footprint relatively small. First we tend not to travel very far from day to day. Many people work on-site, making travel unnecessary. And if we need to go somewhere, downtown Ithaca is only a mile and a half away — one of the main reasons we decided to build here and not on the free site 10 miles out of town.

Our choice of location may seem trivial, but it has significant ecological benefits. Greg Thomas, a former resident and energy consultant, worked out that over three decades, our 60-household village would save about $716,000 in gasoline costs (based on a conservative one round trip per household per day) compared to the free site. And that doesn't even count the environmental benefits of burning less gasoline. Of course, a downtown location would have saved even more, but we would have had to sacrifice on-site organic farming, something we weren't prepared to do (see Chapter One).

Second, the fact that we live so close together makes carpooling and car sharing a natural. A third of EVI couples or families have been able to cut down to one vehicle, and two of our single homeowners are

Jim Bosjolie

EcoVillagers and friends raise the walls in a timber frame duplex in SONG.

completely car-free. It helps that several families make their second cars available to other members who sign up to use them (for a small fee of 30 cents a mile). And one family with two young children doesn't charge money but instead barters car use in return for childcare. Fewer cars make for less pollution and a reduced consumption of all the materials that go into producing and maintaining them.

Third, as a group we use public transportation. The political clout of just 30 FROG families enabled us to lobby successfully for a bus stop at our entry road. Twenty EcoVillagers now take the bus to town for work, shopping, or recreation. Once the Town increases bus service in the near future, bus ridership should increase. This is far more energy efficient than driving individual cars. There is no doubt that the driving habit is hard to break, though. (It just seems easier to hop in the car to run those errands than to bike, walk, or wait for the bus — especially if it's raining.) The value our society puts on independence and mobility fuels our love affair with the automobile and shapes our nation's infrastructure, making some car use unavoidable. Even as a community of environmentalists, most EVI families still own two cars and use them daily. As with most US citizens, transportation is still our environmental Achilles' heel. But we are making headway, and EVI's location is helping us do it.

ON-SITE EMPLOYMENT

On-site employment at EVI saves energy and helps create community — both essential to building a sustainable culture. A recent membership survey showed that more than three-quarters of EVI's wage-earning adults work at least part-time on-site. Not surprisingly EVI boasts a wide range of workers, including childcare providers, environmental educators, farmers, graphic artists, "green" builders, a naturopathic doctor, software engineers, therapists, writers, and more.

On-site employment is great for the environment. For one thing, people don't have to commute to work. For another, they can share resources such as copy machines and high-speed Internet access, reducing the overall costs associated with the purchase and operation of office-related equipment.

But having people working on-site does more than save various kinds of energy. It also reinforces the vibrant sense of community that brings us together. On any given day, we may have upwards of 80 percent of our population on-site. (We have 60 children, from newborn to high-school age, and 102 adults: 17 stay-at-home parents, 12 retirees, 5 currently unemployed workers, and 68 employed workers.) Everybody mixes, making for a richness of interaction that is reminiscent of a hunter-gatherer tribe or small New England town.

INTERNAL ECONOMY

We are increasingly seeing an internal economy develop at EVI — one that is partially money based and partially based on barter. Not only that, but the money that comes into the village has a multiplier effect inside the community as it travels "around the block." For instance when Jared started a new business in computer ergonomics, he hired Megan to create his logo and business cards, Jim to create his website, and Steve to set up his database. Once Jared was up and running, he gave Krishna (a science writer) a free consultation when he complained of eyestrain. Krishna, in turn, traded at least an equivalent amount of time reviewing the manuscript for this book. Later on Mike, a software engineer who typically spends eight hours a day at the computer, hired Jared to do a consultation for him. And some of the money from Mike's consultation went to help pay for our family's CSA share at West Haven Farm. Having the money that is made here stay here is an added benefit of living in a close-knit community.

Of course, by providing more on-site services for each other, we further reduce the amount of commuting that we need to do, saving both time and energy. Plus we support each other in "right livelihood" (satisfying work that reflects our values). Place-based work sites are good for us and good for the planet.

LAND USE

Conservation of land is fundamental to the EVI vision. In fact EVI is intended to provide a viable alternative to suburban sprawl. We conserve 90 percent of our 175-acre site as open space for organic agriculture, woods, meadows, and wetlands. That leaves 10 percent for development. We build our homes in dense clusters, and each of our several neighborhoods requires only 3 to 4 acres for their 30 homes, Common House, and parking. We still have room for a planned EcoVillage Education Center and perhaps an office building. We hope to increase the 55 acres currently set aside in a permanent conservation easement to a much larger portion of the land, thus ensuring plenty of open space for future generations.

HABITAT RESTORATION

Now that EVI is established and stable, habitat restoration has moved up on our list of priorities. We intend to restore the land around us to health and to increase its biodiversity. Right now abandoned hay fields make up most of our land, and useless round bales sit forlornly in our hedgerows, testifying to the depleted soil brought on by decades of poor farming practices. (Farmers won't even take our hay in trade for mowing the fields for us — the nutrient value is far too low. One farmer told us that the hay wasn't even worth hauling away!)

We have already received a small grant from the US Department of Agriculture (USDA) and are using it to restore an initial 12-acre (4.8 hectare) parcel. The grant money pays John (our on-site farmer) for the time he spends establishing the native plants we are slowly reintroducing to the site.

Ironically most habitat restoration work uses herbicides and pesticides to clear the land of invasive species. Our strategy takes a different, more long-term approach. Restoration takes place over several stages and uses completely organic methods to bring the land back to health. First we carefully cultivate the land and then plant a series

What Didn't Happen to West Hill

The 175-acre West Hill property that is now our home could have looked entirely different. In 1991 Lakeside Development Corporation owned the land and planned to build 150 homes on 1-acre (0.4-hectare) lots. Ninety percent of the land would have been taken over by roads, houses, and manicured lawns. The remaining 10 percent would have been left as open space to satisfy a requirement of the Town of Ithaca. The areas left would have been the ones too wet or steep to build on.

Developments like the ones proposed by Lakeside are gobbling up land all over the US There is little room left for wildlife, agriculture, or simple open space. People are completely dependent on cars to get to work, take their children to school, or find recreation. And it can be very lonely living in a bedroom community. Yet this is the "American Dream," the model of development we are exporting to communities around the world. ∎

of cover crops to gradually build up the quality of the soil and smother invasive weeds. In a few years we will reintroduce native grasses to attract local endangered species and increase biodiversity.

The native warm-season bunchgrasses that we plan to establish provide excellent habitat to a variety of birds and animals. They grow in clumps and send up graceful plumes that reach 4 to 6 feet (1 to 2 meters) in height. Ground-nesting birds (bobolinks, eastern meadowlarks, and blue-winged teal) nest in the spaces between the grass stems. And predators such as short-eared owls and northern harriers live and hunt in its concealing network.

With this project, as with many others, nothing has been as easy as it first seemed. Work went slowly in our first year. The farm's tractor was incompatible with the special no-till drill that was needed to plant the seeds. A long wet spring pushed the work into the summer months, which was the busiest time for West Haven Farm, leaving John with no time to plant the cover crops.

But our commitment is there. And while it may take time to work out the kinks, I am looking forward to spotting bobolinks among the tall graceful plumes of Indian grass and switchgrass sometime in the next five years. And we hope that our experience will make it easier for other restoration workers (nature preservationists, ornithologists, and land trusts) to also "go green" in their restoration work.

WATER CONSERVATION

Water conservation doesn't usually seem important in our lush green region, but one summer's drought made us acutely conscious of water use. Even our one-acre swimming pond dropped about three vertical feet (one vertical meter). Our water consumption levels are far lower than that of typical US households.

First, we limit the amount of water we use in our day-to-day activities. Some people have composting toilets, and all our conventional toilets use only 1½ gallons (5.7 liters) of water per flush. Our faucets are low flow. Outside we mostly landscape using plants that require little water and mulch heavily to conserve what they do use. And gentle cohousing peer pressure encourages people to water their gardens only during the cool part of the day.

Second, we use various methods to collect and redirect rainwater. Neighborhood drains and swales collect rainwater runoff from our roofs and direct it to the pond. We use pond water on our community garden and as drinking water for our sheep and chickens. Some households in FROG have retrofitted their roofs with gutters and connected them to rain barrels to store water for their family's garden. And half the households in SONG feed their rainwater runoff into an underground cistern. Through water conservation and rainwater collection, we're learning to make the most of this precious resource.

Food

When it comes to food EVI "goes green" as much as possible, growing organic fruits and vegetables and buying bulk organic foodstuffs for what we don't produce ourselves. Gardening provides some of our food. We maintain a large community garden. Edible landscaping around our homes further builds the habitat-to-food connection. Small gardens and south-facing trellises grow grapes, kiwi, beans, peas, and other climbing vines. But by far the bulk of our produce comes from West Haven Farm.

We make good use of the farm's bountiful harvests, often basing Common House meals around what is seasonally available (see "Liz's Famous Fried Tofu" in Chapter Four). And we preserve huge quantities of its produce for later use. One summer the 500 pounds of tomatoes that we canned provided a tasty base for stews, soups, and spaghetti sauce throughout the winter.

What we don't produce, we buy. EVI shops through United Natural Foods, a regional distributor offering inexpensive bulk organic foods. Their long delivery truck arrives once a month, barely making it around our turnaround. A host of women and children unload and sort the huge bags of grains and beans and boxes of pasta. Some items are destined for the Common House; others go to our families for individual use.

Our commitment to growing and buying mostly organic is a fundamental aspect of our larger commitment to becoming more sustainable here at EVI. Organic farming methods enrich the soil rather than deplete it. By supporting organic food production — either here at EVI or through our bulk food purchases — we are supporting our own health and the health of a planet that is in desperate need of help.

PERMACULTURE

When we started planning EVI in 1991, almost none of the participants had even heard the term "permaculture," much less understood what it meant. However, much of EVI's design actually incorporates the values and principles behind this philosophy. In fact, the Winter 2004 issue of *Permaculture Magazine* (published in the U.K. and distributed throughout North America and Europe) featured a cover story about EcoVillage at Ithaca. The author of the article, Hildur Jackson (founder of the Gaia Trust and the Global EcoVillage Network), called EVI "one of the two best examples I have seen to date of an ecovillage that approaches mainstream standards."

So what is "permaculture"? Permaculture is a multidimensional philosophy that applies nature's principles to the human habitat. It aims to create sustainable human ecosystems that mimic the diversity, stability, and resilience of natural systems, while being economically viable. People who apply permaculture principles aim to care for the Earth as well as meet basic human needs, such as food, shelter, education, employment, and community. They see this as one integrated, living system. Permaculture designers combine a detailed knowledge of the land and a wise use of resources to create spaces that serve human needs and are in keeping with natural processes.

In the summer of 1997, EVI sponsored two weekend workshops, both taught by permaculture designer Dave Jacke. One simple technique he taught, called "sheet mulching," was adopted by many residents — even those who had not attended the workshop.

Sheet mulching creates new topsoil from layers of various materials that gradually break down to form fertile, friable earth. And fertile earth is certainly what we need. When we first moved into FROG its soil was a rocklike, glacial till that had been heavily compacted by construction equipment. In fact the ground was so hard that it literally took a pickaxe to break it up. Sheet mulching is helping to change that.

Mulching materials are applied in layers. A soil supplement such as green sand is sprinkled on the ground. A layer of corrugated cardboard forms the second layer. Earthworms love to nest in cardboard's corrugations and will gradually break it down with their tunneling. A layer of compost goes on top of the cardboard layer, followed by a final layer of garden mulch. Once all the mulching layers are in place, perennials can be planted by simply cutting a hole in the cardboard.

The gardener has an easier time of things and the soil gets improved. The cardboard suppresses weeds, the mulch absorbs and retains water, and a layer of topsoil rapidly forms that would take nature decades to create.

We used sheet mulching on our relatively small garden plots, but permaculture can be used on much larger tracts of land. When SONG residents hired Dave Jacke in 1998 to help them create a site design, he spent days out on the land. Jacke examined the wildlife trails near the future SONG site. He took note of water and wind flows, and he assessed the potential for community gardens.

Once Jacke had the lay of the land, he presented his recommendations. He suggested that we tuck the SONG neighborhood up near the woods, which would block the strong north winds in the winter. He strongly felt that SONG buildings should stay off a dividing ridge that separated the field into different habitats. That would leave room for wildlife to follow natural pathways to the forest above. He also recommended that we leave "the Crux" intact (an open area between the two neighborhoods), since it was such a crucial space for people to gather as a village. With Jacke's recommendations in hand, SONG carried on with the construction phase of its development.

In the fall of 2004, another visitor taught us more about permaculture concepts. Kiyokazu Shidara, the founder and director of the Permaculture Institute of Japan, lived at our ecovillage for a month. In exchange for allowing him to study EVI, he offered several permaculture workshops to residents. He helped to influence SONG's landscaping choices and made important suggestions for future development of a third neighborhood and the Education Center.

We now also have two residents who are trained in permaculture methods, and I hope we can continue to integrate permaculture with future development at EVI.

DIVERSITY OF MODELS

The scale of EVI's site plan allows us to create a diversity of models and use a "learn as we go" approach as we bring the whole development to life. The site plan contains an entire village, including several cohousing neighborhoods, an education center, a village center, and expanded farming. Each new experiment will undoubtedly have its own pluses and minuses, but over time we'll be able to perfect the aspects that work well. And our successes and mistakes will benefit others, too. As we work toward manifesting the whole vision of EVI, we will keep aiming toward a greater degree of both ecological and social sustainability.

Green Building

Neighborhoods at EVI demonstrate the use of some basic "green design" principles. First we reduce our physical footprint by densely

SONG, Verse 1

Fall 2001 — It is a cool fall day and time to start on the foundations of the first 14 homes at SONG — in true EVI style, we've nicknamed this part of the project "Verse 1." After dinner at the Common House, we'll gather at the SONG site for an "Eco-Block™ party."

No, an "Eco-Block™" is not a new type of plastic child's toy. It's a specially fabricated foam building block or "insulated concrete form"(ICF). ICFs are made of expanded polystyrene, are much lighter than standard masonry blocks, and have a high insulative value. Blocks vary in height and length — the ones we are using are 16 inches (40 centimeters) high and 4 feet (1.2 meters) long. ICFs have an R-value of 21 or higher and are fire, earthquake, and termite resistant.

Once snapped together, the hollow core blocks create a wall-like form similar to the wooden forms constructed when pouring a conventional concrete foundation. The construction crew will reinforce the forms with rebar and pour concrete into the hollows. But unlike conventional wooden forms, which are torn up and discarded, ICFs become a permanent and highly insulating component of the foundation.

We will be assembling the forms for transfer to the foundation trench. I stake out a flat surface to work on, and a friend and I take turns snapping the blocks together. We use gloves to protect our hands, but they really aren't necessary.

This is my kind of construction project! Build an insulated foundation in a couple of hours with a work crew made up of 15 adults, 3 young kids, 1 baby in a backpack, and 2 dogs. I am totally in my element, filled with a secret delight. The work is repetitive — but oh, such results! I feel like a five-year-old again, when my favorite activity was building cities out of wooden blocks.

Summer 2002 — Chris and Monnie have done much of the design on their timber frame home, and now Sarah Highland (a local contractor) is overseeing its ☞

clustering our homes. And our shared living/working space at the Common House (dining hall, sitting room, guestroom, children's playroom, and shared laundry room) makes it possible for us to build smaller, more compact homes.

Second we incorporate energy-saving design elements into the homes themselves. We orient our homes to face due south to maximize solar gain. Large south-facing double- or triple-glazed window

construction. When it is time to raise the walls, 20 of us — and a reporter from the local paper — show up to help. The beams, hand-notched by Sarah, are huge, and I wonder how we will ever raise them up to ceiling height. But Sarah has planned well, organizing our unskilled crew to accomplish the seemingly impossible.

What an empowering experience! I'm put on a team of five women and, with two of us on ladders, we manage to heave the beam into place. To me it seems like a miracle, until I step back and watch as the next team does the same thing, and then the next. We finish in record time. And the following week, a fine photo of Chris appears in the local paper, showing her in front of her new home as an entire wall gets raised in the background.

SONG, Verse 2

Winter 2002 — An enormous truck has pulled into the SONG parking lot, loaded with straw bales for one of the new "Verse 2" duplexes. The timber frame is already in place, and we'll be unloading the truck and putting the bales in storage until they can be used.

I look at the owners of the two homes that will be built. Joe and Graham are both beaming. The two (along with Joe's wife Michelle) have worked hard to pioneer the use of straw bale building at EVI. And they've run into many obstacles along the way. But now we're unloading the straw bales, and it all seems worthwhile. We joke about how hot they'll be in the winter, teasing them that they'll have to open all their windows.

Each of the previous three vignettes highlights a different green building technique. But "green building" does not just refer to ICFs, timber framing, or straw bales. "Green building" encompasses a whole philosophy of design that incorporates ecologically friendly buildings with careful land use and design. ∎

walls absorb heat and bring in as much sun as possible in the cooler months. (When we first moved into our homes, I joked with a reporter that our homes were too sunny, knowing that someone who lives in this cloudy climate can never get enough sun.) Roof overhangs reduce solar gain in the summer, helping to keep things cool and comfortable. Each duplex shares one exterior wall, reducing the overall surface area of the building and saving substantially on heating/cooling costs. Shared heating systems maximize the efficiency of the boilers. At SONG earth berms add insulation to the north wall of the basements, with lookout windows on the south side making the space attractive and livable.

Energy savings are impressive. At FROG, we use approximately 40 percent less gas and electricity than other typical homes in the northeastern US And it is relatively easy to save an additional 20 percent, simply by setting the thermostats lower at night and using less hot water. It is too early to tell yet, but it is likely that SONG's more advanced technology will make energy savings there even more impressive than at FROG.

Third, we use ecologically desirable materials in the construction and finishing of our homes. Construction materials are always changing

Jim Bosjolie

About half of SONG's homes have photovoltaic panels that generate electricity from the sun.

as technology advances, and it requires a great deal of research to become informed about available options. For both FROG and SONG, special committees took on the research and reported back with their recommendations to the larger group, which then made the final decisions. Right from the design stage on, we had to make numerous difficult choices as we balanced healthy, ecologically desirable materials with affordability.

Heating systems were one of our first concerns. At FROG one of the many discussions revolved around heat recovery ventilators (HRVs). At the time the devices (which recover waste heat as a building is ventilated) were still quite expensive. Our committee calculated that it would take 30 years to save enough money to pay for their initial cost, and because they were not a primary part of the heating system, it didn't seem worth it. Six years later, however, when SONG was coming on stream, HRV technology had advanced and the price had dropped. So SONG recommended HRVS, particularly for their larger units.

Framing materials were another concern. FROG residents opted to use fairly standard stick frame construction, albeit with double walls that were filled with blown-in cellulose insulation (made from recycled newspaper). SONG, however, opted to use structurally insulated panels (SIPs), a relatively new material that was little known when FROG was being built. SIPs are the opposite of ICFs, in that the foam insulation sits on the inside of its 4-by-8-foot (1.2-by-2.4-meter) panels, sandwiched between two pieces of oriented strand board (OSB). (OSB is made from low grade wood and reduces the harvesting of large trees.) SIPs are quite environmentally friendly, even though they are not natural building materials. An entire wall can be built in a day and the house closed in quickly, resulting in fewer moisture problems. SIPs conserve wood and create airtight building seals. But SIPs are made with formaldehyde glue — their main drawback. The glues that are used vary in their composition, however, and we were able to purchase the least toxic variety. Both framing systems, though different, are structurally sound and work well in their respective neighborhoods.

Other materials requiring our consideration included insulation (a key consideration in our cloudy, Northeast climate), appliances, paints and varnishes, to name just a few. We had to think about indoor air quality. In every case our resident committees put in many research hours. They considered the amount of "embedded energy" in each product (the amount of energy it takes to manufacture and transport goods and materials). They tried to find local suppliers where possible and selected appliances that minimized energy use. They chose paints and varnishes that would not out-gas, helping to keep indoor air quality high. And they tried to anticipate the future, recommending that we plan for retrofits. So, in both neighborhoods, we roughed in our plumbing and wiring in such a way that we could easily retrofit alternative technologies as they become available (photovoltaics, solar hot water heaters, or graywater recovery systems, etc.). All of our research, discussions, and choices have paid off. Both FROG and SONG are well sited, energy efficient, and ecologically friendly in their composition.

FROG and SONG: Choices and Consequences

Perhaps not surprisingly FROG and SONG took different paths on the way to completing their neighborhoods. I would say that FROG, although heavily involved in decision making on design, had a very controlled design and construction process with managers who were clearly in charge. EVI's first resident group (FROG) was fortunate to have Jerry and Claudia Weisburd of Housecraft Builders as our development managers. In many ways the two were a perfect match for our group. Both an architect and a builder, Jerry had an A-Z knowledge of housing development and the ability to keep a tight rein on costs. Claudia was highly skilled in strategic planning and group process, and she had an uncanny knowledge of legal matters (although she was not a lawyer).

The two had 20 years of experience in building affordable housing in the Ithaca area, shared our environmental concerns, and had even had the experience of creating their own cooperative community. Together they formed a formidable team, and they guided us skillfully through the intricacies of designing and building the first cohousing community in New York State.

Although some people chafed at their firm leadership, we needed it. The Weisburds set clear deadlines for us, covering everything from house design to materials choices to the design for the Common House. And it was their track record with our local bank that convinced Tompkins Trust Company to take on the risk of financing our project.

During the design process, we asked Jerry to produce compact, passive solar homes that would feel light and spacious. And I think he did remarkably well. FROG's five basic house designs vary from a 900-square-foot (84-square-meter) one-bedroom design to a 1,650-square-foot (152-square-meter) five-bedroom design. Almost all the homes have a large, triple-glazed window wall on the south side and a cathedral ceiling, making the space feel light and open. And there are mezzanines, open to the living room below, that can be used as office space.

Homes in FROG are very standardized, with few custom features. Jerry and Claudia set clear deadlines, and we knew that if we didn't make a decision on time, they would make it for us. The result was less individual creativity, fewer cost overruns (although there were some), and a more standardized product. Our homes are smaller and, on average, less expensive than their SONG counterparts. And they have fewer "green" features, such as photovoltaics (solar electric panels) or composting toilets. Unlike our SONG neighbors, FROG residents had neither the satisfaction nor the headaches of "building your own."

SONG's design and build process took a much looser approach that allowed for more creativity and owner-builder participation than did FROG's. But it also traveled a bumpier road. After searching for an experienced development manager in vain, Rod Lambert and I finally took on the project, agreeing to work until the project reached the construction stage (see Chapter Six). Although we were relatively inexperienced, we did work hard and effectively on getting Town approvals and on putting site design, house designs, marketing, and financing in place.

Just getting through the design stage was a challenge. Mary Kraus (an architect from Massachusetts who specializes in designing compact homes using green building materials) produced the schematics for the first incarnation of SONG. However, when the original SONG group fell apart and a new group came together, they decided not to rehire Kraus, mostly due to the difficulties of maintaining a long-distance relationship. Instead Rod Lambert helped homeowners to customize the original schematic designs. Once that process was complete, another architect finalized the designs.

When SONG was ready to move from design to construction, Rod's and my part as development managers was over. Rod went on to help build the homes, but I let go of "my baby" with a sigh and some relief. No longer would I wake up at night, trying to solve some difficult development problem.

SONG hired construction manager Mike Carpenter to see them through the construction phase. Mike had a wealth of experience with quality building and brought his knowledge of local contacts and background in solar technology to the project. He and the SONG residents teamed up in a highly participatory process that included the construction, financing, and subcontracting for the whole project, as well as the management of the subsidized housing. Many SONG residents also contributed substantial "sweat equity" to the construction of their homes, and two couples built homes entirely on their own.

The degree of intense participation at SONG proved to be overwhelming for many of the residents with no housebuilding experience. Individual choices had to be made from a myriad of products for every aspect of construction. What kind of framing did they want? What kind of roofing and flooring? What kind of finishing? Would they buy new or salvaged? It was endless. And with no one person or developer firmly in charge, finances and timelines sometimes slipped.

Without a clear group consensus on standard home size or features, it was also easy for SONG residents to get seduced by "house envy" or "feature creep" — adding a bow window here, a meditation loft there — without necessarily realizing how the costs would add up. Unfortunately, many people found that when their homes were finished, they were much larger than was needed and cost substantially more than the original projections. This has led to ongoing emotional and financial stress for some SONG households.

Even with all the ups and downs of the process, though, SONG homes have unmistakable personality, reflecting the individualized taste, choices, and often labor of their owners. As Rob Champion, who not only built

> After a fierce downpour yesterday, the warmth of the sun is bringing out tender new leaves on the honeysuckle. Daffodils make a sunny splash in my neighbor's south-facing front yard, though I'll have to wait a couple of weeks for mine — my front yard faces north and is shadowed by our house. But I notice that maple flowers are blooming bright red against a blue sky. And peepers at the EcoVillage pond keep up a steady chorus, alternating with birdsong and construction noise from the SONG site. Today I could enjoy a walk on the land without wearing a jacket. Spring has finally arrived!
>
> — Journal entry
> Spring 2002 ∎

his own home with his wife, but also worked on several others, commented: "There's something of a rite of passage in building your own home. It's soulful. I'm becoming aware of how meaningful this is to others as well as to me. Building your own shelter is an activity that has been largely removed from us, like growing our own food."

As with many aspects of EVI, the different approaches of the two neighborhoods offer plenty of lessons to ponder. Perhaps a third neighborhood will take a middle road, having more centralized management and overall control but room for owner-builders to customize their homes, too.

Recycling

No discussion of sustainability would be complete without mentioning the importance of reusing and recycling. At EVI we have a well-established and detailed recycling program. And, as the following vignette shows, recycling fits in seamlessly with our day-to-day activities and interactions.

JULY 2002

It's recycling day again. I fetch a garden cart from the shed across the street and load up compost, paper, glass, metal, plastic, and half a bag of trash. Thank heaven for the carts — they let me move everything in one trip, with very little effort. It's another gorgeous summer day, sunny and pleasantly cool.

I admire the flowers in my neighbors' gardens as I pass. Each week brings something new as the flowers proceed majestically through the season, changing from the first spring crocuses and tulips to the deep purple iris of summer and fall. Right now the white daisies and bright gold sundrops are on their way out, the roses are in full bloom, and huge sprays of lavender are at their peak. Lavender has such a heavenly scent, and I stop to stroke one of its blossoms and savor the smell on my fingers. Little white butterflies that land only on the lavender circle the plants like a mist. If I were an insect, that's what I would choose, too.

I wheel my cart behind one of the carports to the compost area that we all use for our kitchen scraps (minus anything meat based that could attract rodents). People are getting sloppy about covering their scraps, I notice with annoyance. For compost to turn to "black gold," it has to be treated right.

"Brown" matter goes over "green." Basically you chop up large pieces of kitchen waste (such as corncobs or bagels) and crush any eggshells so that everything will compost faster. And then you cover it all up with brown matter, such as leaves, hay, or other mulch. If the mix isn't right, it won't heat up. But when the mix is good the compost easily heats up (reaching 140 to 160 degrees Fahrenheit [60 to 71 Celsius]) and turns into very rich humus. The finished product has no smell and is an excellent addition to our home gardens. I dump in my contribution to the compost and cover it over. And then, after stopping to chat with friends, I'm off to the dumpster.

The common dumpster sits on the other side of the Common House. After much soul-searching we recently upgraded to a larger size, and we now fill a 108-cubic-foot dumpster every week. Not bad for a community of 160 people. Although this is about a quarter of what other US housing developments of this size generate, in my view there is still plenty of room for improvement. .

The decision to upgrade has posed a challenge for me. It makes me want to cut back even further on my own household trash. (I know I tend to be lazy about washing plastic bags for reuse, and I find that plastic constitutes most of our trash.) But it also makes me want to find out how much waste the whole community puts out week by week.

I'd like to find a student who is willing to enlist a few volunteer families to weigh their trash, recycling, and compost every week and record the findings. That would be useful data, providing us with a baseline for future comparison and acting as an incentive for us to further reduce our output now and as an ongoing commitment. For now, though, I better get a move on.

I wave hello to Rob, who is up on a ladder busily building the SONG carports. He tells me that building is like an outdoor adventure course, except you have something to show at the end. You get to be outside all day, he says, taking some risks and being creative. He is clearly in his element. I say goodbye and walk to the recycling shed.

The shed sits at one end of the carports and has a huge sliding barn door. We have large bins for paper and cardboard and others for #1 and #2 plastics. Still others are set up to take metal and glass containers. And bicycles hang on pegs on the wall.

On my way back from the recycling shed, I decide to visit the reuse room — a closet in the Common House that serves as the repository for donated clothes, shoes, and toys. I'm delighted to find a fairly new pair of women's hiking boots in my size. I remind myself to bring up the jeans I've decided to give away, so that someone else can use them.

As I am standing on the Common House porch, I notice a big basket from the farm. A label on it proclaims, "Enjoy!" Inside I find a few snow peas left over from the CSA distribution. I happily scoop them up and sample one for good measure. They're a little limp from being in the sun for a day or two, but they taste like summer, and my mouth feels green and lush just biting into one. Still munching, I return my cart to the shed.

Some kids are playing up by the swing set, and I ask them if they'll help me feed the chickens. I'm a little embarrassed to ask, since I've lived here for over five years and have never tried it. I wonder if it takes a special technique. If so, the kids will know, I think. Morgan, who has just celebrated her fifth birthday, says she'll help, and we chat about her birthday on our way to the chicken run.

The chickens make us laugh. Morgan shows me how to break up small pieces of food and throw them on the ground. Watching the chickens rush toward us is a little like watching somebody trying to run at top speed with a watermelon between their legs. The five chickens that are out today gobble up my stale blueberry pancakes as if they were starving! All of us — Morgan, the chickens, and me — are enjoying ourselves immensely. I make a mental note to save more bread and do this again. I thank Morgan for her help and head on home.

Although you could say I've just done a chore, it hasn't really felt chore-like. I've had a chance to enjoy the sights of the neighborhood, chat with friends, and have a good laugh with Morgan. I've also made a useful contribution to the health of the planet by reusing or recycling some items and feeding the earth with my leftover scraps. And I've learned how to feed chickens!

Influencing Friends and Neighbors

The things that we do can have a remarkable effect on others. One person's example of "green living" can ripple out and influence others to change their lifestyles. For example, when our family of four moved into EVI, we had two cars. Both Jared and I commuted to work on different sides of the city, and the children were going to different schools with very inconvenient bus service. It was easier to drop them off than to endure their groans about having to get up at 6 a.m. and walk half a mile in the snow to the bus stop. Then there was grocery shopping after work, track practice for Jason, the gym for Jared, and a variety of other stops. We were a typical US family with typical transportation needs.

I started to notice other families at EcoVillage who seemed to manage with just one car, although it was often quite a juggling act. So when my car died about two years later, after putting in a serviceable 175,000 miles (282,000 kilometers), it seemed time to try the grand experiment. Could we live with just one vehicle?

Well we tried it out. Jared and I got familiar with our respective bus routes to work, and the kids took the city bus more often. Frequently I was the chauffeur, dropping Jared at work and Jason at the high school, and then driving up to Cornell for my workday. Daniel was part of a carpool that went to the Alternative Community School (ACS), and Jared fulfilled our carpool obligations on his flex day off. Every Sunday night we negotiated who got the car on which days for the following week. It worked pretty well, but it was still a lot of driving.

As I drove home I often saw our next-door neighbor Arthur Godin (the general manager of our local food co-op) biking home. After a while I realized that if he could do it, then I could, too. So one day I packed the contents of my briefcase into my backpack and hopped on my bike.

I glided down West Hill at 30 miles per hour (48 kilometers per hour). This was going to be easy! I biked through town in traffic (not as much fun), then biked up East Hill, a shorter but steeper rise. Halfway up I was panting and wondering what I thought I was doing. But I felt so great at work all day that I knew it was worth it. Getting home, however, was a different story.

West Hill is very long and has about a 2-mile (3-kilometer) continuous rise. The only way I made it was by concentrating on a tree 50 yards (45 meters) away and telling myself that if I could get to it, then I could rest. By the time I got to the tree, I didn't want to stop; I just wanted to keep going to the next landmark. It took time, but I just kept going, with sweat pouring down in rivulets from my forehead. Eventually I made it up the grade. I was exhausted but also very proud of myself. After that first day I started biking several times a week, and it did get easier with time.

Jared was so impressed with my efforts that he decided to try biking to work, too. He needed to look professional at his job and knew there was no shower there, so he was a little worried about how it would work out. But after a couple of days, he relaxed. Already an avid recreational cyclist, Jared didn't find the ride terribly strenuous — he didn't even sweat much. From then on he just rolled his work clothes up into a neat bundle and stored them in his panniers. He arrived at work looking happy, energized, and not rumpled at all.

When we started the ACS carpool again after the summer, I was bummed out, since it meant I would have to drive a couple of days a week again. Daniel suggested that he and the other boys could bike down to school (close to the bottom of West Hill) and back. We talked to the other parents about the idea, and they encouraged their kids to give it a try — although there was quite a wall of resistance at the start.

The experiment worked very well. It was fun for the kids to be more independent and to zoom down the hill at top speeds in the morning. And they all rose to the challenge of getting home — even if it meant walking partway. Daniel became an excellent cyclist and often continued on an additional 5 miles (8 kilometers) to another friend's house after school.

The ripple effect didn't stop there, either. Other people started biking, too. Steve (another neighbor) started biking downtown to catch his bus to work, using the convenient rack on the front of the bus for his bike on the way home. Francis, a hardy and dedicated SONG member with a PhD in transportation planning, bikes to work at Cornell throughout the winter.

Since I took up biking I've started to feel its health benefits. On the days when I bike, I work more efficiently and feel happier and more relaxed. People tell me that I glow. I've lost weight without trying and improved my muscle tone, making me feel very fit. And all the while I get to enjoy the changing seasons and the feel of the sun and wind on my face. I even get to watch deer grazing in the fields as I pedal along, still panting, up the long hill.

So thank you Arthur, for starting a trend. You showed me that one individual can influence many others simply by setting a positive example.

Our family still has a car, but I am hoping that eventually we will be able to get rid of it, too. I would like to see our current informal car-share system expand to a fleet of reliable EVI vehicles that can be borrowed for short or long trips.

Influencing each other to live a greener lifestyle is part of what makes EVI "so ecological." But so are many of the other measures that we have put in place here. Whether we focus on energy reduction, "green" building, organic farming, or recycling we are constantly refining our practices to create a more eco-friendly place in which to live and work.

CHAPTER 8

CREATING THE "VILLAGE"
IN ECOVILLAGE

Labor Day Weekend 2003
*Saturday — It is a glorious blue-sky day, and we have several
activities planned for the weekend. After the many ups and
downs of building SONG and creating a Village Association,
we are finally holding our long-awaited "Village Celebration."*

*Right now dozens of men, women, and children are
hard at work hammering boards. One two-year-old happily
bangs away with a plastic hammer, undaunted by the fact
that his nail is not going in. Rod Champion (SONG resi-
dent-builder), with help from Todd Ayoung, has designed
and bought materials for a simple bridge that will span the
15-foot (4.5-meter) ravine between FROG and SONG.*

*By the end of the morning the new bridge will be finished,
and we will no longer need to walk through the parking lots
to visit each other's neighborhood. But the bridge has a far
greater significance — it also provides a symbolic joining of
the two cohousing groups into one cohesive village.*

*Sunday — Seventy of us gather by the bridge and begin
to walk a giant figure eight around both neighborhoods.
The interconnected circles represent eternity. We sprinkle
cornmeal as we walk, honoring the Native American tradition of blessing the land and its non-human inhabitants.
I find myself walking with several women friends, singing,
"Now I walk in beauty" (a song based on a Native prayer).*

*Once the circle-eight is complete, we return to the bridge
and form a tunnel with our hands. We continue singing,
and everyone passes through the tunnel to the other side of the*

147

bridge. We form a large circle between the two neighborhoods, and each person shares a word of hope for our new village.

Maria Gasser, a longtime FROG resident, speaks for many of us when she says, "It has been too hard to carry the whole EcoVillage vision alone as one neighborhood. It is such a relief to have our neighbors in SONG bring energy and enthusiasm to community projects."

Before we plant a cherry tree for the whole village, we each write down something we are ready to release that might hinder our personal or collective growth. Taking the exercise seriously, I surprise myself by writing down not one but three things. I put my slip of paper in the bottom of the planting hole along with the others. And it works! I feel some old resentments melt away.

We fit the cherry sapling into the ground, and ten children shovel earth around the roots, tamping it down to secure the tree in its new home. Like the tree, our life as a village is ready to grow.

How do 60 households from two different neighborhoods become a village? As pioneers of the first linked cohousing community

Jim Bosjolie
Building a bridge between FROG and SONG.

in the US, we had to invent the process ourselves. We needed to find ways for FROG and SONG to become part of a larger identity known as "the village," without either forfeiting its individual status — not an easy task. And we had to address many issues having to do with shared responsibilities, shared space, shared leadership, and even shared social conventions (such as the appropriate time for skinny-dipping in the pond). There was a lot of friction, as well as goodwill, as we all moved into a new stage of our life together.

Getting Us Together

In the process of getting together and forging a village identity, the most difficult issue by far involved the "Common House Sharing Agreement." The agreement was meant to clarify how members of the second neighborhood could use the FROG Common House before the SONG Common House was built. The whole issue became highly contentious when a few members from SONG implied that they might not want to build a Common House at all. Two FROG members then insisted that stringent financial measures be taken if SONG did not build its own Common House within a certain time frame.

The budding trust between the two groups shattered as acrimonious words went back and forth over e-mail and at meetings. The vast majority of people in both neighborhoods were excited to be shaping a village together. But so many people's feelings were hurt over the Common House debate that it seemed as if we would have to start from the beginning to rebuild trust.

There were also tensions within each neighborhood. A few people at FROG preferred the status quo and felt that the 30 families at SONG were taking over what had once been a favorite open field. Likewise a small number of SONG residents were disrespectful of the considerable work that FROG members had done in launching the first cohousing neighborhood, not only at EcoVillage but also in New York State. Their competitive message seemed to be, We can do much better than they did. If we were ever to become a cohesive village, we clearly needed to move beyond conflict.

Rather than let issues fester, we chose to focus on concrete solutions. First we made sure both groups were communicating. We held two forums to talk about what was going on. Aptly titled "Exploring our Differences, Deepening our Connections," the forums gave us all a chance to explore resentments or perceived inequalities between the neighborhoods and to solve problems together.

We also formed a nonprofit Village Association to look after all matters having to do with the village. The Association owns the roads, the water and sewer systems, the pond, and the land between the neighborhoods. A Village Board actively plans for meetings and takes legal and fiscal responsibility for the village. Meetings are held monthly as part of a FROG or SONG meeting. All residents belong to the Association and pay village-wide dues that help maintain the infrastructure. The founding of the Association helped to clarify our shared responsibilities.

But by far the best solution was also a simple one. We did things together. We shared frequent village-wide meals, work parties, and celebrations. And it is these shared experiences that helped us to merge into a village, while still maintaining unique identities as neighborhoods. One village-wide event that brought us together concerned "The Crux," a small area that nestles between FROG and SONG.

The "Crux of the Matter" Party

SEPTEMBER 2002

The sky is cloudless, and it is really hot out — at least 92 degrees (33 Celsius). We've all been invited to a "Crux Party," partly for fun but also to plan what to do with the area between our two neighborhoods. Dubbed "The Crux" by our permaculture landscape designer Dave Jacke (see "Permaculture" in Chapter Seven), the area has the best view on-site but is currently undeveloped.

In the center of our little village, "The Crux" looks out over the pond and fields to the blue hills beyond. It could be a lively, beautiful site for people to gather. We could have picnic tables here, a meandering stream, a small pavilion, an outdoor performance area, a basketball court, an arts and crafts area, an herb and flower garden, a bus shelter, and even more. But right now a row of carports, a gravel parking lot, and a weedy back lot are all that exist here. And the carports block the view to the pond. Ironically the parking lot offers the best views at EVI — not exactly the image or ambiance that we want to create in the heart of our community. It makes sense to plan something new for this area.

I see that the organizers have attracted kids as well as adults from both neighborhoods, and I'm impressed. They've put out a table loaded with chips, salsa, lemonade, and watermelon slices. Chairs cluster invitingly in the shade, and there's a water balloon game going on. Teams of two toss the full balloons back and forth, moving farther and farther apart as they try to prevent the balloons from bursting. The last three balloons pop at the same time, splashing water all over the pairs, who howl with laughter. A circle game called "A Big Wind Blows" starts up and draws in young and old players alike. It's a brilliant idea to make this a fun event. It has gotten people out here and experiencing the feel of the place.

When it's time to move on to the envisioning process, Steve Gaarder presides over a sand tray representing the one-acre site. He has etched roads into the sand and parked small toy cars in boxes standing in for the carports. His model gives us all a clear idea of the area we'll be considering.

Steve summarizes the history of thinking on "The Crux," and Elisabeth hands out questionnaires to each household. The questionnaire includes a little more historical background, some basic questions of preferences and concerns, and a chance to sketch our own great ideas about how we could develop the space.

"Everyone who completes a questionnaire will get a prize," Elisabeth tells us.

"What's the prize?" a chorus of voices asks.

"A piece of homemade sushi, a henna tattoo from Graham, or a foot rub from Bill," comes Elisabeth's answer. That's motivation enough to fill out a questionnaire on the spot! Soon people are busy drawing and chatting with each other about ideas.

But it is not all fun and games. There are serious implications no matter what route we decide to take. Greg (a member of the SONG finance committee) draws me aside to talk about money. He is worried. SONG's recent cost overruns have pushed the common costs (money spent on development costs other than the housing such as management, infrastructure, and consultant fees) through the roof. How will SONG finance the additional amount needed to move the existing carports and/or the road through "The Crux"?

I have another concern. How will spending money on "The Crux" affect repayment to EVI's lenders? It took FROG, SONG, and EVI over a year to reach an agreement over cost overruns. The "ISLAND Agreement" stipulates that any cost overruns on village-wide infrastructure will be split three ways. If SONG can't meet their obligations on "The Crux," then the EVI lenders, who have been waiting for their payback for a very long time, could be hit badly.

The tension over finances is very familiar. Almost all of the money used to develop EcoVillage has come either from the residents' pockets or from the original risk takers who loaned us money to buy the land. Only a very small amount has come from grants or donations, memberships, tours, and garage sales. Setting priorities among competing financial needs is one of the hardest community tasks we face. Greg and I agree not to bring up these controversial issues now. Instead we will address them in our questionnaires and with "The Crux" planning committee. Today is meant for nurturing group playfulness and creativity.

The two of us drift off and mingle with our other neighbors. The sushi is delicious, and the henna "tattoos" bring out midwife Graham's artistic side. Bill, an attorney, confides that he wants to take a reflexology class to learn more about how the foot relates to the rest of the body, so that he can give even better foot massages. Who would have thought our community could have such fun in this godforsaken weedy little lot?

There's a vigorous game of basketball going on in "The Crux" parking lot, and my feet tingle from a foot massage as I carry tables and chairs back into the Common House and put away some of the leftover sushi. As I leave the Common House, I notice that the Earth Flag flying over the entry has gotten all tangled up. About a dozen yellow jackets have taken up temporary residence in its smooth folds, and I gently but firmly shake them out. It feels great to unfurl the flag and see again its beautiful image of our blue-green Earth. I look down at the children playing in front of the Common House and think, This is for you.

The "Crux of the Matter" Party got us working together on our shared space and helped us bond as a village. Learning to share leadership has also brought us closer together.

Sharing the Load, Sharing the Glory: The Benefits of Shared Leadership

Leadership often functions best when it is shared. Unfortunately our culture seems to either exalt or revile its leaders — giving them the status of superhero or demon — rather than allowing them to be simply human. We certainly need leadership if we want to get anything done. But rather than vesting it in one individual, we can view leadership as a role that needs to be performed. Within that definition many people can become leaders and take on different roles at different times.

THE "WHAT" OF LEADERSHIP

There are many leadership roles at EcoVillage. My role of director for the nonprofit requires that I take leadership in helping to shape and implement the overall EVI vision. The role of the Board of Directors requires that its elected members take leadership in carrying out its mandate. Similarly the role of the Village Association requires people to provide leadership in relation to our village-wide responsibilities. Then there are the requirements of the working structures of the two neighborhoods. Beyond that there are committee chairs and work teams. With so many functions operating simultaneously and so many positions to fill, almost everyone takes on a leadership role at one point or another.

But leadership roles exist in other areas, too. In fact the "burning souls" in our community initiate much of what happens here at EVI. They are usually the most willing to provide energy and ideas to make something new happen. Since our goal is to create a model of a more sustainable culture, every aspect of living is up for grabs. Does someone care passionately about open space? They can learn about habitat restoration and land trusts. Is education someone's reason for being? They can start programs to teach sustainability in the classroom. Is group process really someone's gift? They can offer workshops in consensus and mediation. The list is endless. People have the opportunity to blossom. And as they offer their talents to the community, they add immeasurable richness to the whole.

THE "HOW" OF LEADERSHIP

My work as a paid grassroots organizer has given me a unique perspective on leadership. For my entire adult life I have worked for consensus-based nonprofit groups that are oriented toward social change. Occasionally a group would have a paid staff of two or three, but often I have been the lone paid staff person.

My role trained me to consult widely with others and listen well, to synthesize viewpoints and define a direction, and to focus group energy on achieving a goal. And it trained me to be as unattached to outcomes as possible, to trust in the wisdom of the group, and to at all times uphold a larger vision.

Riding the waves of a group's emotional psyche was devastating at times and exhilarating at others. But I learned that the more I could see my role as facilitator and coordinator, the easier it was for me to be patient and trust the process.

So now I liken leadership to a magician's scarf trick. When a magician pulls a continuous piece of silk out of the hat, it flows smooth and cool through the fingers and lightly passes on. Similarly when I figure out what needs to be done and learn how to do it, I try to pass on the skills and responsibility to someone else.

PROCESS VERSUS ACTION

In any group dynamic there seems to be a built-in tension between process-oriented people and action-oriented people. Our project at EVI is no exception. As someone who believes that both good process and good results are crucial, I am smack in the middle but able to see both sides.

I remember working with two young college graduates to help the budding EVI group look at the process-versus-action issue at our first Annual Meeting in January 1992. We drew two pictures. One showed a rocket ship sitting on a launching pad. A group of people was gathered around its base, talking. The caption beneath read, "Will the rocket ever get launched?"

The second drawing showed a rocket ship starting to take off. A group of people was struggling to hold it down. The caption below read, "We have to stop them! If they launch now, they won't have a clue about where they are going, and they may run out of fuel."

I still chuckle at those cartoons, because they are such an apt portrayal of the process-versus-action dilemma. The first picture illustrates the position of process-oriented people who talk things through until they are sure every detail is in place. For them process is more important than action. The second picture illustrates the position of action-oriented people who just want to get going, even if they don't necessarily know where they're heading or if they have the resources to support their flight. For them action is more important than process. What was true at our Annual Meeting in 1992 is still true now.

Fall 2003 – Summer 2004

Eleven years after we first produced the two cartoons, the process-versus-action drama is playing out once more, this time in the SONG neighborhood. Once the construction of the west end was finally completed, a landscape committee of well-motivated, action-oriented people wanted to plant trees in their somewhat barren neighborhood. They felt it was important to get something planted before the onset of winter, so they found a sale and bought 20 trees. Then they went door to door to some of the neighbors, asking what kind of trees each family wanted.

People at the other end of the neighborhood were incensed. Angry comments flew hard and fast. "But you haven't consulted the whole community on this issue!" "You can't just ask individual households what they want. It also affects community-wide views." "We need to slow down and reconsider." The landscape committee felt unappreciated and left in a huff, and a new committee formed in its place.

Since the disagreement, the new committee has spent many months bringing landscape issues to the community meetings. Meanwhile winter arrived, and the original trees were heeled-in to the ground, so that they wouldn't die. No one knew whether or not they would survive until it was time to replant them.

By the following summer, the issue was still not resolved, although the group was making some progress. And there were new issues, such as where a community garden should be located. At that point Jay Jacobson and I were called in from FROG to mediate between the SONG landscape committee and the SONG process steering committee.

In my opinion the drama of the trees tested the SONG group's ability to find a balance between process and action. The first group wanted to get something done quickly — perhaps too quickly. The second group spent many, many months trying to get the group's input — perhaps too many months. There really is no one right way to do things, but this particular controversy certainly highlighted both ends of the process-versus-action continuum.

Sadly the controversy also led to a deep rift in the SONG community for a time. In my view, what was going on at the surface wasn't what the conflict was really about, anyway (see "A Personal Conflict" in Chapter Five). The underlying issue had to do with trust. But it also had to do with the group's ability to accomplish a task and use an inclusive process to do it.

I am pleased to say that by fall 2004, SONG had resolved some (but not all) of its landscaping issues. There was great rejoicing as the first trees were planted, offering grace and beauty to the second neighborhood.

When Joan Bokaer and I co-founded EcoVillage at Ithaca in 1991, we had to deal with the process-versus-action dynamic, too. It turns out that the rocket ship analogy applies to groups as small as two. Joan's strong vision and charisma provided the rocket fuel for the project, and I helped to bring the whole group on board. Joan had a tendency, though, to decide independently on a course of action and take off, leaving the group behind in the dust. Part of my role became to seize the controls before she headed off, so that the group had some time to discuss her plans. Despite the fact that I slowed down her style, she often thanked me for intervening.

In order to deal effectively with the process-versus-action dynamic, the action-oriented people who are ready to get things done need to have patience with the process-oriented people as they work out a viable plan. And, at some point, the process-oriented people need to put an end to the discussion and let go, so that the rocket ship can take off.

WORKING AS A TEAM

Teamwork has been an integral part of the process since EVI's inception and has helped weave the strong fabric of our village. For one thing, Joan and I worked well together. Our work styles were complementary: Joan had charisma and a strong idea of what she was doing, and I was strong on group process and empowerment. Together we inspired each other to take big, bold leaps of faith.

Jim Bosjolie

After months of heated discussion with the group,
SONG landscape members plant the first of many trees.

It is compelling to map out a vision for the future (especially one that embodies your deeply held values) and then take action to make it happen. When we started, neither Joan nor I had prior development experience. Joan was an elementary schoolteacher, and I was a grass-roots organizer. We had no training in planning, architecture, finance, real estate, marketing, environmental design, or any of the myriad fields that would have been helpful. We did, however, have substantial people skills in communication, group development, teaching, and organizing. Working as a team, we were able to co-create something exciting, complex, and marvelously alive and growing.

Our shared leadership was actually a key factor in our success. The old saying about two heads being better than one certainly applied to us. That saying could easily have been expanded to "Two hearts are better than one," and even to "Two sets of resources are better than one." The two of us also had "beginner's mind," which probably worked to our advantage: Neither of us had any experience with the kind of work we were doing, which meant we didn't have any preconceived ideas of how to proceed, either. Finally it also helped that we were both women, able and willing to nurture and support each other through very challenging situations. In fact our experience convinced me that passion, dedication, and resourcefulness are among the most important attributes to have when bringing a dream to life.

Joan and I also drew on the talents and experience of the people around us. When new people came to the project, we found out what they enjoyed doing. And we determined what they wanted to learn about. Before long the newcomers would be immersed in a newly forming committee that made full use of their particular skill set.

The strategy was mutually beneficial. By inviting people into the process, they quickly became part of the community. But, perhaps more importantly, they helped broaden and deepen the scope of the work. The more expertise people brought and were willing to share with the community, the more we were able to accomplish as a community.

Leadership at EVI has never been a solo act. After the pre-construction phase of SONG was completed in the spring of 2002, I decided to take some time off. I had spent 11 years of total dedication getting EcoVillage off the ground and had worked most weekends and many evenings. I was deeply exhausted. I also thought that it would strengthen the whole organization if I left for a while and gave others a chance to take up the slack. Since I worked with so many academics, I decided to call my five-month break a "sabbatical."

I had a glorious time. I reveled in living in this beautiful place and, for the first time in years, no meetings were hanging over my head. I started writing this book and took some delightful trips. I traveled to Costa Rica to visit my brother, and I went to California to attend a nephew's wedding and take a backpacking trip in the Sierras. Jared, Jason, Daniel, and I even took a bike trip from Vermont to Montreal. I loved the stimulation of seeing new places and meeting new people, and I loved my cozy nest at home, as well. By the time I went back to work in September, I felt recharged at the cellular level.

I was delighted to find that nothing had fallen apart in my absence. Alison, a part-time paid assistant, had stepped in to take major responsibility for some of my work. Laura and Greg had taken responsibility for the SONG subsidy program. Elan had kept track of our educational work, and Michelle had kept our visitors happy and well cared for. A number of other people had looked after everything else. I felt grateful and somewhat humbled by how well the village did without me.

Once I was back at work, I found that I had new energy for tackling the land debt — the most long-lasting problem of all. In a flurry of confidence, I initiated the "Debt Free in 2003" campaign. Although I still did much of the work, our small core fundraising team motivated the entire community to accomplish our ambitious goal. Each team member made a significant contribution of time and energy, and it was our mutual strategizing and support that enabled the campaign to succeed. I was reminded again that the strongest organizations are ones in which the leadership is spread out widely. I could almost feel the muscular growth of the many shoulders now carrying the work forward.

RIPENING INTO LEADERSHIP

One of the most gratifying aspects of living at EcoVillage is that I get to watch people grow into their larger selves. Dozens of individuals at EcoVillage have felt passionately about an issue and convened a team of neighbors to act on it:

- Martha Stettinius helped save West Haven Farm by fundraising for an adequate deer fence.
- Laura Beck took on the huge, ongoing task of recruiting and orienting people for the subsidy program. And she is now

working with Linda Glaser to ensure that our village becomes more accessible to the elderly and people with disabilities.

- Katie Creeger started an organic berry farm and regularly works with volunteer students to clear invasive brush from the land.
- Greg Pitts took on some of the most difficult management tasks in SONG and brought them to completion.
- Bill Goodman has helped both neighborhoods and the nonprofit work their way through thorny legal and financial questions, always with a steady hand.
- Tina and Jim Nilsen-Hodges, busy as they were with teaching Montessori school, found time to convene an EcoVillage Kids' Council.
- Rachael Shapiro took on the task of organizing EVI's biggest fundraiser of the year — renting out residents' homes over Cornell's graduation weekend.

The list could go on and on. It is truly exciting to see what one person's focused work can accomplish and to see how different individuals ripen into leadership.

I celebrate the strength and beauty of our collective leadership. Every person in our community can offer some of the qualities, skills, and passion needed to manifest the EcoVillage vision. Without each contribution, the project would never succeed.

But a community's life is never static, either. Sometimes, in order to move forward, we need to take a look back. And that is what Phebe Gustafson helped us do.

Revisiting the Vision

During 2004 Phebe helped the community revisit its original vision for EcoVillage at Ithaca. We had originally met Phebe and her husband Wayne in 2001, when the two came to EcoVillage to visit and fell in love with the community. A graduate student at Antioch University in Seattle, Phebe was working on her MA in Whole Systems Design. While here, she decided to focus her thesis on an envisioning process for EVI's future education center.

The couple returned to Seattle, but Phebe's idea catalyzed the formation of a focus group, which Elan and I convened here at EVI. Meanwhile, back home in Seattle, Phebe developed a process called

"Living the Questions" for us to use to study the topic of the education center. Over the course of five sessions, Phebe posed the questions to the group and then collected and transcribed our taped discussions. The process led us through many thoughtful explorations, albeit few conclusions. And Phebe completed her MA and graduated. But her work at EcoVillage had just begun.

Phebe and Wayne moved to EVI in March 2002 and started building a house in SONG. Phebe continued to search for her niche in the educational side of things and often felt frustrated that her role was not clear. She eventually found her place.

Making use of the "Living the Questions" model she'd already developed, Phebe helped the whole community to refocus on what it means to live here. First she convened a working group to map out an effective process. Phebe's husband Wayne signed on, as did a contingent of EVI old-timers, including Monty, Jay, Elan, and me. Together we planned the sessions (both work and play) that would help everyone in the community express their thoughts and feelings about life at EVI.

Once the plans were in place, all we had to do was get on with things. Requiring five months from start to finish, the community had its first session in January 2004 and began by "Telling the Story of EcoVillage." We went on from there and ended with a final session in May 2004, in which we celebrated the specific tasks we had accomplished. Along the way, we revisited our collective history and reviewed and revised the original "Guidelines for Development."

The exercise was amazingly transformative! Not only was it a powerful way to integrate the many newcomers to the village, but it also tapped into the deep wisdom of those who had spent years at the helm. It renewed our strong intention to create a healthy, vibrant community. And it sharpened our ecological focus. As we revised the "Guidelines for Development" we were energized anew by the original bold vision. As a result, vital creative energy bubbled up for the next phase of projects. With Phebe's help the community had deepened its understanding and intentions in ways that will ripple out for years to come.

Over the years our shared experiences, shared work, and shared leadership have all helped to bring us closer together as a community. Our reconsideration of the whole EcoVillage vision made us feel like an extended family. With each year that passes, the "village" in EcoVillage becomes stronger.

CHAPTER 9

LEARNING AND TEACHING

Visitors to EcoVillage at Ithaca often enjoy walking down the winding pedestrian streets, getting a peek at the Common House, and hearing about our ecological focus. If they are lucky, they may get to taste fresh strawberries from the farm or take a dip in the cool pond. They may partici-pate in cooking a community meal or feel the warmth of the caring interactions between children and adults. What they may miss entirely, however, unless it is made explicit, is the profound way that education permeates the project.

E VI started out as an educational project in 1991. It is designed to be a living example of a more sustainable way of life — one that demonstrates both social and ecological alternatives to the status quo. We are particularly interested in whole-systems thinking that focuses on the intersection between human and natural systems. Our educational style can best be described as experiential, project-based learning.

As residents we are engaged in a fascinating social experiment. We have endless opportunities to test out methods of strategic planning, consensus decision making, conflict resolution, and creative parenting. And we can experiment with such things as community celebrations, green building, native landscaping, and alternative transportation. We truly are a learning community.

At the same time we are eager to share what we learn with the broader public. Although most of our teaching takes place with college students, we also host visitors of all ages and backgrounds. And we are educa-tional partners with others who are creating a wave of new approaches to solutions-based learning.

Community Education: Learning from the Inside Out

As residents at EVI, almost every aspect of our lives involves learning, whether we learn as individuals or as a group. Sometimes our learning comes about as a result of self-reflection. Most healthy people will occasionally take a critical look at their behavior, but living in community seems to accelerate the process. In fact I sometimes say that we live in a cauldron of personal growth here. As we learn to relate thoughtfully with the other 160 children and adults in our community, we inevitably discover clashes in values, lifestyles, personalities, and preferences. The key is not only to be open to others, but also to look closely at our own behavior. If something isn't working, it's important to question how we might be contributing to the problem and take responsibility for making creative changes (see Chapters Five and Six). And we need not do the work alone.

Plenty of support groups at EVI help people grow through self-reflection. As we saw in Chapter Six, we have had a variety of active support groups at EVI. Each group focuses on something different, but they all foster personal growth within a supportive group context. Our support groups add deep meaning and texture to our relationships with each other.

Rachael Shapiro

Three friends — Allegra, Allesia and Ariana — and a frog.

Because our lives are so interwoven, we also have myriad opportunities to learn as a whole group. One such learning experience had to do with pets and wildlife. When we first moved into our homes in EcoVillage, some of us were quite concerned about the ecological impact of having dogs run loose on the land. Although we didn't have a set of rules governing pet behavior, dog owners were encouraged to keep their dogs on a leash or at least under voice control. As it turned out, only one of the dozens of dogs that have lived here frequently killed wildlife. Cats, however, posed a significant problem.

Cats that go outdoors tend to hunt, and they can devastate bird species — particularly those that nest on the ground. Yet many pet owners see their pets as family members and hate to restrict their freedom. So we circulated a number of scientific articles to educate residents on the dangers that predatory cats pose to bird species. Since then most people who own outdoor cats have agreed to keep them inside during the nesting season. We have still not adopted rules about

May Day this year is warm, intermittently sunny and rainy. We are dancing around the Maypole — old and young together — dancing around the tall pole, weaving ribbons that have faded from years of use. My fellow dancers, aged 5 to 65, are strikingly beautiful — eyes sparkling and heads encircled by bright wreaths of forsythia and daffodils. We dance to the lilting sounds of flute, guitar, and hammer dulcimer being played by a few of our neighbors. Our ceremonious dance honors the joyous energy of Eros that springtime brings. The tall Maypole represents the masculine element, the woven ribbons the female.

As we disperse after our dance, children and adults together wander over to the nearby pond, where toads are busy with their own springtime ritual. We watch in fascination as the male toads perch on reeds in the water and serenade the females with piercing calls, their little throat sacks puffing up into transparent balloons. The females, bright orange and twice as large as the males, are in great demand.

In an age-old, watery mating ritual a small gray-green male clings piggyback to a female. As the female emits a long string of black eggs, the male fertilizes them with a milky cloud of seminal fluid. Within minutes the shoelace-thin strand of eggs puffs up with water and becomes jelly-like and translucent. This is Nature's fertility dance and a perfect teaching moment for all ages, giving us a chance to closely observe the beginning of a new cycle of life. ■

pets. But due to a group learning process, most residents voluntarily restrict their pets' activities during the critical seasons of spring and early summer.

Some group learning experiences occur during times of conflict. One such conflict arose when a pair of geese chose to nest on the island in our swimming pond. The geese caused a bigger flurry of e-mails than any other controversy in our history! A number of very vocal residents felt that the geese should be chased off — because they might pollute the pond and the beach with their feces, or because they might attract other geese, or because they might endanger swimmers.

One man sent an e-mail saying that he planned to shoot the geese at sunrise the next day unless he heard any objections. That e-mail, of course, brought horrified cries from those residents who loved wildlife and saw the geese as sentient beings deserving our respect.

So what did we do? Various residents did some research on geese and circulated their findings. Some found articles that characterized geese as pests, while others found information that geese are birds that mate for life. We also circulated articles that discussed the laws that protect nesting birds and the permits needed to remove them. And we learned that once geese lay eggs, it is almost impossible to scare them off. Finally one resident, Pam June, convened a forum to discuss what we had learned and to express our feelings about the geese.

As a result of so much internal education, the group sentiment changed and people accepted the geese, at least temporarily. One woman who had been vociferous in her opposition started sending out daily e-mails about "Poppa goose," noting that he was very adept at chasing off other geese and thus protected our pond from further incursions. Swimmers took turns cleaning up the beach with a pooper-scooper, and eventually we erected a string fence around the beach to keep the birds out. By gathering information, airing our different viewpoints, and doing a little creative problem solving, we saved the day. And the geese? Well, they carefully shepherded their four goslings away from the swimmers, and all was well. (Now we just have to figure out what to do for next year!)

Group learning does not necessarily have to be about the practicalities of life, either, as Jay Jacobson articulated in his comments to the working group that was planning our re-envisioning process (see Chapter Eight).

Spiritual progress usually has been a matter of individual effort. Aspirants found a teacher, a monastery, or a desert and devoted years to understanding themselves and their relationship to God. That may have led to many personal transformations, but only infrequently to the evolution of whole groups of people. Now, with [the] increasing capacity of humans to destroy ourselves and our environment, the next important phase in human evolution may be what is called "group work."

It probably goes without saying that EcoVillage is an ideal crucible for group work. How does a group of approximately 100 adults get to know each other, trust each other, and row in the same direction, rather than in different directions [and] with perhaps many not rowing at all?

For me, re-envisioning the "why we are here" part is not only [about] recommitting ourselves to the vision of building clustered, comfortable, energy-efficient houses, but it is [also about] learning how to work through differences and find where we each fit in and can play a role, both in day-to-day life and [in] formulating our future direction.

In Jay's view the work we do as a community at EVI is also a significant spiritual act.

It must be said that trial and error accounts for some of our group learning, too. Of course we can study examples in books or get advice from experts on a variety of issues. But sometimes we are inventing the very things that researchers have yet to study. And sometimes we are too busy to research. That's when we just pick a strategy and see how it works, which is what happened when we were setting up our work teams.

When the first neighborhood was completed, we set up work teams to deal with community chores (see "Famous Fried Tofu ..." in Chapter Four). Each adult was asked to join a team for a few weeks, then rotate onto another team. We thought it would be a wonderful way for people to gain skills in a number of areas without getting bored by repetition.

The method actually led to a chaotic mess. Just as one team was finally learning the ropes of their assignments, it was time to rotate to another area. Worse, we found that not everyone is good at everything.

People who didn't know how to cook for themselves (let alone a neighborhood) were in charge of community meals. People who were challenged by changing a light bulb were in charge of fixing the malfunctioning boiler in our rather complex energy system. It was a setup for disaster.

It took us a while to wise up and let people choose a team that reflected their natural inclinations, and *stay* with it. Not surprisingly the meals began to taste better; the physical plant stayed in good shape; and the Common House sparkled. We had finally figured out a method that worked!

In a more current example of the trial and error method of group learning, the cook team has been experimenting with ways to make mealtimes quieter and more relaxed. (This is a desirable but tricky project, given that up to 80 adults and children all eat together in one room at the same time.) We have tried "family style" meals, at which people are served at tables rather than lining up buffet style. We have tried serving our youngsters at a separate children's table. To keep the noise down, we have tried saving group announcements until after most people have finished eating. And we've tried dividing up our weekly community meals, so that one meal night is for FROG residents and one is for SONG residents. The last strategy is an attempt to keep numbers manageable and still provide three meals a week to those who want them.

We haven't come up with one surefire solution, but as we experiment with these and other options, we will gradually fine-tune what works and what doesn't. Certainly we wouldn't even have begun to make changes if people hadn't told us they were unhappy with the original setup.

Now that we have two neighborhoods, suggestions for change often come from the whole village. One such occasion occurred when SONG residents were still sharing the FROG Common House. People from both neighborhoods often complained that people rarely took time to hang out in the common area. So, in a simple but profoundly successful switch, the "Design Lab" committee put couches and a rocking chair next to the front door of the Common House, in place of a dining table.

The move changed everything. With a cozy nook to settle into as soon as you enter the building, the whole place became friendlier. And it got livelier, too, as people started to strike up casual conversations at any hour of the day. Once again a small structural adjustment had led to a satisfying cultural shift.

The residents of EVI learn from the inside out in a variety of ways, but we also share what we know with others.

Sharing Our Learning

At EVI we aim to create a learning environment that is deeply transformative and empowering. The world needs people who are whole in mind, body, and spirit and who are capable of being both thinkers and doers. Students of all ages thrive in an educational environment that includes a sound theoretical framework, cooperative learning strategies, hands-on practical application, and a deep examination of values and principles. With an emphasis on whole-systems thinking, we examine both the world's problems and their potential solutions. This type of multidisciplinary, experiential education can be a remarkable, energizing force in society.

EVI was founded under the auspices of the Center for Religion, Ethics, and Social Policy (CRESP) at Cornell University, which has a long-term affiliation agreement with the university. CRESP is a nonprofit organization whose mission is to "foster vital and caring communities to provide a foundation for a world of peace, mutual understanding, and respect for all life." It also provides an umbrella under which budding groups can develop into full-fledged nonprofit organizations. EVI's mission fit right into CRESP, and our association with it gave us an important toehold at an Ivy League university from the start.

In 2002, after a decade of working mostly with Cornell students and professors, we branched out to develop a joint partnership with the Environmental Studies Department of Ithaca College. The partnership received a three-year $149,000 matching grant from the National Science Foundation (NSF) to develop curriculum on the "Science of Sustainability" (an integrative approach that looks at how human and natural systems affect each other). The grant led to tremendous growth at both institutions.

I like to think of EVI's educational outreach as a series of concentric circles. The innermost circle consists of our intensive one-on-one work with individual students (interns, graduate students, and those doing independent studies). The next circle consists of the semester-long courses that we teach at EcoVillage. Tours and conferences make up the next circle, followed by additional circles having to do with media coverage and other outreach.

Our organization offers a rich field of study and can appeal to a broad range of people interested in studying almost any aspect of human endeavor. All facets of human existence may be examined, including work, play, parenting, housing, food production, and energy use, to name but a few. Each of these facets is looked at from the perspective of creating a sustainable culture. We also seek to preserve and enhance the natural environment and to learn more about coexisting with nature in creative ways. And we encourage self-reflection and inquiry. It is no wonder that EVI has attracted a great deal of interest among students and professors alike, as well as among visitors of all stripes.

WORKING WITH ELAN

Elan and Rachael Shapiro and their children moved to EcoVillage at Ithaca in 1996. Rachael and I soon became close friends, often finding time to bike, ski, or hike once or twice a week. And Elan and I had known each other during my San Francisco days, largely through my work with Interhelp (an international network of people who bring psychological and spiritual insights into their social change work). Elan saw EVI as a place where he could teach and also integrate his passion for ecology and community. And I knew that we were already on the same page when it came to educational outreach.

In 1998 we received an unexpected large donation, and I hired Elan to work 15 hours a week as an educational coordinator. Elan brought his skills as an educator, counselor, and deep ecologist to the work, as well as his infectious excitement about learning. He also brought a strong commitment for reaching out to the broader Ithaca community.

With Elan on board our educational work took on a sharper focus, and we expanded beyond our usual tours and guest lectures. We held two "Envisioning Education at EVI" sessions with educators from around the county. And we proactively began to cultivate like-minded professors and students at Cornell.

The envisioning sessions helped us find our place. We needed to find out what educational niche EVI could fill and how we could best complement the work others were doing in the field. So we deliberately designed the sessions to reach out to a variety of nonprofits,

September 2002

My biweekly meeting with Elan on educational coordination is scheduled at noon, but we are both a little late. I've been working at the farm harvesting veggies, and Elan has been busy helping the builders at his new home in SONG.

We begin our meeting with a personal check-in. This is a very busy time for Elan. He and his family just got back from vacation, it's the first day of school for his kids, and their van broke down. He's wondering if they should replace it or try to start a more effective car pool at EcoVillage. Elan is thrilled to be learning some hands-on construction skills, but he's also trying to juggle his counseling practice and educational work. I have just returned from my sabbatical and fill Elan in on the details (see Chapter Eight). Our check-in takes about 20 minutes. But no matter — we have started to reconnect as friends, and that will smooth the way for working together.

Once we get down to business, we discuss the NSF grant in detail, including finances, course scheduling, and a text on sustainability. We even take a dip in the pond and talk as we swim lazy laps. Elan poses a very important set of questions: What do we want to accomplish over the course of the grant? What outcomes will most help EVI, Ithaca College, the students, and the broader Ithaca community? And how will we measure success? These are stimulating questions, and I very much want to help define the answers. As we stroll back to my house, we decide we'll set another meeting in a few days' time. We schedule in some fun time, too — maybe we'll take a long bike ride or go for a hike together.

Although some people like to keep their work and personal lives separate, I don't. I delight in having friends who are also colleagues and enjoy working mostly out of my own home. I like that I can have meetings by the pond or on the porch of the Common House. It helps me to feel integrated. On the flip side, of course, I sometimes feel overwhelmed. And there really is nowhere for me to go to get away from it all — calls about EVI can come at any hour, or important visitors may casually drop by my home. Mostly, though, I feel blessed to be immersed in my life's work in a place where people care deeply about each other, where stimulating ideas crop up daily, where I feel profoundly connected with the land, and where I can experience the strong collaborative spirit that is so much a part of my community. ■

environmental organizations, and schools. And we received a favorable response. As Janet Hawkes (then executive director of Cayuga Nature Center) commented: "EcoVillage has a big story to tell. It's not just local or regional; it's national and international in scope. You are creating a whole new concept of living, with cohousing and ecological living combined."

The sessions had some spin-offs, too. We presented a popular "Sustainable Living Series" in partnership with Cooperative Extension. The series offered monthly public workshops that, in turn, grew into three ongoing "Living Lightly" study circles. We were on our way.

Our careful cultivation of Cornell faculty also bore fruit. In fall 2000, Elan and I were offered the opportunity to team-teach part of a graduate course in Environmental Management through the Department of Rural Sociology. The 18 graduate students represented 10 different countries, including several in Africa, South America, and South-east Asia.

We held our two teaching sessions at EcoVillage. We gave students plenty of time to interact with other residents and tour the homes. They even got to peel off the outer skins of onions at West Haven Farm, while hearing about the joys and trials of small-scale organic farming. And our exam questions were challenging. Students had to grapple with the pluses and minuses of the environmental and social choices that EVI has made over the years. And we asked them to come up with strategies that would best spread the word about the whole ecovillage movement. Invitations to teach did not end there, however.

In spring 2001 Ithaca College (IC) professor Garry Thomas arranged for Elan to teach a pilot course to 20 students on "Sustainable Communities" through the Department of Anthropology. The course integrated academic learning with weekly field trips and service-oriented projects at EVI. Its success helped cement a strong relationship between Ithaca College and EVI and ultimately led EVI and Ithaca College to apply for a joint National Science Foundation grant.

EVI also hosted students from Cornell at the same time the Ithaca course was in session. Elan, Jay, and I worked with Cornell professor Jack Elliott from the Department of Design and Environmental Analysis to offer enriching student projects for his course in Ecological Design.

Our dual responsibilities were a major breakthrough and also a bit overwhelming. We were coordinating students from the two colleges at once in about eight different projects that ranged from composting and greenhouse design to landscape planning for our entry road and improved signage around the village. But our work was also exhilarating. We were reaching out further into the larger community and bringing our EcoVillage experience to more people. I was grateful that we had Elan to help us as we expanded our educational horizons.

INTERNS

EVI's interns find us; we don't find them. To date about a dozen interns have worked at EcoVillage in as many years. Some have been full-time, while others have worked with us for a few hours a week over a semester. What astonishes me is that these highly motivated, very bright young people have invariably contacted us, without any effort on our part to attract them.

We have welcomed interns from all over the US and beyond. Several have come from New York State, including students from Bard, Cornell, Ithaca College, and Wells. Some have come from further afield, such as Florida (New College), Washington State (Evergreen State University), and Ontario, Canada (Fleming College). We have even had a Humphrey Fellow (an international, mid-career professional) from Senegal!

Tim Allen, whose help was invaluable at the start of the project, worked with us full-time at the start of the EVI project and received a stipend through the Brethren Volunteer Service. Now, more than a dozen years later, he has purchased a subsidized home at SONG and is reaping the concrete results of his labor. Aside from Tim all our other interns have worked as volunteers, often bartering with EVI residents for room and board in exchange for childcare or housework. Fortunately many student

Walking the Talk

On Rachel Carson Way, the winding gravel road leading up to the Common House, a dozen students are wielding loppers and pitchforks, as they remove beautiful but invasive purple loosestrife and honeysuckle. Their work is part of the "Community Plunge" program. This community service program at IC matches incoming freshmen with various local nonprofits for a half-day of volunteer work. We're lucky to have them. It's a nice spin-off from our academic association with IC. A few residents work side by side with the students, and together they make a small but important dent in the ongoing task of controlling these invasive plants. It is a win-win learning situation. ■

interns are able to receive college or university credit for their work in lieu of payment.

One outstanding young man joined EVI as an intern in the 2003 spring semester. Zach Shahan, a student from New College, had to adjust to our snowy Ithaca winter, as well as to the ups and downs of community life. But he managed to stay cheerful and worked long hours, primarily as an assistant to Elan.

Zach handled many of the logistics for the first course taught under the NSF grant. He copied course readers and ferried students back and forth between Ithaca College and EVI. And he acted as an important liaison between the students and their adjunct professor (Elan) in their experiment of creating a "learning community." Zach's feedback and advice helped to shape the course, giving him a strong sense of empowerment. As he noted: "Students are opening up to things they can do in the world and to people who are energetic, motivated, and respectable members of society. They are seeing these people confronting issues in a successful way. Students are finding out that you can do something useful with your life, rather than just make money."

COURSES ON SUSTAINABILITY

The NSF grant funded the development of four courses at EVI. Elan Shapiro developed the first course and set a high standard from the outset. Elan built substantially on the previously offered "Sustainable Communities" course, making it even more multi-layered. The resulting ambitious four-credit course examined all facets of ecologically oriented communities, while creating a learning community among the students themselves.

Course requirements were rigorous, with both personal and academic components. The personal component included such things as keeping a journal, a semester-long ecological practicum, "personal sustainability" practices such as meditation or yoga, and participation in group discussions and decision making.

On the more academic side, reading assignments were hefty, and students were expected to integrate their learning into papers and oral reports. In addition, students chose one of several hands-on project areas to work on. The projects included alternative transportation, a resident energy and water use assessment, or the development of a sustainable landscape guide for SONG. Each project had a corresponding resident who served as a team leader and helped the students to focus their work on what would be most useful for EVI.

At the end of the semester, students spent two full evenings presenting their work to the community, who received it with great interest. The course was a great success, with several students reporting that the course had changed their lives.

EVI resident Jon Harrod taught "Energy Efficiency and Sustainable Energy," the second course funded by the NSF grant. Jon found that he learned a lot by teaching about energy. He was able to go beyond his primary job as a "green" heating and insulation contractor and examine the broader social, political, scientific, and economic dimensions of energy use. The class concluded that "the technologies we need to make the transition to a sustainable energy future are already here and already cost effective."

Jon loved the work, even though the bureaucratic requirements of academic life were not something he enjoyed. He has since collaborated with a physics professor at Ithaca College to teach a freshman seminar that addresses energy and sustainability issues.

Photo courtesy of EVI

Elan Shapiro left, with his students in the "Sustainable Communities" course.

The third NSF-funded course was team-taught by IC professors Susan Allen-Gil and Garry Thomas. Students in the innovative "Environmental Futures" course compared the ecological footprints of SONG and a downtown neighborhood in Ithaca. (The ecological footprint measures the amount of land needed to continuously sustain one person's needs for such things as food, shelter, clothing, fuel, waste absorption, etc.)

Although results were not very precise, the analysis did confirm the findings of earlier studies that pegged EVI's ecological footprint at about 40 percent less than the typical footprint in other American neighborhoods. One finding identified airline travel as a key factor that raised EVI's energy usage. If none of us traveled by plane, then our average footprint would be more like 50 to 60 percent less than that of other US residents. Now, as I find myself traveling to give presentations at conferences around the world, that fact keeps coming back to haunt me.

"Sustainable Land Use," the fourth NSF-funded course was also taught by Elan. Three EcoVillage educators — who collectively have backgrounds in plant physiology, permaculture, organic gardening, environmental education, and service learning — helped to teach the course collaboratively. The teaching team has made good connections with local land stewards, including forester, author and Native American Mike de Munn, who conducted two inspiring field trips as part of the course (attended by both students and some EVI residents). Kiyokazu Shidara also helped teach us all how to study the potential of the land, water, and meadows surrounding the village.

The Footprint Challenge

Our ecological footprint may be relatively small — at 14 acres (5.7 hectares) per person, rather than the 24 acres (9.7 hectares) typical of the general US population — but it could stand to be even smaller. Right now our resource use is roughly equivalent to that of someone living in New Zealand or Brazil. To be truly sustainable, we need to match the resource use of someone living in Jordan or Turkey.

And if we look at our footprint from a bigger perspective yet, then it's obvious that we still have a long way to go: Even if every person in the world matched EVI's footprint, we'd still need approximately three planets to support us all! The good news is that we have already begun to make changes and are moving in the right direction to meet the footprint challenge. ■

STUDENT PROJECTS AT EVI

Course work is not the only way that students can learn at EVI. Students from Ithaca College and Cornell also undertake a variety of practical projects that benefit both the EcoVillage community and the two schools. The design of a "green" bus shelter was one such project. And the task was definitely not trivial.

The design project arose as a direct result of the second "Sustainable Communities" course, in which the "alternative transportation" group identified EVI's need for a "green" bus shelter. Working with Rob Licht (a local artist and builder who taught at Ithaca College), several Cornell students spent a productive summer researching and designing an EVI bus shelter.

As majors in architecture, natural resources, and engineering, the students brought an impressive array of skills to the table. They discussed the project with the major stakeholders —EVI residents, TCAT (our local bus company), Ithaca's town planner and engineer, and the New York State Department of Transportation. They studied "green design" principles and looked at building materials. And they came to terms with some pretty stringent design requirements. They also invited EVI residents, as active participants in the design process, to attend two student-led forums.

The students had their work cut out for them. The building would have to be moveable, in case TCAT eventually agreed to bring the bus stop closer to the village. The project budget would cover only materials costs, and most materials had to be recycled or reused. The shelter needed to incorporate passive solar features and be aesthetically pleasing. Finally it had to be as vandal-proof as possible.

The students came up with a fascinating design. The building included a cozy indoor waiting area, a sod roof, and a place to store bicycles. There was also a place for mailboxes that was out of the wind, and a handy recycling bin in which to toss unwanted mail. Residents eventually opted to finance a simpler, less expensive bus shelter that would exclude the mailboxes. But the students learned a lot from their hands-on experience.

And the shelter project isn't over yet. The Village Association has set aside money to hire a construction coordinator to gather materials and actually build the structure, along with resident and student help. Once completed, it will offer a wonderful "green" statement at the EcoVillage entryway and provide a cozy place to wait out of the wind.

It will also be a tangible testament to the collaboration between EVI and the many students who worked on the project.

Other independent study projects at EVI are ongoing. One project has to do with designing practical applications for photovoltaic panels, including a solar-powered system to pump rainwater from an underground cistern. A Cornell engineering course, taught by resident Frances Vanek, studied the feasibility of wind power at EVI. The project will be continued by IC students in a subsequent independent study project.

Yet another student project had IC students work with Mark Darling, with the physical plant of the College. They designed a pedestrian pathway so that IC students could safely walk from the campus to downtown Ithaca. This, too, is likely to be a multi-semester project, with each group of students building on the prior work done by their peers.

Over the years, we've learned a number of lessons about our study projects.

1. Students respond very well to hands-on projects that combine theory with practical application, while offering them a chance to make a real difference — in fact many have been longing for that kind of engagement all their lives. Excitement can quickly turn into frustration, however, if the projects do not address the complexity of the interplay between academic and village cultures. Our experience dovetails with the service learning movement that is becoming increasingly valued on college campuses. Service learning emphasizes how much students can learn through hands-on involvement with local organizations, while also "giving back" to their communities.

2. It is essential to have a resident who is dedicated to coordinating the students' work and providing an interface between the students and the village, thus ensuring that everyone's time is used productively. Ideally the coordinator should be paid for his or her time.

3. It is best to offer a "real-life" project that responds to a genuine community need. The students then get to make a real contribution and also receive feedback and support from the people they are helping.

4. Group size matters. Ideally a project group should consist of three to six students.

5. Multi-semester projects are more likely to make a lasting difference to the community than are short-term projects. Students can take more care with long-term work and approach it more deeply. To be successful, the long-term goal needs to be clearly articulated. Projects should be well documented, so that each new group of students can build on the results of the last group. Short-term goals (which might include different phases for research, design, and implementation) should be within the scope of what both the students and the residents can handle.

   For instance, I worked with the "Alternative Transportation" group in the spring, which surveyed and interviewed residents on their transportation habits and needs. From this semester-long project one concrete project was completed (an electronic ride share system), and another was generated (a green bus shelter). This led to a design project in the summer, and to a future hands-on building project.

   Even with this relatively successful project area, we have encountered significant glitches. The electronic ride board was something that many residents requested. Wells student Alice Lo and many others worked hard with members of the resident "geek team" to build a practical model. When they presented it at the end of the semester, community members cheered. However, over time we found that most residents never used it — perhaps because the people offering rides had less motivation to go online than did people requesting rides. Often behavioral change is the hardest step of all!

6. Surveys, interviews, hands-on work days, forums for discussion, 3-D models, and final presentations are all good ways for students to interact with residents. (It doesn't hurt to motivate residents to attend forums by offering dessert!) But if we want to engage significantly with a student project, our community can only handle one to three substantial projects at a time. More than that leads to burnout and frustration.

   If project developers follow the guidelines, then tremendous synergy can occur between the students' desire to learn and be of service, and the EcoVillage community's desire to teach and become ever more sustainable. And as we get better at providing real-life environmental projects, everyone benefits.

GRADUATE STUDENTS

EVI has provided fertile ground for graduate students wanting to complete their studies. Over the last 13 years, six people have completed their MA theses about some aspect of life at EVI, one PhD has been completed, and another PhD dissertation is in the works. Tendai Chittewere, a doctoral student in anthropology, spent 15 months living in our community in order to fully understand the residents and their motivations for living at EcoVillage.

In her research, Tendai (originally from Zimbabwe) wanted to explore why middle-class people were moving from all over the US to form an environmental community. Tendai formulated her line of inquiry this way:

> As an anthropologist, my particular questions centered on American environmentalism, consumption, and class. How does this community foster environmental change, and make people conscious of environmental problems? How does living at EcoVillage make people feel about each other? Why did some people move out? What are the environmental, social, and financial costs associated with this community? Through my research, I hope to shed a light on one group's efforts.

Jared Jones

Tendai Chittewere and her husband Matt.

Tendai quickly became a well-loved member of the community. She attended meals, yoga classes, and lots of community meetings. She also interviewed 99 percent of EVI's current and former residents.

Tendai's research found that most EcoVillage residents are very happy with their new patterns of living. People here enjoy the strong sense of community, the common meals, and the work teams. And they appreciate having a safe place to raise their children as they also learn to be better stewards of the environment. Challenges do exist, though, regarding the financial costs of living here. And some people expressed frustration with our consensus-based decision-making process.

In Tendai's view the traits that help to make EcoVillage a successful community include people's willingness to be open and to work with others. "Tolerance and patience are great skills," Tendai told us. "I was so impressed with people's desire to work through differences and solve problems."

Whether we are working with students, developing and teaching sustainability courses, or creating other educational outreach programs, EVI's influence on individuals and groups continues to grow. It is an exciting time to be involved in sustainability education, and EVI is right in the thick of the excitement.

Partnership Education: Creating the Basis for Institutional Change

EVI's experience with learning and teaching about sustainability continues to expand outward as we partner with like-minded educational institutions and others to bring about systemic change. We are beginning to feel the first swell in what promises to be a tidal wave of interest in sustainability issues. The wave is already making itself felt on college campuses — not really a surprise, since major cultural shifts often begin there. The 60's peace movement began on campuses across the nation, as did the 70's antinuclear movement and the 90's anti-globalization movement. Today, with people becoming more aware of our precarious ecological situation, environmental sustainability is becoming the new movement. As educators in sustainability, EVI is both riding the wave and helping to create it.

THE NSF GRANT

In 2002 EcoVillage at Ithaca formed a partnership with the Ithaca College Environmental Studies department. We applied for and received a joint NSF grant to develop curriculum and teach courses in the "science of sustainability." IC assistant biology professor Susan Allen-Gil was a "burning soul" in the writing of the partnership grant and also brought her enthusiasm, scholarship, and dedication to the work of coordinating it. "Students need to learn not only about ecological problems," she said, "but also about positive solutions. They need to have hope for the future."

Ithaca College and EVI matched the three-year, $149,000 NSF grant with funds and in-kind services, making it the largest grant with which EVI had ever been involved. The grant included money for equipment, as well as funds to pay EVI educators and to cover release time for several faculty from Ithaca College to coordinate the program. Coordinators from IC included Susan Allen-Gil, Tom Shevory (a political science professor), and Garry Thomas (an anthropologist); Elan and I made up the EVI contingent.

The grant has been an ideal stepping stone for EVI to grow more fully into its educational mission. EcoVillage is set up to be a living laboratory in which students can immerse themselves as they apply a whole-systems approach to their sustainability studies. The grant has made it possible for us to extend our educational resources to a greater number of people and to tap into the considerable expertise of our residents. Over a dozen residents, representing a wide range of academic and professional skills, have been or will be involved in teaching courses, giving guest lectures, or supervising student project teams. And every one of them sets a powerful example by living the message they are teaching.

SPREADING THE WORD

The sustainability message is spreading, bringing about some dramatic and positive changes at the institutional level. Ithaca College has committed to teaching about and working toward environmental sustainability campus-wide. And they have a sympathetic administration to help them succeed, including IC's innovative provost Peter Bardaglio and IC president Peggy Williams. In an Associated Press interview, Williams stated, "It is our goal to become one of the nation's leading proponents of sustainability, to practice what we preach, and to produce leaders in many fields who will find solutions for meeting the needs of their generation without shortchanging future generations" ("Conference on Sustainability a Step in College's New Direction," by William Kates, an article that appeared on Newsday.com, April 6, 2004).

The College has already taken some steps in fulfilling their commitment to sustainability. They have hired a consultant in Sustainable Management Systems who is helping to address the "triple bottom line" (human, economic, and ecological) in all College activities.

- IC's Business School is in the process of becoming a model for the teaching of sustainable business practices. The College has already raised half of its projected $14 million budget for a state-of-the-art building to house the school. Provost Peter Bardaglio notes that the building is planned to be "LEED platinum" (the highest "green" building certification that exists), and one of only two in the country on a college campus. "The building, as well as its design and construction, will be used as a learning tool for students and visitors alike," Bardaglio told me.

- In February 2004 Ithaca College hosted a Sustainability Summit. Local community leaders and representatives from IC and other colleges attended the summit. Businesses and regions committed to sustainability also sent representatives.

- And there is interest in creating a Sustainability Institute, which would focus on multidisciplinary approaches to teaching and practicing sustainability.

It is still too early to tell exactly what steps the College intends to take in the classroom, but some ideas have already been suggested. Curriculum initiatives might include guest lecturers, a first-year seminar course such as "Sustainability 101," and possibly even a major or a minor in Sustainability Studies.

Meanwhile EcoVillage has committed to increasing its teaching capacity. By developing a core team of educators, we are going to be able to offer more college level courses, as well as high-quality adult education workshops. Student housing (which would allow for on-site work and study) is also on the agenda. In the long term, we plan to build an EcoVillage Education and Research (EVER) Center. Such a center could complement any facilities developed by Ithaca College.

The sustainability message is not limited to academia, however. Our county is getting into the act, too. Recent interest has incubated into a formal proposal to create a "Sustainable Tompkins County." In

September 2003 an exciting workshop brought together 40 local leaders from government, academia, business, and the nonprofit sector. The group discussed how the functions of various governing bodies around the region could be redesigned to promote long-term sustainability.

Dynamic guest speaker Ed Quevedo from Palo Alto, California joined us. Quevedo is director of Environmental Management and Sustainability Programs at WSP Environmental and had worked with "Sustainable Sonoma County". Quevedo encouraged attendees to identify the major environmental, social, and economic challenges faced by our region; and to brainstorm the first steps toward implementing a regional sustainability management plan for the greater Ithaca area. The workshop — organized by Ithaca College, EcoVillage and the Town of Ithaca — brought together one of the largest, most diverse collaborative groups to have met and worked at City Hall in years. Many EcoVillagers contributed to the formative stages of the sustainability initiative. Elan served on the active steering committee, and several other EcoVillagers served as facilitators of the circles or wrote guest editorials for the local paper.

Subsequent to the workshop, Gay Nicholson (former director of the Finger Lakes Land Trust) was hired to conduct an initial feasibility study for Sustainable Tompkins County. Her creative approach brought in dozens of county business and civic leaders to address sustainability in a series of discussion circles. The circles gave participants a chance to explore the concept, envision a positive future for the region, and identify achievable projects. "Sustainability cafés" held at local restaurants and coffeehouses opened up the discussion to the public.

By 2005 Sustainable Tompkins had five forming project groups.

- The "Planning and Land Use for Sustainability" group brings together planners, designers, architects, and public officials to discuss local and regional issues related to sustainable development. The group has created a vision for sustainable residential development in Southwest Park, now under consideration by the Town of Ithaca.

- The "Healthy Generations" group (made up of health professionals and others concerned with building stronger, healthier communities) is working to connect healthy living with sustainable neighborhoods and intergenerational activities.

- The "Green Resources Hub" group (made up of green builders and renewable energy advocates) is looking at ways to effectively exchange and disperse useful information and resources.
- The "Communicating Sustainability" group (made up of artists, writers, and other communicators) is looking at ways in which the creative arts can communicate the sustainability message.
- The "Sustainability Indicators" group is exploring the community indicators that can measure the effect of a local/regional sustainability movement.

Additional classes and events are also helping to inform people, including a six-week series on "Green Building Workshops" and a "Sustainable Technology Showcase" (which plans to bring together businesses, entrepreneurs, and investors in green technologies for a day-long conference).

It is gratifying to know that EVI helped to initiate the countywide effort. Various residents, including Elan and our housemate Dan Roth, continue to take important leadership roles in the new organization.

Although I am intrigued with the array of activities, EcoVillage keeps me so busy that I have chosen not to get heavily involved. However I have decided to take on a time-limited project to co-facilitate two daylong retreats for the Sustainable Tompkins Coordinating Council. It is one small way to ride the waves of this sustainability movement as it ripples out toward the region.

How Change Happens

How did our small grant partnership team help shape a college's mission and also create a new countywide initiative in just two short years? Good timing, well-placed support, and a great deal of creativity made the changes possible. First our timing happened to coincide with an upsurge of interest in sustainability. Although we didn't entirely create the interest, we certainly took advantage of it to spread the message.

We also had good support, both at the college level and at the regional level. A few key administrators at Ithaca College were supportive, and our faculty partners had both vision and persistence. The consultants we brought in were well-respected and inspiring teachers on sustainability issues: Barbara Anderson founded Penn State's Center for Sustainability. Ed Quevedo helps major businesses toe the "triple bottom line." And Environmental Studies professor David Orr from Oberlin College is perhaps the most eloquent spokesperson for sustainable transformation in the academic world.

Finally we used a number of creative initiatives to get the word out about sustainability. At EVI and Ithaca College, we were able to infuse the curriculum with sustainability issues.

- We offered multiple faculty development workshops that fostered dialogue between EVI educators and IC faculty on curriculum and pedagogy.
- We gave out $1,000 "seed grants" to IC faculty to develop or modify courses to include a sustainability focus. To date we have given out ten grants to IC faculty in diverse disciplines, with generally excellent results.
- We offered six "mini-grants" worth $1,000 each to EVI educators to have them develop modules or projects that both furthered sustainability research at EVI and could be used by IC faculty to enrich existing courses.
- We helped to mentor EVI educators who had no prior background teaching at a college. And we assisted IC professors to reach out beyond the confines of the classroom and take a more holistic approach to teaching sustainability.
- We offered a series of "Sustainability Salons" on campus. Short presentations, small group discussions, and a menu of festive local foods helped create an informal culture of sustainability. The Salons also gave IC faculty a chance to showcase their thinking on diverse aspects of sustainability.

The team worked hard to overcome institutional barriers and communication gaps between EcoVillage and Ithaca College. To work effectively with us, our IC colleagues had to accommodate to the more informal culture of our volunteer-based community. And at EVI, we had to work with traditional academic expectations as we created courses and projects that worked in our setting and reflected our values.

The partnership approach to teaching the science of sustainability has been incredibly effective, and I am eager to see what the coming years bring. It is certainly a rare and wonderful occurrence to drop a small pebble in a pond and watch the ripples spread out and become waves.

Aside from our work here at home, EVI is also involved in sustainability education at the international level.

International Ecovillage Education

THE GLOBAL ECOVILLAGE NETWORK

The Global Ecovillage Network (GEN), of which EVI is an active member, was founded in 1995 and links dozens of ecovillages and thousands of traditional villages around the world. The organization informs and educates its members (and others) on issues relating to sustainability, and promotes the development of communities committed to living in harmony with the natural world. GEN also holds conferences, workshops, and study sessions around the world to bring together like-minded people already involved in ecovillage living and to educate those who are interested in the ecovillage movement. The meeting I attended at Findhorn in 2004 was one such conference.

THE FINDHORN CONFERENCE

In spring 2004, at the initiative of Hildur Jackson, two dozen people from 15 different ecovillages on six continents gathered in a beautiful stone manor at Findhorn, Scotland. Our goal? To formulate a standardized introductory training session about ecovillage design that could be taught in ecovillages around the world.

Under the able guidance of facilitators, the diverse group took a multifaceted approach to the deliberations, using a combination of presentations, discussions, brainstorming, meditation, poetry, dance, humor, and celebration. We also used a diagram from the groundbreaking *Ecovillage Living: Restoring the Earth and Her People* (Green Books, 2002), edited by Danish ecovillage activists Hildur Jackson and Karen Svensson.

Filled with exceptionally beautiful photos and articles from ecovillages around the world, the book begins with a colorful wheel depicting "The 15 Elements of Ecovillage Living." The wheel focuses on three elements — the social-economic, cultural-spiritual, and ecological dimensions of ecovillage life — and provided us with an excellent jumping-off point for our discussions.

Many of the elements of the proposed curriculum seemed obvious, given Hildur's "wheel" and the years of experience that Findhorn and other ecovillages had in offering similar training sessions. But there were areas of disagreement, too. I proposed and others strongly agreed that economics — including an analysis of the global economy — needed its own quadrant. We also had intense discussions about the role of spirituality. Eventually we all agreed that spirituality ought to be given room as a subject area, even though it also infused the whole ecovillage philosophy.

Some of the discussion focused on social issues. Several European communities, for example, highlighted the importance of looking at issues of gender, love, and sexuality. So these considerations were added to the mix.

Other discussions considered issues of semantics. For instance, some people questioned the use of the word "permaculture" and wondered whether or not a broader audience would better understand the term "sustainable design." (It seemed clear to me that whatever curriculum mix we arrived at would ultimately be modified anyway — due to dif-

Findhorn, May 2004

It is a cool day in late May. I am wandering in a stunningly beautiful forest garden at Findhorn, Scotland. Large beech trees, hundreds of years old, lend an air of ancient wisdom to the space as I follow a well-worn path and descend into a magical rhododendron dell.

Rhododendrons in full bloom grace the dell in shades of dark red, pink, bright orange, white, and gold. I even see bushes of light purple and violet. Bright yellow buttercups, orange and golden poppies, and tall graceful bluebells shine like stars amid the long green grass. Bushes laden with creamy azaleas perfume the air with their sweet fragrance.

I sit on a generous tree stump in the middle of the dell, my eyes and spirit intoxicated with nature's beauty. My heart fills with joy, and I feel tremendous gratitude for the gardener who, for decades, has carefully cultivated this space. My mind circles back over the very full time I've spent here at Findhorn, the spiritual community and ecovillage formed over 40 years ago near Inverness.

Findhorn has been hosting a gathering of ecovillagers and educators from all over the world, and I was invited to take part. One session was set up for ecovillage educators who want to offer ecovillage design training workshops in their communities. The second session was set up for teachers who take US students for a semester abroad to ecovillages around the world. ☞

ferences at individual ecovillages and to differing skill levels and back-grounds of the trainers — so why quibble? Still, since we were trying to come up with a standardized training module, it was crucial that we take the concepts and make them ours as a group.)

For Hildur — the matriarch of the group who had spent years think-ing, writing, and acting on the principles depicted by the wheel — the process of letting go was not easy. (Hildur, along with her husband Ross, was a founding member of GEN and is one of the driving forces in the international ecovillage movement.)

One morning Hildur told us about her dream from the previous night. In the dream she had a young baby. She realized in terror that she had forgotten to feed the infant. Imagine her relief when she dis-covered that a group of people was holding and feeding the baby and that it was gurgling and happy.

We have heard presentations from a variety of ecovillages. Countries as far-flung as Australia, Brazil, Denmark, England, Germany, India, Italy, Mexico, Portugal, Scotland, Senegal, Thailand, and the United States sent representatives. I have been struck by how different each ecovillage is and how each varies in size, mission, structure, and appearance.

Of course, not every ecovillage could send representatives. Some of the more sustainable ones are traditional indigenous villages that are revitalizing their cul-ture and taking a stand against globalization. Some are new experimental villages based on spirituality, new social forms, or ecological commitment.

Although working with two newly formed groups has not been entirely easy, I smile as I think of my several dozen new friends and colleagues, each committed to living and teaching the same principles upon which EVI is also founded. No mat-ter where we come from or how we define our mission, together we create a varied community as colorful as the bushes in the rhododendron dell. Each ecovillage is unique yet related: We share the common purpose of creating a harmonious and sustainable way for people to live together on this planet.

Once again I am filled with gratitude for the beauty and hope that each of these communities offers, and for the wisdom of the indigenous people who have been our forebears. We need to draw on that ancient wisdom now, to relearn how to live in balance with each other and with the natural world. ∎

Hildur's poignant dream reminded me of the similar situation that Joan Bokaer faced at the EVI Envisioning Retreat. She, too, had had to give up her "baby" (her vision of EVI), so that a larger group could claim it as its own. It takes an act of courage to release our attachments to our dreams and allow others to nurture them. I admired both Hildur and Joan for their willingness to recognize that it was time to let go and let others help carry the dream.

The truth is that others were already carrying the dream, albeit in different ways. Ecovillages from Findhorn (Scotland), Auroville (India), Crystal Waters (Australia), and Zegg (Germany) had all pioneered multi-week courses in ecovillage design. Others, like EVI, were experimenting with semester-long courses that focused on one main topic or were testing out other forms of teaching. Each group had its own take on how to develop the ecovillage vision.

It was interesting to me to compare EVI's accomplishments to those of other ecovillages. Most were years ahead of us in providing intensive residential courses, facilities to house and feed guests and students, and skilled trainers with years of experience. Our mainstream ecovillage, on the other hand, was doing pioneer work by establishing an ongoing partnership with our local colleges and university. But whatever way we carried the dream forward, we all shared the same goals.

The Findhorn gathering fit beautifully into EVI's ongoing commitment to sustainability education, and I was very thankful to have been a part of it. By the end of our time together, we had not only come up with the outline of a training module on ecovillage design, but we had also strengthened the ties of the broader ecovillage community.

EcoVillage at Ithaca really is all about education, whether we are working at a personal level as residents, locally with our educational and governmental institutions, or internationally through organizations such as GEN. Our work will be ongoing for many more years. There is still so much to learn and so much to teach.

CHAPTER 10

SPREADING THE WORD

In a remote area of Nepal, the houses of Tamang (ethnic) villagers remain clustered. Villagers keep cordial relations with their neighbors and help each other. When I visited the farm at EcoVillage, I saw many people working together, just as in a Tamang village, where they take turns helping each other. If someone becomes sick in the village, they help the family out, just as you do. They celebrate many festivals jointly and eat together as in your Common House. When a guest comes to the Tamang village, he or she is introduced to all the villagers and treated with special respect. I was surprised to see the same culture here.

— Mira Rana, director of
Educate the Children (Nepal)

EVI's experiment in sustainable living speaks across linguistic and cultural borders. Perhaps the human-sized scale of our village communicates with some fundamental level of experience common to the whole human family. Perhaps the connection we have with the land reminds people of something they already know deep down. Or maybe the culture of belonging that we foster here is so clear as to need no translation. Whatever the reason, the EcoVillage model resonates with people all over the world.

Our ties to the world community are strong and deep. We welcome visitors from many countries to our village here at home, maintain ties with our sister community abroad, take part in international "eco-events," and respond to media with information about EVI. We are interested in what relevance our ecovillage model has to fast-paced modern cultures in countries such as Japan and Spain. And we are eager to learn what traditional cultures can teach us about sustainable living. We focus on what we hold in common, how we are connected, and how we can cooperate to bring about a more equitable and sustainable world. Ultimately we are engaged in a global dialogue.

EcoVillage at Ithaca already has much in common with people elsewhere in the world.

The People Connection

The people who visit us at EcoVillage often feel an immediate connection to our community. We host visitors and tour groups from all over the world. Whether our guests are from China or Russia, Denmark or Japan, they tell us that EVI looks just like the rural villages in their home countries. Mira Rana, for example, was so taken with the similarities between EVI and her village in Nepal that she wrote an article for the *EcoVillage Newsletter*.

Rana is the director of Educate the Children (Nepal), an organization engaged in rural development with a special emphasis on women's education and income-generation programs (see Chapter Six). In 2000 she visited EVI as Pamela Carson's guest and was moved to write:

Liz Walker

Adji Arame Thiaw was a key organizer at the Third International EcoCity Conference and came to the US seven years later as a Humphrey Fellow.

I like EcoVillage very much because it is located in a beautiful place and all houses are attached. The land is saved to be used for other purposes.... The common playing center for children is very practical. Here the children can develop psychological and mental power, learning to share with each other and become socialized amongst themselves. This will greatly help their future.

I had an impression that people of the Western world are more individualistic and less cooperative. I found that EcoVillage people are friendly and cooperative with each other and live in harmony. Every house is accessible for all villagers and you share cooperatively (for example, some cars are for everyone's use).

Another exciting thing for me at EcoVillage is the common kitchen. It was like a big family kitchen with everyone eating in one place as they do in rural Nepal; the only difference was the facility. In Nepal we sit on the dusty floor and eat with our hands. In EcoVillage the kitchen was clean and beautiful with nice furniture and utensils.

The similarities between EcoVillage and a Tamang village include vegetable farming, animal-keeping, living cooperatively, celebrating festival[s] and holidays, and sharing the pains and joys of life together with families next door.

The attributes held in common by our ecovillage and a Tamang village are typical of small communities anywhere and constitute a precious resource. In communities where everyone knows everyone else (as in the small Vermont town where I grew up), people seem to develop a sense of cooperation and tolerance. Individuals who, in larger cities, would be homeless or institutionalized tend to receive practical help (such as food, clothing, or shelter) without being singled out as "too different." Residents hold town meetings to discuss local issues at length. Both elders and children are respected. People know and protect the value of each other's property. People feel accountable to one another and possess a strong sense of community.

EcoVillage is part of a growing movement of people around the world busy reclaiming the traditions that connect us to each other and the earth. People are beginning to say no to the increasingly homogeneous, consumer-driven, globalized culture that is strongly promoted by multinational corporations. Instead they are saying yes to traditions that bring a sense of purpose and belonging. Peasant farmers in the *Via Campesina* movement, for example, are saving indigenous seeds that might otherwise disappear as a result of widespread genetic engineering and seed patenting by corporations. And at World Social Forums, tens of thousands of people from all walks of life discuss how to create a world that is equitable, cooperative, and ecologically sound. (And the people are having an effect. *The New York Times*, commenting on worldwide demonstrations against the US invasion of Iraq, has identified world opinion as "the second superpower." See Patrick E. Tyler's article, "Suddenly it's US and the Rest of the World," in the February 17, 2003 issue.) As EcoVillagers we celebrate the values that are bringing people together internationally.

We also have a responsibility to embody the same values here at home. We live inside the "belly of the beast" — the most powerful nation that has ever existed. What we do in our own backyard matters. If we can help raise the consciousness of our fellow citizens, if we can offer a haven of deep connections between people and the natural world surrounding us, if we can demonstrate the connections between the wisdom of traditional villages around the world and a fulfilling modern lifestyle, then I believe we are on the road to success. People talking to people can make all the difference in the world.

EcoVillage at Ithaca has developed another "people connection" through our sister village abroad.

Sister Village
SEPTEMBER 1991

When we first started EVI, we were very fortunate to be approached by Serigne Mbaye Diene, a leader from the village of Yoff, a 500-year-old traditional fishing village in Senegal. Serigne was getting his doctorate in international nutrition from Cornell and had heard that we were starting an ecovillage. In a flash of intuitive brilliance, Serigne understood that what we were attempting to do was of tremendous importance to his village.

"You're doing what we've always done," he told us. "We have lived in a sustainable community for 500 years. But now the city of Dakar is encroaching on us; there are no jobs; and our young people are moving to the city. People watch TV shows like *Dallas* and think that's the way all Americans live. And [then] that's the way they want to live, too."

Serigne proposed that EcoVillage at Ithaca and Yoff become sister villages. With his ability to bridge our two cultures, Serigne wisely understood the mutual benefits such a pairing would bring. Yoff residents would get a tremendous boost from having US citizens visit the community to learn, bolstering their confidence in the value of their traditions. And we would have the eye-opening experience of seeing a truly sustainable culture in action (one that had already lasted 500 years). In turn, our knowledge of appropriate technologies might help solve some of the community's growing problems with garbage and sewage disposal. We enthusiastically accepted Serigne's proposal at our first annual meeting, in January 1992.

THE YOFF DELEGATION, MAY 1992

In May 1992 a delegation from EVI went for a visit to Yoff and came back excited and amazed at the dramatically different culture. In this devoutly Muslim "village" of 40,000, the elders made the decisions. Extended families lived in densely clustered compounds in homes made from local sand mixed with cement. There were almost no cars, and many streets were just pathways of sand.

Homelessness and hunger were virtually unknown. People lived on the millet, peanuts, and vegetables they grew in their own gardens and on the fish they caught from the sea. Food was shared with whomever was hungry, and unemployed men could work on any fishing boat in return for a share of the catch.

On Fridays, after prayers, local elders mediated conflicts under the dabouliya tree. Crime was not tolerated, so there was no need for police. Instead, since everyone knew everyone else, people felt a strong sense of accountability. If there were incidents of crime, such as thievery for example, the thief would not be allowed back into the village. There was a relaxed sense of safety, caring, and extended family connections that permeated the village. We share that feeling at our ecovillage, yet on a much smaller scale. We have much to learn from a society that has lived nonviolently for hundreds of years.

At the same time, the traditional way of life in Yoff was under tremendous social and environmental assault. Unemployment was running at about 75 percent, and the population was exploding. Women typically had six children, and men often had two or more wives. The fish harvest was rapidly diminishing, mainly due to huge foreign trawlers. Plastic garbage was everywhere. And agriculture was being threatened as fertile land fell victim to the sprawling growth of nearby Dakar. Yoff was under siege. Clearly the whole complex set of social networks that defined the culture was in danger of unraveling unless a healthier economy was established.

In 1995 Richard Register, a pioneer in the EcoCity movement, approached Yoff and EVI to find out if we would be willing to co-host the Third International EcoCity Conference. Both parties happily agreed.

THE THIRD INTERNATIONAL ECO-CITY CONFERENCE

L'Association pour la promotion économique, culturelle, et sociale de Yoff (APECSY), a grassroots organization in Yoff, and EVI joined forces to plan the conference, to be hosted by the City of Dakar and its traditional villages of Yoff, Ngor, and Ouakam. APECSY organized housing, food, media contacts, security, and an advisory committee to participate in the program. EVI publicized the event internationally, served as the communication hub, and arranged for the program of international speakers.

The mayor of Dakar committed city funds, the use of a conference center, and staff time to help with logistics. Joan Bokaer and Serigne Mbaye Diene acted as central organizers, while a number of the rest of us assisted. Richard Register, who had spearheaded the first two EcoCity conferences, was a welcome consultant.

Held in January 1996, the conference was a stunningly productive exchange of experiences and ideas, shared work, and newly begun friendships. Approximately 120 visitors — government officials, city planners, architects, scientists, engineers, artists, students, farmers, and activists — from some 27 countries gathered with 260 of our African colleagues. Races, religions, and languages contrasted and communicated across a world of differences. But the differences were small compared to our common need to rethink and reshape humanity's built environments. Over our ten-day stay, we would experience a snippet of life in an African village, learn from one another, and further define an International Ecological Rebuilding Program.

The conference itself was scheduled over five days. Each day we explored a different theme, beginning with "Lessons from the Past" and "The Ecological City." Later in the week we looked at other themes, such as "Social, Political, Economic, and Educational Issues," "The Natural Environment," and "Agriculture."

Sixty presenters from around the world gave fascinating presentations (translated simultaneously into English, French, and Wolof) on topics pertaining to each day's theme. We heard about Curritiba, Brazil, a model of ecological planning, and about traditional villagers in the Sarawakian rainforest of Malaysia, who are struggling to keep their identity in the face of logging, Westernized education, and the economic lures of the city. There were talks about "transit villages" on new urban rail lines (allowing residents to conveniently hop on the train to go to work, shop, or play) and urban development patterns from Perth to Vancouver. And we heard an analysis of the political and economic context of Africa — a continent still struggling to emerge from 500 years of slavery, colonialism, and exploitation.

The conference also held workshops. Jon Katz, for example, held one lively meeting to talk about how to develop Yoff's additional land. Planners and architects, permaculturists, and engineers from all over the world had a chance to talk to their counterparts in Dakar. Local planners explained why they wanted to widen the streets of Yoff and make the village more accessible by car, and guest professionals talked about why Yoff should be preserved as a pedestrian village. The workshop highlighted a common dilemma: The professionals from "developing" countries were eager to emulate the patterns of car-centered, fossil fuel-consuming countries, while their professional counterparts from "over-developed" countries were eager to steer them away from such destructive patterns. It was good to see such a full exchange of perspectives on the often difficult topic of future development.

Throughout its proceedings and in the international media it generated, the conference honored traditional village values and sought ways to integrate African village wisdom into strategies for bringing ecological sustainability to the built environment. In a final plenary session, the conference endorsed an international strategy for rebuilding cities, towns, and villages everywhere that included:

- an end to automobile subsidies;
- the reshaping of cities away from sprawl and toward pedestrian-accessible centers;
- the restoration of large natural spaces;
- the revitalization of traditional villages;
- the establishment of biodiverse local agriculture;
- the creation of strong economic incentives for ecologically oriented businesses;
- new funding efforts to support the retooling necessary for ecological building and technology; and
- the establishment of government departments with a whole-systems perspective that could assist ecological rebuilding.

The Ecological building program formulated at the EcoCity conference at Yoff was later presented at Habitat II, the second United Nations Conference on Human Settlements, held in Istanbul in June 1996.

Meanwhile the swirl of daily living in Yoff acted as a constant backdrop to the conference. *Terenga* or "hospitality" is a very strong value in Senegalese culture. We toured traditional villages and attended special dances and feasts, including the annual festival of Mame Ndaire, the female ocean spirit who protects the village. Residents warmly welcomed us into their homes.

The level of the people's openness and generosity reminded me of the Navajos we had met during the Global Walk. As we traveled over the dry plains of the reservation, we had been welcomed with feasts of fry bread

Yoff, Winter 1996

Twenty hours after leaving a blizzard in Ithaca, New York our group arrives to bright sunshine and 80-degree desert heat (27 Celsius) in Dakar, Senegal. A formal line of elders dressed in floor-length robes greets us. We shake hands and try out a hastily learned greeting in Wolof — "Nanga def," we say; "Mangi fii rekk," comes the reply. It is the first of hundreds of times that we will exchange these words during our ten-day visit.

Drums sound their throbbing beat as we come out of customs and into the broad daylight. A hundred people from Yoff gather around to greet us. Two women's dance troupes, dressed in traditional boubous (beautiful floor-length dresses with open, airy sleeves), perform for us.

As it turns out the welcome we receive at the airport sets the tone for the rest of our visit. The people hold special dances every day that we are in Yoff. The women encourage the *toubabs* (foreigners) to dance, and the gathered crowds shriek with encouragement and amusement. Even the young boys use sticks to beat out complex rhythms on anything handy. The dance festivals often last late into the night (1:00 – 2:00 a.m. is not uncommon). Dancing and drumming seem to be the heartbeat underlying daily life in the village.

On our first day our hosts treat us to an afternoon feast and show us how to eat Senegalese style. We settle ourselves on straw mats on the floor, five to eight people to a group. A big platter — heaped with mounds of rice and accompanied by large chunks of fish and vegetables — sits at the center of each group.

The food is delicious and flavored with many unfamiliar spices. As is the custom, each person eats from a pie-shaped wedge of the central platter, scooping up a handful of rice along with some of the fish and vegetable mixture. Our hosts laugh with us as we clumsily dribble rice and fish in our attempts to eat without knives and forks.

In the evening our guide walks with us to the beach. As we move along, the gentle "scuff- scuff" of our sandals on the sand mixes with the occasional ☞

and mutton stew at every hamlet we passed. And we had been invited to festivals of singing and dancing, put on to make us feel welcome.

It is a curious fact that the people with the fewest financial resources are often the most open hearted and generous. Our Senegalese hosts, like the Navajo, were richer in spiritual and cultural resources than we could have dreamed, even though we would consider their standard of living below the poverty level.

sounds of laughter and radio music coming from compounds on either side of the path. Here and there women gather around small braziers, cooking.

The people of Yoff don't seem to sleep much. Even at midnight little groups of children and adults greet each other and stop to talk. And at any time of the day or night I can walk alone down unlit streets and never feel afraid — a wonderful new sensation!

On our second day we revisit the beach in the afternoon, when the fishing boats come teeming in. We watch as everyone helps bring in the long, beautifully hand-carved crafts. Some of the catch will be dried, and some will go to nearby Dakar for sale. But some of the fish is for sale here on the beach. Local women buy directly from the fishermen and then walk gracefully away, balancing their catches in big plastic tubs on their heads. Watching them I feel as if we have entered a different world.

Time definitely seems to travel more slowly here. Nothing happens by clock time; instead events seem to happen after a gradual coalescence of energy that eventually signals "the time is right." Senegalese time can drive us Westerners crazy, until you just relax and let yourself go with the flow. Then it is like magic singing in your veins.

All too soon our visit is over, though Jason (13) and Jon stay on for another two weeks after the rest of our group leaves for home. Jason is a source of great interest to the local youth, who adopt him as an out of the ordinary *toubab* friend. The locals nickname him "Issa," and Jason has the name engraved on a copper bracelet that he wears for years afterward. He is in great demand for teaching children how to fold paper airplanes and origami cranes. And he has the freedom to roam the local bazaars, looking for such things as hand-carved wooden elephants, walking sticks, and other interesting handicrafts. Jason loves to bargain, and by the time he comes home, his suitcase is full of treasures. ■

The conference had a number of fascinating outcomes, some of which could never have been predicted.

- Following the conference, forty people from the three neighboring villages of Yoff, Ngor, and Ouakam signed up for a ten-day "Permaculture Certification" course; as a result some flourishing gardens based on permaculture principles have been established.

- Richard Register and Brady Peeks co-edited *Village Wisdom, Future Cities* (Alonzo Press, 1997), providing a wonderful record of the conference and its achievements.

- Dr. Marian Zeitlin of Tufts University was so excited by her experience at the conference that she decided to retire and move to Yoff. Once there she and Serigne Mbaye Diene helped establish "Eco-Yoff," a new initiative designed to create an ecological expansion of the village.

  Now a co-director of the organization, Marian has continued to volunteer full-time, offering her services as an educator, organizer, and fundraiser. The Eco-Yoff initiative has grown over the years and currently includes dozens of Senegalese traditional villages that are striving to become even more ecologically conscious. And the group now receives some of its funding from the UN and GEN as a "Living and Learning Center." The Center is host to dozens of international students a year, who team up with students from Dakar to research ecological solutions to village problems.

- On a more personal note, Lynn Anderson, coordinator of the Alternatives Library at Cornell (like EVI, another project of CRESP), fell in love with a Senegalese librarian while she was at the conference. Abdoulaye and Lynn got married and now live in Ithaca. Together they actively promote economic and cultural exchanges with Yoff, send library books, and sell Senegalese crafts.

- The EVI-Yoff connection continued when Jerry and Claudia Weisburd worked with the people of Yoff to design and build low-maintenance composting toilets to help resolve the sewage problems of the ever-growing population.

- Seven years after the conference, Adji Arame Thiaw (a key conference organizer) stayed with us at EVI for several months as a graduate student and international Humphrey Fellow, studying nonprofit development. While here she also held a traditional Senegalese feast to fundraise on behalf of a women's micro-credit group in Yoff.

The conference brought about many positive changes to Yoff, but the inexorable forces of Western-style development have continued, creating further economic, environmental, and social stresses. The fish harvest is at risk. "Many times the fishermen catch plastic garbage rather than fish," Adji Arame tells us. "We need to retrain people to move away from the traditional fishing economy and find other jobs." But that's not all. With changes in global climate, the sea is rising, and some of the homes closest to the shore have already been swept away. And the population has more than doubled since the conference. Better health clinics have reduced infant mortality rates and more children are staying alive than previously, leading to rapid population growth.

Despite the recommendations of the conference, much of the new development built to accommodate the increased population has copied the West. Instead of duplicating the intimacy of family compounds and pedestrian streets, people are building single-family homes and wide streets that allow for increased car traffic. And Dakar continues to sprawl outward, bringing crime and fast-paced city living ever closer to Yoff.

The clash of modern and traditional village cultures is unrelenting, as illustrated by Richard Register in a short passage from *Village Wisdom, Future Cities:*

> Looking down a quiet street with children practicing a dance step and older folks walking past a horse-drawn wagon, we can see one or two sheep wandering from place to place. In the background, behind the humble, two-story, sand-colored houses and ancient trees that look ever so small, even fragile, an unbelievably gigantic machine, getting larger and larger, lifts into the sky. It looks larger than an ocean liner. It completely dwarfs the sleepy town.... Suddenly the massive 747 is overhead and its shadow, as wide as the whole neighborhood, is rippling

over the houses, the people, cart, horse, sheep. Thunder consumes this small world. (p. 216)

As Register points out, such an extreme contrast between rural and urban cultures is an underlying reality in city-village relationships everywhere. The villagers in the vignette could never afford a plane ticket on that 747, yet the allure and promise of distant places comes intoxicatingly close with its passage, affecting young people especially hard.

"An enormous issue rises like that airplane here," Register says. "How do traditional villages and rural societies more grounded in sustainable relations with nature keep the young people home?" And he goes on to answer his own question.

"The village can adopt some of the creative aspects of the city, and the city some of the ecological aspects of the village. Both can become more exciting and relevant.... Joining the wisdom of the ancients and the attempt to redesign our cities — the combination is like mixing oxygen and fuel, lighting a lamp to the darkness. What could be more positive, more hopeful, more promising?" (p. 216).

Serigne Mbaye Diene's brilliant initiative to create a sister village connection continues to have ripple effects many years later — a testament to the rich cultural interchange that can happen when different worlds come together, even for a brief moment in time.

Our international connections do not stop with the people of Yoff, Senegal.

The Allure of Village Life

It has been fascinating to me over the years to see the allure our ecovillage has for certain cultures. Japan, for example, has sent several delegations to EVI, ranging from the president of the largest Japanese environmental group to a farmers' group.

Japanese media have also focused on EVI. One national television show came to Ithaca to highlight both "Ithaca Hours" (our famous local currency) and EVI. The crew was quite disappointed to find out that we did not use "Ithaca Hours" for all of our daily transactions! A popular Japanese magazine, *Memo*, did an eight-page story on EVI, including a photo spread that used dozens of gorgeous color shots.

One student's take on our ecovillage showed just how well our human-sized village connects across cultures. Keiko, a Cornell student, was helping me out in the office one semester, and I asked her what particularly interested her about EVI. In answer, Keiko described the Japanese village in which she had been raised. The houses were very close together, she told me, and children played in the streets. Neighbors knew each other well. Green swaths of small farms surrounded most of the village, with the sea bordering the rest. Not surprisingly, fishing and farming were the main occupations. Since Keiko's childhood, her village and hundreds of other such traditional villages had largely disappeared and city living had become the norm. In the fast-paced urban environment, people usually feel little connection to either the natural environment or to their neighbors. In contrast, on her first visit to EcoVillage, Keiko shyly told me, "I feel so at home."

Japanese culture is known for its love of beauty. The careful brushstroke rendering of a plum tree in blossom or a mountain covered with snow evokes a deep connection with the natural world. When this connection is ripped away, a longing remains to reconnect. One of our Japanese visitors, Kiyokazu Shidara (see "Permaculture" in Chapter Seven), who runs a permaculture institute in Japan, told me that he wants to train people to develop ecovillages in his country. I think he'll have a lot of interested students!

People from Japan are not the only ones with a special interest in our ecovillage. Given the number of articles and books that have mentioned EVI, the people of Spain seem to have an equal fascination. Carlos Fresneda, a staff writer for the national Spanish newspaper *El Mundo*, wrote a feature article on EVI and then included us in his book *La Vida Simple* (Editorial Planeta, S.A., 1999). EVI was also included in another book on sustainable development, *EcoUrbanismo/EcoUrbanism: Sustainable Human Settlements: 60 Case Studies*, ed. Miguel Ruano (Editorial Gustavo Gili, S.A., 1999), which covered villages and cities around the world. And in 2001 the crew of the national television program *No Sola Musica* flew to Ithaca to do a story on our ecovillage.

In addition to our links with Japan and Spain, here are just a few examples of other international connections.

- A delegation of architects and planners from Germany and the United Kingdom visited EVI for a special tour.

- A delegation from the Canadian Mortgage and Housing Corporation (the Canadian equivalent of US Housing and

Urban Development) made two special trips to visit EVI. They were looking for examples of sustainable communities as they set environmental standards for Canadian housing.

- The Korean women's magazine *Her World* described EVI in gushing terms as "Heaven on Earth."

- Two Australian authors, Malcolm Hollick and Christine Connelly, visited EVI as part of a cross-continental tour of ecovillages. In their book *Sustainable Communities: Lessons from Aspiring Ecovillages* (Praxis Education, 1998), the authors note, "In our minds, EVI is shaping up to be the most balanced, integrated and viable ecovillage we have seen." I hope that we can live up to this high compliment.

EcoVillage at Ithaca is also lucky to have had a number of residents from different countries at various times: Argentina, Canada, France, Germany, Japan, Nepal, Sweden, Trinidad and Zimbabwe. We also have residents who are second-generation Chinese and Indian. It makes for a wonderful, yeasty mix of cultures — something quite unusual in a small town in upstate New York.

The media has also shown a marked interest in EVI.

Jim Bosjolie

Kiyokazu Shidara, founder of the Permaculture Institute of Japan, visited EVI for a month in 2004. He plans to build an ecovillage outside of Tokyo.

Working with the Media

EVI has enjoyed media attention not only at the international level (already mentioned) but also at the national level. The concept of an ecovillage that was Earth friendly yet attractive and comfortable was so appealing that, long before our first buildings were constructed, articles about EVI began to appear in the US media. The amount of coverage we received over the first couple of years was astonishing.

- Elissa Wolfson, an editor for the national environmental publication *E Magazine*, attended several Land Use Planning Forums and was so impressed that after publishing her article about EVI, she decided to move here.

- Wolfson's article prompted *The Washington Post* to call and do an interview for their Home section.

- Meanwhile USIA-TV requested a 90-second spot that they wanted to broadcast internationally. I wrote the script; an Ithaca College student shot footage; and a Cornell student created a tightly edited spot that aired in 130 countries.

- And Gannett News Service did a story that was picked up by the *Chicago Sun Times* and the *San Francisco Chronicle*, among other well-known newspapers.

As someone who had worked in the environmental movement for years, I was amazed. That amount of press coverage in the first two years, and we hadn't even built anything yet! We were on to something big, and our timing couldn't have been better. We were clearly tapping into two deeply felt needs: the need for a sense of community and the need for environmental change and restoration.

One thing led to another.

- The following year (1994), *American Demographics*, which studies cutting-edge trends, did a cover story on the Gassers, a family who planned to move from their comfortable home in New Jersey to EcoVillage at Ithaca. Editor Brad Edmondson pointed out that this type of environmental commitment represented a trend to which American businesses should pay attention. The *American Demographics* article alone prompted over 125 inquiries from potential residents, as well as inquiries from a number of planning departments as far-flung as Hawaii, Albuquerque, and Saskatchewan.

- Starting in 1994, EVI appeared regularly in the new national magazine *Cohousing*, often through articles that I submitted.

- *Progressive Architecture*, one of the top two architectural magazines in the country, did a story featuring the plans for FROG, our first neighborhood.

- National Public Radio did the first of what would be several stories.

- Local and regional coverage included television, radio, and front-page newspaper coverage.

- *The Cornell Magazine*, an alumni publication with a circulation of 40,000, wrote a great article about EVI.

And things didn't end there, either.

- In 1995 the senior editor of *Popular Science*, Mariette DiChristina, came to EcoVillage for a full day of interviews. In her feature-length article about ecological communities she stated, "A growing recognition exists among architects and planners that the suburbs, which are now home to the majority of Americans, have played a key role in the unraveling of ecosystems and community ties." DiChristina was clearly entranced with the EVI model as an alternative model (even though it was not yet built).
- National Public Radio interviewed me for their show *All Things Considered*.

It was almost getting to be commonplace to be interviewed. I had to laugh when I realized that as a preteen I was so shy I used to write down the potential dialogue for a phone call in advance, worried that I would get tongue-tied. Now here I was routinely coordinating media visits and often acting as the primary spokesperson for EVI. (Sometimes it seems that part of our life's work involves overcoming hurdles that once seemed insurmountable.)

In 1996, it seemed as if everything happened.

- The year started out with the very successful Third International EcoCity Conference, which received excellent international coverage and earned an article in the US-based *Earth Island Journal*.
- In October the first residents moved in, but within weeks we lost eight homes and the Common House to fire. The fire elicited a huge flurry of regional publicity — not exactly the kind of stories we were looking for, but still our disaster helped to put us on the map.

When the neighborhood was finally rebuilt in 1997 and everyone had moved in, there was a media explosion.

- *In Context* magazine and *Co-op America Quarterly* both published articles on EVI in 1997.

- *Utne Reader* wrote a story about the "10 Most Enlightened Towns in America" and named Ithaca #1. Writer Jon Spayde cited EcoVillage at Ithaca and the "Ithaca Hours" barter system as two of the key reasons he chose to visit Ithaca in the first place.

- *The New York Times* sent a reporter to meet with EcoVillagers for two days. The subsequent story, featuring EVI and Cantines Island (another cohousing community in New York State) appeared on the cover of the Sunday paper's Real Estate section. Reporter Mary Vizard wrote, "The most ambitious cohousing project in the country by far is the EcoVillage at Ithaca."

- CNN TV featured EVI in a four-minute spot on its *Earth Matters* program. The narrator concluded by saying, "The community, residents say, may be a model for the new neighborhoods of the 21st century."

- Nickelodeon, a national TV station for children, featured EVI in a specially created program about children in cohousing.

- National Public Radio created a show about EcoVillage for *Living on Earth* — making it the third time we had appeared on NPR.

- *Parenting Magazine* interviewed Rachael and Elan Shapiro for a story on family life in cohousing.

- *Cohousing Magazine* and *Communities Magazine* continued to publish articles about EVI, many of which I wrote.

From there, things slowed down for a while, although in 1999, EVI was featured in an 18-minute segment of an educational video series for PBS on "Preserving the Legacy." The video, called "Sustaining the Earth," included interviews with Elan, Rachael, Jay, and me and was beautifully produced.

The next major flurry of national media occurred when SONG broke ground in 2002.

- On New Year's Day, NPR broadcast a four-minute piece on cohousing and focused on EVI as an example. It aired on Morning Edition and was repeated throughout the day.

- *Mother Earth News* did a story, "From Suburbia to Superbia," in their summer issue.
- And *Residential Architect* included EVI in a feature story called "In from the Fringe."

Recognition of the importance of ecovillages continued to be strong in 2003.

- *Mother Earth News* did a cover story about ecovillages and featured Dancing Rabbit Ecovillage (Missouri), the Los Angeles Ecovillage, and EcoVillage at Ithaca. The article noted that "although each developing ecovillage faces its own set of unique challenges, collectively their positive impacts are being recognized at the global level. In 1998, the UN named ecovillages in their Top 100 List of Best Practices. '*We stand at the junction between two millennia,*' says Albert Bates of the Global Ecovillage Network. '*The past millenium was about building societies that ran on fossil sunlight and militarism. The next one, still a mystery, must be more conscientious and humane, or we won't survive. It's on the shoulders of ecovillage pioneers that the dream rests for peace, security, prosperity, family, and happiness for the coming generations of our children — whether we or they recognize it yet.*'"

EVI has certainly been fortunate in getting the word out, and we recognize that our task has been made much easier by the help we have received from the media.

It is both exciting and humbling to be a part of the ecovillage movement and to know that what we are doing here at Ithaca speaks so deeply and in so many ways to others, wherever they may live. We have come a long way since the Global Walk for a Livable World. And the journey is not over yet.

CHAPTER 11

ASSESSING THE PRESENT, PLANNING THE FUTURE

On Monday evening Jay and I are going through a 14-page "Sustainability Assessment" put out by GEN. Other small groups are working on it, too, as part of a month-long evaluation process. Once finished, we'll all get together and discuss the results.

There are three parts to the assessment: social, ecological, and spiritual. Right now we are focusing on the "ecological" part. We answer detailed questions about "sense of place," food availability, ecological building, transportation, consumption patterns, solid waste management, water and wastewater, and energy sources.

Jay is typically someone who sees the glass as half empty, whereas I see it as half full. What surprises me is that we agree on almost every category. Jay even manages to be more positive than me at one point, which reminds me that we are all open to change.

I'm eager to know our final "score." On a scale of 0 to 50+ (indicates excellent progress toward sustainability), we average 32 — perhaps the equivalent of a B- grade. Not bad, not great.

Later I compare our answers with 12 others who have also filled out the form. Though our answers vary a lot, overall it is clear that EVI excels at the three R's of reduce, recycle, or reuse and at composting and organic food production. We still need work on wastewater treatment, building materials, renewable energy use, and transportation. And we need to improve our knowledge and support of the native

Laura Beck

Dylan gives Monty a bouquet.

plants and wildlife. It's a little sobering that even as an ecologically oriented community we still have so far to go.

A week later I work with Phebe to fill out the "social" section of the questionnaire. It's fun and we laugh a lot — mostly because it is very affirming. According to the community results (averaged out from our total of 14 questionnaires), we come out with very high scores — some of them off the charts — on qualities such as openness, trust and safety, outreach, education, communication, and health care. "Sustainable economics" is the one category that needs more work.

The third and final questionnaire assesses "spirituality." Although EVI did not form as a spiritual community and does not have a common spiritual practice, we rank above 50 on most categories. GEN's definition of spirituality must be pretty broad, though. The categories include such things as "community glue," "community resilience," "peace and global consciousness," "systemic worldview," and "cultural sustainability." According to our assessment results, we need to pay more attention to "arts and leisure" and "spiritual sustainability."

We have accomplished a great deal since we first started EcoVillage in 1991 and have much to be proud of. At the same time we continue to face some major challenges, both as a community and as a nonprofit. There are also many aspects of the overall EVI vision that have yet to be realized. We have enough work to keep us all busy for decades to come. But it is worthwhile and fulfilling work, and I firmly believe that what we are bringing into being here will increasingly benefit others worldwide.

We continue to assess our progress as a community and as a non-profit organization.

How Are We Doing?
ACCOMPLISHMENTS

The ecovillage that started out as a vision is manifesting as a reality. We have bought and paid off the mortgage on a beautiful 175-acre parcel of land. We have established two cohousing neighborhoods, built 60 homes, and developed a vibrant intergenerational community. According to the GEN "Sustainability Assessment," we are making excellent progress on social and spiritual aspects and good progress on ecological goals. And we are learning over time to create a more sustainable culture, filled with shared work, shared decisions, and shared celebrations.

Collectively our ecological footprint is at least 40 percent less than that of typical US neighborhoods. All of our buildings are super-insulated and passive solar; a quarter of them now generate their own electricity from solar panels. Aside from using some innovative high-tech building materials, we have also experimented with natural building materials and techniques, such as straw bale, timber frame, and the use of local woods.

We produce a great deal of our own food during the growing season. West Haven Farm is a thriving model of organic farming, and the berry farm is making slow but steady progress.

Our outreach efforts continue to bear fruit. Our educational programs are beginning to take off and have already created important ripple effects, nudging local colleges and the Tompkins County region in the direction of sustainability. We continue to build important international ties. And we have generated an astonishing amount of national and international interest in EVI, resulting in a great deal of media coverage and public recognition. We can rightly be proud of all our wonderful, tangible accomplishments.

However, just stating our accomplishments can obscure the areas in which we still struggle. Most challenges that we face have to do with issues of money or time.

CHALLENGES
Affordability

Affordability, which affects both residents and the nonprofit, remains a complex and sticky issue that won't go away soon, since it is embedded in the larger society of which we are a part. The initial cost of homes, ongoing maintenance costs, and taxes are always on the rise. The Ithaca housing market is heating up, and that affects house prices at EcoVillage. FROG homes that originally cost $90,000 to $150,000 in 1996 are selling at $130,000 to $175,000 or more just eight years later. SONG homes, originally intended to be even more affordable, now range from $120,000 to $300,000. The steep rise in home prices echoes what is happening in desirable locations around the country, but as a low-income person myself I find it deeply alarming.

I have devoted the last 14 years of my life to co-creating EcoVillage out of idealism and the desire to create an inclusive community, while receiving very little financial compensation for my work. I understand that people have to protect their assets, and it would be artificial if house prices in EVI stayed static, while those in the Ithaca area continued to rise. But I wonder if we have created a beautiful haven that will eventually be affordable only to upper-middle-class and wealthy people. It would be deeply ironic for me if that were the case.

Why do homes at EVI cost so much? When people buy here, they not only buy a home, but they also become members of a caring community, with access to beautiful open spaces, a Common House, an organic farm, and stimulating educational opportunities. As an appraiser once told me, those "intangibles" add at least $20,000 more per home — an amount that will only continue to rise in tandem with the baseline price of homes in the Ithaca area. In addition, as more people come and go in our community, home prices escalate with each resale.

Unemployment and low wages are also of concern. As in the rest of the country, some people in our community are unemployed or underpaid, creating an ongoing financial strain. Also many couples with young children choose to have one parent stay at home. While this creates a nurturing environment for the children, it can also create extra pressure for the remaining wage earner of the family.

Sometimes people's dreams of having extra time to participate in community activities or live a simpler life evaporate as they struggle to keep up with mortgage payments. The problem is exacerbated for those who chose to build larger homes with more amenities, only to realize later that a smaller, more affordable home would have offered them more freedom. Given so many financial pressures, it is no wonder that community-wide financial decisions are very difficult to make.

As a community we struggle with deciding where to put our limited resources. Should we put money into making our neighborhoods more accessible for the disabled and elderly? Should we fund a wind turbine to generate our electricity? Should we hire a part-time maintenance person? Should SONG build its own Common House or should we continue to share common space? We have gradually learned to slow down when it is time to make such important decisions, and to take time to gather all opinions and options. It's hard work!

We have generated some partial solutions to our thorny affordability issues. One of the biggest solutions was to subsidize 20 percent of the homes in SONG. By using a grant from the Federal Home Loan Bank, six homes in SONG were created as affordable housing for people whose income was 50–80 percent of the median income for this county. But we also have smaller ways of addressing affordability.

When discretionary items are added to the budget, we frequently give people an option to opt out of paying extra. This gives everyone a feeling of choice, and allows people who are experiencing financial strain a chance to pay less without feeling guilty. (All such arrangements are kept strictly confidential.)

We also have a "flip tax" that applies in both neighborhoods. A portion of the profit made by a home resale (20 percent in FROG; 50 percent in SONG) goes back to the neighborhood to support other affordability measures.

And SONG, as part of a community land trust, is further safeguarded. The land that the homes are built on belongs to the nonprofit, and presumably will not greatly appreciate in value. We continue to seek solutions that will make EcoVillage more affordable to residents.

The EcoVillage nonprofit struggles financially, as well. Being a living model, EVI is quite different than a typical service-oriented nonprofit or educational institution. Our holistic approach tends to exclude us from many of the often-narrowly defined grants available from foundations and government agencies. Thus our bare-bones operational budget tends to be funded through individual donations, memberships, tours, and a few small fundraising events throughout the year.

In my role as director, it has been difficult to find enough time to both fundraise for and coordinate the multiple layers of work needed to run the project (everything from building neighborhoods to hosting visitors to working with the media, among other things). As the sole staff person, there are simply not enough hours in the day!

As a grassroots organizer, I have always prided myself on being able to accomplish a lot on a very small budget. If I have to choose between spending time fundraising to pay myself a regular salary or taking the time to get the work done, then I generally find that it feels more fulfilling to do the latter. However, I am beginning to see the limitations of this approach.

Now that the land has been paid off, it is time to "grow" the organization. I've convened a fundraising committee, and over the next two years, I hope to make some major strides forward in our fundraising abilities, which will enable us to bring in additional paid staff. Our first priority must be to put the nonprofit on a solid financial footing, and a larger staff could greatly increase the scope of our activities and make us more effective in what we do. Challenges associated with the issue of time fit closely with those associated with money.

Time

Time constraints affect everyone at EVI. Many of us feel stretched by our multiple responsibilities. There are neighborhood and village-wide meetings to attend and committees and work parties that need participants. As we grow and develop, complex community issues also arise and need to be resolved. Then there are all the tasks associated with making a living and having a family. And some people in our community have high-powered jobs. If they were less driven, then they would have more time to enjoy a slower-paced life and contribute more to community and educational activities.

Of course time pressures are not unique to EcoVillage. In general North Americans face more of a time crunch than do individuals elsewhere in the world. With our penchant for hard work and productivity, most people only get a week or two of vacation a year — far less than Europe's typical four to eight weeks. As with the affordability issue, the time issue has both a community and a cultural component.

Over the years we have developed some strategies for ameliorating chronic time crunch. We share several community meals a week and offer informal opportunities for shared childcare — both of these are basic cohousing conventions here. And we have many community protocols figured out.

We've also refined the amount of time we spend at neighborhood meetings. FROG, with eight years of shared living experience, typically only meets once a month for a few hours, plus an additional work party or neighborhood gathering. SONG, which formed more recently, still meets twice a month for half a day and has very active committees.

And we're starting to get a handle on a few other chores. We are gradually replacing some former, very demanding volunteer positions (such as visitor coordinator or maintenance coordinator) with part-time paid positions. The move offers a few extra employment opportunities on-site and helps prevent burnout of some of our key volunteers.

To a certain extent we also are developing a culture that supports healthy work habits. We encourage people to set limits, take breaks when needed, and ask for help. In some cases, we applaud people who typically work more than their share when they decide to say no to more responsibilities. (This trend is a healthy one, in my view, and goes along with encouraging shared leadership.) In other cases, people save commuting time by working on-site in self-created businesses.

Simplifying and sharing also save us time. As we simplify our lives, our demands for goods and services go down. And by sharing resources such as cars and recreational equipment and reusing clothes and toys, we further cut down on expenditures. Both strategies end up saving us time, since we are not as driven to earn ever more income.

Of course money and time issues are not our only challenges, but they do tend to underlie most other areas that still need strengthening. As noted in the "Sustainability Assessment", our ecological side could use more attention. Our finances certainly determine how much we can spend on new items, such as renewable energy equipment or on new initiatives, such as creating an on-site biological wastewater treatment facility. And time constraints undoubtedly affect how quickly we are able to begin new projects, such as creating model permaculture sites or educating ourselves about the flora and fauna on our site. As is often the case, things are seldom as straightforward as they appear on the surface. Issues of affordability and time may be our greatest challenges, but they are not the only ones.

Diversity

In some ways our community is very diverse: We have all ages here, and our residents represent every income level from struggling to wealthy (although most are solidly middle-class). Our ways of making a living are also quite diverse. Spiritually we represent many different faiths. And we have several lesbian couples and one gay man as residents. People in our community come from many different nationalities, which is unusual in upstate New York. Some of our residents have disabilities, ranging from environmental illness to muscular dystrophy to the early stages of Alzheimer's disease.

One of our challenges, however, is to create a more racially diverse community. In a 2002 demographic survey 86 percent of the village was Caucasian; 2 percent was Black; 5 percent was Asian; and 5 percent was Mixed Race. Although this is not a bad start, we have a ways to go to more accurately reflect US racial diversity.

To me it would be wonderful to have an even stronger mix of cultures and traditions here.

We also have an ongoing challenge in creating a more diverse community. It's not an easy task, however. One lesbian couple from a Latina background strongly considered living here, but sadly decided that they didn't want to live in a community with a relatively small number of minorities. Aside from increasing diversity, we also need to improve our community's accessibility.

Accessibility

Various kinds of accessibility are an increasing challenge. As our population ages it is becoming clear that we need to strengthen physical accessibility in all areas of the community. There is already a general agreement to improve the pathways that are difficult for people with limited mobility, and we hope to design a very accessible third neighborhood. In addition, architectural students from the State University of New York at Buffalo have worked on ideas to make our multi-storied homes in FROG more accessible.

We also need to make our community as friendly as possible to those with environmental illnesses. With three residents with severe multiple chemical sensitivity (MCS), as a community we have learned much more about toxins in our environment. Two homes in the SONG neighborhood were especially constructed for these residents. We strictly limit the burning of wood as a way to control outdoor air quality. And we've replaced toxic Common House cleaning and laundry products with non-scented, biodegradable alternatives. But some individuals in our community still use home cleaning or cosmetic products that can cause strong reactions in our neighbors with MCS. It's all part of the process of learning to be sensitive to others' needs.

It is my hope that we will eventually find creative solutions to all our challenges. And rather than just reflect the problems of the larger society, perhaps we can experiment with a variety of responses that can lead in helpful new directions.

By now it should be clear that EcoVillage at Ithaca has a very large vision. Although many aspects of that vision have manifested or are well underway, there are many projects as yet unfulfilled. Following is a partial list of what we still hope to accomplish.

Dream Projects

AGRICULTURE AND LAND STEWARDSHIP

A vibrant and full range of agricultural activity was part of the original EVI vision. West Haven Farm and the berry farm have already brought much of the plan to fruition. But we'd still like to realize the whole plan and establish a large organic orchard, so that we could produce our own fruit and nuts on-site.

We'd also love to establish a farm stand that would attract visitors and give us an outlet for the sale of organic produce, berries, fruit, and possibly homemade goodies and crafts. Our teens could run the stand, providing themselves with worthwhile summer jobs.

Some villagers have also considered expanding our animal husbandry to include the raising of more sheep, chickens, goats, and even llamas!

Land stewardship is another fundamental aspect of the EVI vision. Although we have already begun habitat restoration on a portion of the land, we hope to increase our support of the natural areas surrounding us. In some cases that will mean restoring native species; in others it will mean removing invasive plants. It may also mean thinning some of the trees in the woods to allow for better growth and species diversity. We will move slowly, though, and only make changes when we have a firm understanding of the land and the flora and fauna that live on it.

CAREFUL PLANNING FOR FURTHER DEVELOPMENT

Since we have committed ourselves to building on no more than 10 to 20 percent of the land, we need to revisit how we want to use the remaining acreage set aside for development. There is a lot to consider. How many more neighborhoods do we want to build, for example? And how do we minimize the ecological footprint for any future buildings? What exactly do we want to develop anyway? Is it feasible to combine the functions of a Village Center (for community gatherings, indoor basketball games, dances, and performances) with an Education Center (for classes, workshops, and conferences), for example? And how do both of those needs fit with people's desire for more office space and possible housing for cottage industries? Besides all that, what do we do about providing housing for students and interns?

Whatever we end up doing, it all needs to fit into the one field still available for development. It also needs to pull the village together practically and aesthetically, and connect harmoniously to the rest of the landscape. Thankfully there are professionals who can assist us.

I've invited architect and village designer Greg Ramsey to EVI for a four-day planning charette to be held in the fall of 2005. (A charette provides the opportunity to bring together creative design ideas from many people, then winnow them down to a workable design solution.) Ramsey's company, Village Habitat, has designed other award-winning projects that reflect EVI's values of open space, clustered housing, integrated agriculture, and a strong sense of community. My hope is that, as an outside expert, Ramsey will help our group (with its diverse range of opinions) to coalesce on a unified site design. The design will then lay the groundwork for future development.

As with so much else having to do with EcoVillage, I have had to learn the rudiments of yet another profession — planning — in order to help our group move to the next stage. And although it is definitely stimulating to learn a bit about so many different disciplines, sometimes I long to work in a field that I have already mastered!

ECOLOGICAL INNOVATION

"Green" is good, and we'd like to go even greener in our energy production and heating methods, our wastewater treatment methods, and our modes of transportation. It would be wonderful to have more of our electricity generated from "green" sources on-site. Right now about half the homes in SONG use solar electric panels that are connected with the grid. Given that our climate is very cloudy in the winter, however, it would be good to have some wind generation, too.

As mentioned in the education chapter (Chapter Nine), some Cornell engineering students did a preliminary study on wind potential at EVI. The results were promising, although the initial investment would be expensive, and a more detailed follow-up study is planned.

It would also be great to improve on some of our heating methods. Currently all homes in FROG are part of a mini-district heating system. That is, they are linked up through underground pipes that connect to four "energy centers," and natural gas fuels the boilers that provide hot water to the system. The system is designed for easy retrofitting to renewable energy sources. We have yet to determine, though, which renewable energy source will best suit our needs or how much we can afford to invest in switching over.

Aside from improving on our energy production and heating methods, it has been a long-held dream to create our own wastewater treatment facility. There are several options available to us, including a greenhouse system known as a "Living Machine." In such a system, the liquids left over from composted human waste are filtered through a series of tanks filled with aquatic plants. The natural processes of the plants purify the water, just as they do in bogs and wetlands, and the end result is pure, clear water. The system is pricey, however, making it likely that we would opt for the less expensive wetlands system.

It would also be great to build a graywater treatment system. Graywater is the household wastewater generated from such activities as showering, doing laundry, and dishwashing. FROG homes are already outfitted with dual piping, so that black water (sewage) can be separated from graywater. Now all we have to do is create a filtration system to cleanse the graywater. Of course any on-site wastewater treatment method must clear some substantial hurdles, including Town approvals, financing, good design, and ongoing maintenance.

Another longstanding eco-dream has to do with modifying our modes of transportation. Some of us would love to do away with many of our individual cars and replace them with an extremely fuel-efficient fleet of cars. We'd even like to experiment with alternative fuels, including bio-fuels or solar-generated electricity.

Some residents have already started the process. There are half a dozen hybrid cars (gas and electric) on-site, and another car has been converted to bio-diesel. Several of us will also be working with students from both a Cornell course and from an IC course to study the feasibility of several of us creating a village car fleet.

EDUCATION AND ECONOMIC DEVELOPMENT

As our project matures, we want to be able to share even more of our experiences with students and the public. But we have a lot to do if we hope to live up to our full educational potential. We will need reliable financial resources to fund curriculum development, teaching, and administration if we are to develop ongoing programs. We definitely need additional housing for interns and workshop participants.

June 12, 2004

It is one of those sun-drenched days in early summer that is so clear it seems to ring. Light magnifies the colors of the freshly opened spring flowers, and the blue hills cut undulating silhouettes on the horizon. There are two events planned at EcoVillage today — a memorial service; and a performance by several Native American groups that will include storytelling, dancing, and a concert.

The memorial service is for Mary Webber. She and Bill moved to Arizona in 1999 to be closer to children and grandchildren, and fortunately Mary had several good years with her family before developing lung cancer. Bill has brought some of her ashes back to EcoVillage. Seeing him here today is bittersweet and brings back a flood of memories.

A group of us walks down to the farm and gathers in a circle next to the young fruit trees. There are sweeping views of the hills across the valley, and Cornell (Bill and Mary's alma mater) is clearly visible from where we stand. The ceremony that follows is simple and moving.

Deena plays a hauntingly beautiful guitar piece, and Janet Shortall (a minister and good friend of Mary's) offers each of us a chance to speak. Mary is remembered fondly and tearfully for her radiant smile, her profound commitment to social justice and racial equality, her courage, and her love. When it is my turn, I remember the reassuring sound of her bright laughter. And I describe how, although as director of CRESP she was technically my boss, Mary became a mentor and friend. ☞

And, as mentioned earlier, our long-term dream for an EcoVillage Education and Research Center (EVER Center) would provide enough space for classes, workshops, and conferences — and possibly even an alternative high school.

Education is potentially a promising cottage industry for the community. It could generate enough money to employ a number of residents, who could share our accumulating knowledge about sustainable living with a broad audience. Other "green" businesses may also develop over time and employ a greater percentage of EcoVillage residents.

We have much left to do. And the work is exciting — full of growth and challenges. As with everything else, our only limits are money, time, and our own imaginations. I have learned that the only way to be truly

Deena plays another haunting guitar piece as we scatter Mary's ashes among the young peach trees. I can't believe that I am holding her remains in my hands, or that I have to say goodbye. Mary and Bill helped ensure EVI's future when they forgave their loan. And the permanent conservation easement we established in return was close to Mary's heart. She called it "a gift for the 7th generation." It seems fitting to be scattering her ashes on this land — land that will indeed grow organic food and provide open space for future generations to enjoy for years to come. My tears drip down onto the ashes, but at the same time it feels good to bring her home.

In the evening Mark Thunderwolf, a member of the Wolf Clan, stands on the Common House porch playing soul-stirring music. He invokes the spirit of the trees from which each of his 20 flutes was made, as well as the spirit of the wolves that he has befriended.

As his music soars over the hushed crowd sitting on the grass, the sky turns to pink, with gold-shot clouds. Bullfrogs croak in harmony from the pond, and a distant group of dogs sets up a chorus in reply. It feels as if the land itself is being consecrated and gathered in a vast embrace that includes the gorgeous sunset, the music, the animals and the humans, and now a flock of geese that flies overhead, catching sky colors on their wings. ∎

sustainable is to move slowly and thoughtfully forward, keeping our vision in mind at all times, and celebrating our small accomplishments along the way.

Ecovillages and the World: What We Have to Offer

What do ecovillages have to offer the world? I see us as incubators of a new culture, one that values cooperation in the most profound sense: cooperation between diverse peoples and cooperation with nature. We are part of a vast wave of change, made up of billions of people who want to be free from war, environmental destruction, and economic slavery. Along with other growing movements, we are taking the brave step of trying to live out our ideals.

Ecovillages are not inventing anything new. Instead we offer a place to bring together the best practices of land preservation, organic agriculture, green building, renewable energy, and all the aspects of living in community.

We learn from each other how to better work, play, resolve conflicts, make decisions, support each other, and celebrate. We attempt to integrate the wisdom of indigenous cultures and small communities everywhere, while living modern lifestyles and often using the latest technologies.

Ecovillages also have a commitment to teach what we are learning to the broader public. For if we are going to change the world, it is crucial that we reach out and share our commitment, our sweat, our despair, and our joy.

The stories I have told here are threads in the living quilt that is our community. Whether we are raising our voices in exuberant song, praying for and receiving guidance, or gathering together in sorrow or joy, there is a larger purpose at work here.

We are touched by Spirit. It is as if a gentle hand is guiding us through the work and sacrifice of creating something larger than ourselves. Spirit is here in the quiet of an evening walk on the land, in the sparkle of children playing, and in the bounty of fresh flowers and vegetables from the farm. Spirit is here in the strong sense of love and connection that unites us. Spirit is with us as we take the next evolutionary step and learn, one lesson at a time, how humans can live well on Earth without destroying it. Each of us brings something special to offer the world. What gift will you bring?

GLOSSARY OF ACRONYMS

ACS: Refers to the Alternative Community School, a small public junior high and high school attended by some EVI young people.

APECSY: Refers to L'Association pour la promotion économique, culturelle, et sociale de Yoff, a grassroots organization in Yoff, Senegal.

CH: The Common House or community center of a cohousing community.

CLT: Community Land Trust is an organization that supports land preservation, affordable housing, and organic farming.

CRESP: Refers to the Center for Religion, Ethics, and Social Policy, a nonprofit organization affiliated with Cornell University that assists projects working to promote peace, justice, and sustainable communities. EVI started as a project of CRESP.

CSA: Community Supported Agriculture, a farm in which consumers buy advance shares in the harvest and share the risks and benefits of the farm's operation. West Haven Farm is an organic CSA farm.

ETC: Refers to the nonprofit organization Educate the Children, founded by Pamela Carson to raise money in the US to support impoverished children in Nepal. The organization later grew to include women's empowerment programs.

EVER Center: Refers to the proposed EcoVillage Education and Research Center.

EVI: Derived from "EcoVillage at Ithaca" for ease of usage. Used interchangeably with "EcoVillage" to refer to the ecovillage community. May also refer to the nonprofit organization that oversees the entire EcoVillage project. Use of the term does not diminish the fact that there are hundreds of ecovillages around the world.

FROG: Refers to the First Resident Group, the first cohousing group to form and build a neighborhood at EcoVillage.

GEN: The Global Ecovillage Network is a nonprofit organization that coordinates a network of ecovillages around the world. EVI is a member of GEN.

HRV: Refers to a Heat Recovery Ventilator. An HRV is a fan system that introduces fresh air into the home and exhausts stale air out of the home. In the winter, heat from the stale air is recovered and used to warm the cold incoming air. In the summer, cool air from the home is recovered and used to cool the hot incoming air.

IC: Refers to Ithaca College, which partners with EVI on many educational projects.

ICF: An insulated manufactured product that becomes a permanent component of a building. Designed to replace the traditional lumber forms, such as those used when pouring concrete foundation walls. Derived from "Insulated Concrete Forms."

ISLAND Agreement: The Infrastructure and Land Agreement made between EVI, Inc., FROG, and SONG that spells out each group's specific financial responsibilities for land and infrastructure.

LUPF: The Land Use Planning Forums undertaken by the community to determine how best to develop the EcoVillage land.

MCS: Refers to Multiple Chemical Sensitivity.

MIT: Refers to the Massachusetts Institute of Technology in Cambridge, Massachusetts.

NIMBY: Refers to an attitude in which people resist the presence of institutions or projects (such as halfway houses or gas generation plants) near to where they live. Derived from "Not in My Backyard."

NOFA: The Northeast Organic Farming Association, an association of organic farmers from the northeastern area of the US.

NSF: Refers to the National Science Foundation.

OSB: Refers to relatively inexpensive manufactured wood panels, typically used for roof and wall sheathing. Wood from fast-growing sustainable trees (such as aspen and southern yellow pine), is formed into uniform strands that are oriented in cross-directional patterns (to maximize strength), mixed with wax and binders, and pressed into layered sheets. Derived from "Oriented Strand Board."

PVC: Refers to a type of thermoplastic resin used in such manufactured products as water pipes, floor tiles, etc. Derived from the chemical name "polyvinyl chloride."

SIPs: Refers to the relatively inexpensive manufactured panels that are used in a variety of building applications, including roofs, walls, and floors. The panels consist of a rigid insulating core between two facing structural "skins" (often made of oriented strand board). Derived from "Structural Insulating Panels."

SONG: An acronym for the Second Neighborhood Group at EcoVillage.

SOUL: Refers to a partnership of six people who raised $120,000 to pay off a loan held by an unhappy lender. "SOUL" stands for "Save Our Unlimited Land."

VA: Refers to the Village Association, the not-for-profit entity that owns the infrastructure at EVI and coordinates village-wide decisions between FROG and SONG.

YIMBY: Coined by an EVI resident to refer to an attitude in which people would welcome the presence of a water tank near to where they live. Derived from "Yes in My Backyard."

ECOVILLAGE AT ITHACA TIMELINE

1990
- The Global Walk for a Livable World draws participants from six countries for a nine-month walk from Los Angeles to New York City.
- Joan Bokaer develops the vision for an ecovillage to be created in Ithaca, New York.

1991
- Joan Bokaer speaks about the EcoVillage vision in Ithaca, drawing about 100 interested participants.
- The Envisioning Retreat at Ithaca takes place in June, jump-starting the formation of the EcoVillage organization, under the aegis of the Center for Religion, Ethics, and Social Policy (CRESP), a nonprofit associated with Cornell. Joan Bokaer and Liz Walker serve as co-directors, with Tim Allen as staff associate. Committees continue to meet after the retreat.
- In August, Liz Walker and Jon Katz move to Ithaca.
- The newly formed EcoVillage group decides to purchase the West Hill property and adopts a Statement of Purpose. Joan and Liz begin to put financing in order to meet the purchase price.
- EcoVillage lecture series begins and continues for a full year.
- Ongoing media attention about EVI begins.

1992
- In January, EVI receives nonprofit status and holds its first Annual Meeting. Election of Board of Directors and adoption of bylaws.
- EVI and Yoff, Senegal begin a sister village relationship.
- The first cohousing group (FROG) holds its first meeting in March.
- A delegation from EVI visits Yoff, Senegal in May.

- Land purchase completed on summer solstice. A year-long land use planning process begins in September and results in the "Guidelines for Development" and a visual "Envisioning Plan."
- McCamant and Durrett of the Cohousing Company hold a workshop for the newly formed group, and give public lecture about cohousing.

1993

- First MA thesis about EVI's land use planning process completed by Cornell student.
- Two Cornell classes take part in semester-long projects at EVI.
- FROG hires Jerry and Claudia Weisburd as development consultants.
- First harvest from West Haven Farm.

1994

- FROG hires Housecraft Builders as design-build team for first neighborhood.
- Town approval process begins.
- 200 trees planted by residents.
- Mayor of Dakar, Senegal visits as planning begins for Third International EcoCity Conference (jointly organized by EVI and APECSY).

1995

- Final site plan for FROG approved by Town.
- Labor Day groundbreaking draws 200 people.
- Infrastructure in place, including road, sewer, water, and pond.

1996

- Third International EcoCity Conference held in Yoff, Senegal.
- Joan Bokaer retires as co-director of EVI.
- Second neighborhood group (SONG) begins to form under the guidance of Liz Walker.
- Mary and Bill Webber forgive their $130,000 loan and interest to EVI. Fifty-five acres set aside as a permanent conservation easement, to be administered by Finger Lakes Land Trust.
- First families move into FROG in October.
- Major construction fire destroys eight homes and the Common House.
- SOUL partnership forms to buy out unhappy lender.

1997

- SONG hires architect Mary Kraus.
- EVI holds two permaculture workshops with Dave Jacke.
- Future development committee formed to help group resolve complex issues on becoming a village.
- FROG neighborhood completed, and 30 households move in.
- Major media coverage continues.

1998

- Village-wide design process continues, with consensus on major financial and legal issues (the ISLAND Agreement and "Crux of the Matter").
- Elan Shapiro hired as part-time educational consultant for nine months.
- EVI named a finalist for the World Habitat Award.

1999

- SONG hires Liz Walker and Rod Lambert as co-development managers.
- Affordable housing options fail and all but three SONG households drop out.
- PBS video "Preserving the Legacy" features EVI in an 18-minute segment.

2000

- EVI secures low-interest $100,000 loan from Equity Trust Fund to plan SONG infrastructure. Many new households join SONG.
- Longtime EVI resident Pamela Carson dies.
- Elan and Liz are hired as adjunct faculty for a Cornell course on Environmental Management.
- Martha Stettinius spearheads a fundraising effort to build a deer fence at West Haven Farm.

2001

- Elan Shapiro teaches a 14-week course, "Creating Sustainable Communities," at EVI for Ithaca College students.
- Mike Carpenter is hired as SONG construction manager.
- EVI celebrates 10th anniversary on Labor Day weekend.

- SONG receives final Town approval. Groundbreaking on SONG infrastructure begins September 20.

2002

- EcoVillage doubles in size. The first 14 homes (Verse 1) in SONG completed, and Verse 2 is begun.
- EVI becomes the first cohousing project in the US to construct two neighborhoods.
- EVI receives $112,000 grant for affordable housing from the Federal Home Loan Bank, in partnership with Tompkins Trust Company and Better Housing for Tompkins County. The money will be used to help subsidize six units in SONG.
- EVI receives grant from USDA to restore wildlife habitat on 12 acres of land.
- EVI and Ithaca College form partnership on the "science of sustainability" and receive a matching grant of $149,000 from the National Science Foundation.
- Liz Walker takes a five-month sabbatical.

2003

- SONG homes completed.
- Residents build a bridge over the stream between FROG and SONG as part of a celebration marking the completion of SONG and the start of the Village.
- The "Debt-Free in 2003" campaign successfully pays off the rest of the mortgage on the land.
- The Town constructs a water tank on EVI land.
- Educational work takes off, with two Ithaca College courses taught by EVI residents.

2004

- Ithaca College, EVI, and the Town of Ithaca help launch "Sustainable Tompkins County" initiative.
- Ithaca College holds a "Sustainability Summit" and makes a major commitment to sustainability.
- GEN holds an international gathering at Findhorn, Scotland to launch the development of an introductory ecovillage design curriculum.
- Memorial service and scattering of Mary Webber's ashes.

INDEX